RESEARCHING THE PUBLIC OPINION ENVIRONMENT

SAGE SERIES IN PUBLIC RELATIONS

SERIES EDITORS
Robert L. Heath and Gabriel M. Vasquez

Embracing ideas as old as the rhetorical heritage of Western Civilization and as new as theoretical models that draw on social science, the **Sage Series in Public Relations** comprises the work of academic and professional practitioners. Combining theory and practice, authors seek to redefine the field through thoughtful examinations of the breadth and depth of public relations. Books in the series may emphasize theory, research foundations, or practice, but all focus on advancing public relations excellence. The series publishes work devoted to the principle that public relations adds economic, sociopolitical, and cultural value to society, particularly those societies based on democratic ideals.

Books in this series:

Communication Planning: An Integrated Approach
  Sherry Devereaux Ferguson

Ongoing Crisis Communication: Planning, Managing, and Responding
  W. Timothy Coombs

Researching the Public Opinion Environment: Theories and Methods
  Sherry Devereaux Ferguson

SSPR
Sage Series in Public Relations

RESEARCHING THE PUBLIC OPINION ENVIRONMENT
Theories and Methods

Sherry Devereaux Ferguson

Sage Publications, Inc.
International Educational and Professional Publisher
Thousand Oaks ▪ London ▪ New Delhi

For information:

Sage Publications, Inc.
2455 Teller Road
Thousand Oaks, California 91320
E-mail: order@sagepub.com

Sage Publications Ltd.
6 Bonhill Street
London EC2A 4PU
United Kingdom

Sage Publications India Pvt. Ltd.
M-32 Market
Greater Kailash I
New Delhi 110 048 India

Printed in the United States of America

Library of Congress Cataloging-in-Publication Data

Ferguson, Sherry Devereaux.
    Researching the public opinion environment: Theories and methods /
by Sherry Devereaux Ferguson.
        p.   cm. — (Sage series in public relations: v. 3)
    Includes bibliographical references and index
        ISBN 0-7619-1530-3 (cloth: acid-free paper)
        ISBN 0-7619-1531-1 (pbk.: acid-free paper)
        1. Public opinion.   2. Public opinion polls.   3. Mass media and public opinion.   I. Title.   II. Series.
        HM1236.F47   2000
        300.3'8—dc21   00-008509

This book is printed on acid-free paper.

00   01   02   03   04   05   10   9   8   7   6   5   4   3   2   1

Acquiring Editor: Margaret H. Seawell
Editorial Assistant: Sandra Krumholz
Production Editor: Astrid Virding
Editorial Assistant: Victoria Cheng
Designer/Typesetter: Janelle LeMaster
Cover Designer: Candice Harman

Contents

PART II: MONITORING AND ANALYZING THE MEDIA

PART III: RESEARCH METHODOLOGIES

PART IV: THEORIES ON THE IMPACT OF THE MEDIA

This book is dedicated to
five generations of women in my family:

Verna Claire Gunn

Maureen Claire Devereaux

Barbara Ann Champagne, Desirée Marlene Devereaux,
and Maureen Claire Smith

Alexandra Maureen Hendriks, Christin Anne Prinster,
Ashley Claire Smith, and Cameron Devereaux Velut

Ashley, Courtney, Lydia, Mara, Melissa,
and Victoria Champagne

Emilie and Erica Ferguson

Alexandra Claire Prinster

Introduction

Politicians, government leaders, and chief executive officers (CEOs) face the challenge of coping with a volatile public opinion environment. Whereas presidents and prime ministers once enjoyed a relatively lengthy honeymoon period with their constituencies, they now find that they are under attack within 6 months of entering office. The "immediacy" of the new media has collapsed the time available for decision making to unrealistic parameters, creating panic in leaders who are expected to be all-knowing. Every politician fears stepping off a plane and being faced with a crowd of reporters who shout, "What do you think about . . .?" In reality, the leader may think nothing, being totally uninformed on some event that occurred while the person was traveling from one destination to another. Increased access to information means that ever larger segments of the population learn about crisis events and political developments at the same time as, or even before, their leaders.

The response of government heads and CEOs has been to establish sophisticated intelligence systems that track the opinion of key publics on high-profile issues. Some have also developed early warning systems that identify emerging concerns. Some public relations employees, charged with the task of scanning daily newspapers and television news, quake at the possibility that they may have missed two lines in a prominent news source (or sometimes even in an obscure community or ethnic newspaper). Once the omission is discovered, reaction from the top can be swift and punitive. The turnover of press secretaries within government reflects the importance that executives attach to the function of staying informed on matters of public opinion. Press secretaries do more than make statements to the press. They also monitor the efficiency of their information-gathering structures—their means of obtaining immediate feedback on what people are saying in the press, on the Internet, and through other public venues. The number of media-monitoring and Internet-monitoring firms has mushroomed as interest in issue tracking has increased.

Governments, media, and corporations also invest large sums of money in surveys and polls. Even when organizations do not conduct their own surveys on public issues, the majority appear to recognize the benefits of becoming sophisticated consumers of surveys commissioned by other groups. Government monitors big business, and big business monitors government. In the same way, focus groups have acquired tremendous popularity in recent years as public, private, and voluntary sectors seek to understand their constituencies and clientele. Some consulting firms have developed less well-known methodologies such as stakeholder assemblies. Organizations use this knowledge of stakeholder opinion to feed into their policy-making processes, to frame their corporate communication strategies, to learn more about how key publics perceive the leadership of the organization, and to evaluate their programs.

This book fills a gap in the academic literature. No other academic book brings together concepts related to theories of public opinion, media monitoring, survey and focus group research, and scanning and monitoring practices. Many books, however, address individual topics of relevance. For example, Sage is the dominant publisher in the area of survey techniques, with books such as Bourque and Clark's *Processing Data: The Survey Example* (1992); Bourque and Fielder's *How to Conduct Self-Administered and Mail Surveys* (1995); Edwards, Thomas, Rosenfeld, and Booth-Kewley's *How to Conduct Organizational Surveys: A Step-by-Step Guide* (1996); Fink and Kosecoff's *How to Conduct Surveys: A Step-by-Step Guide* (1998); Fowler's *Improving Survey Questions* (1995) and *Survey Research Methods* (1993); Fowler and Mangione's *Standardized Survey Interviewing: Minimizing Interviewer-Related Errors* (1990); Frey and Oishi's *How to Conduct Interviews by Telephone and in Person* (1995); Lavrakas's *Telephone Survey Methods* (1993); Litwin's *How to Measure Survey Reliability and Validity* (1995); Mangione's *Mail Surveys: Improving the Quality* (1995); Schuman and Presser's *Questions and Answers in Attitude Surveys: Experiments on*

Question Form, Wording, and Context (1996); and Weisberg, Krosnick, and Bowen's *An Introduction to Survey Research, Polling, and Data Analysis* (1996). Fink has published numerous monographs in this area, including *How to Analyze Survey Data* (1995a), *How to Ask Survey Questions* (1995b), *How to Design Surveys* (1995c), *How to Report on Surveys* (1995d), *How to Sample in Surveys* (1995e), *The Survey Handbook* (1995f), and *The Survey Kit* (1995g).

Other books exist in the area of focus group testing. Popular texts include Barbour and Kitzinger's *Developing Focus Group Research* (1998); Krueger's *Analyzing and Reporting Focus Group Results* (1997a), *Moderating Focus Groups* (1997b), and *Focus Groups: A Practical Guide for Applied Research* (1994); Morgan's *Focus Groups as Qualitative Research* (1997); Morgan and Krueger's *The Focus Group Kit: Volumes 1-6* (1997); Stewart and Shamdasani's *Focus Groups: Theory and Practice* (1990); and Vaughn, Schumm, and Sinagub's *Focus Group Interviews in Education and Psychology* (1996). Books that treat Q methodologies include McKeown and Thomas's *Q Methodology* (1988).

Locating a book that covers the topic of media monitoring is more problematic. Merriam and Makower wrote *Trend Watching: How the Media Create Trends and How to Be the First to Uncover Them* (1988), and Fan wrote *Predictions of Public Opinion From the Mass Media* (1988). An early work by Aguilar (*Scanning the Business Environment,* 1967) established the terminology for scanning and monitoring.

Yeric and Todd's *Public Opinion: The Visible Politics* (1996) and Price's *Public Opinion* (1992) are interesting academic treatments of public opinion. Yeric and Todd's book includes discussion of the classical public opinion literature, development of individual opinions, tools of public opinion polling, citizen impact on public policy, and public opinion and public issues.

To obtain instruction on how to analyze media coverage, classical treatments such as Berelson's *Content Analysis in Communication Research* (1952), Holsti's *Content Analysis for the Social Sciences and Humanities* (1969), and Gerbner, Holsti, Krippendorff, Paisley, and Stone's *The Analysis of Communication Content: Developments in Scientific Theories and Computer Techniques* (1969) are the best. Dyer added useful insights in the area of computer analysis with his book *In-Depth Understanding: A Computer Model of Integrated Processing of Narrative Comprehension* (1983). Sage published works by Weber and Krippendorff in the 1980s. Berger's *Media Research Techniques* (1991) includes a short chapter on content analysis of the media, as do numerous methodology textbooks published for use by communication students. Generic in their applications, none of these treatments discuss examples specific to analysis of public opinion data.

The final category of works (relevant to the topic of monitoring public opinion) comprises books dedicated to issues management and strategic planning. These books tend to reflect management and communication literature. Older works include Brown's *This Business of Issues: Coping With the Company's Environments* (The Conference Board, 1979); Chase's *Issues Management: Origins of the Future* (1984); Buchholz, Evans, and Wagley's *Management Response to Public Issues: Concepts and Cases in Strategy Formulation* (1985); Heath and Nelson's *Issues Management* (1986); Ewing's *Managing the New Bottom Line: Issues Management for Senior Executives* (1987); and Heath and Associates' *Strategic Issues Management* (1988). The Quorum Books Division of Greenwood published Renfro's *Issues Management in Strategic Planning* (1993) and Mahon and McGowan's *Industry as a Player in the Political and Social Arena: Defining the Competitive Environment* (1996). Ferguson authored *Mastering the Public Opinion Challenge* in 1994 (published by Irwin), and Heath updated his earlier book in 1997 (*Strategic Issues Management: Policy Options*).

In 1999, Ferguson published *Communication Planning: An Integrated Approach*. This book emphasizes the importance of using stakeholder opinion as a basis for strategic planning in organizations. In the same way as *Mastering the Public Opinion Challenge, Communication Planning* stresses the importance of drawing on many different sources in seeking to understand how key publics perceive the organization, its leaders, and its issues. In conclusion, the previously mentioned books represent the range of literature that is relevant to the topic of public opinion monitoring. In seeking to inform readers on the rationale, purposes, and methodologies involved in public opinion research, *Researching the Public Opinion Environment* adds important new perspectives to the literature.

The book is divided into four parts. Part I examines theories and systems relevant to public opinion research. Chapter 1 reviews the classical debate regarding the role of public opinion in democratic society and the modern debate regarding the purposes and ends of public opinion research. Taking a populist perspective, Chapter 2 discusses the importance of listening to key publics, the sources that feed organizational intelligence systems, components of such systems, and approaches to setting up the intelligence function in organizations. The chapter assumes that corporations are as interested as governments in learning more about how people perceive their organizations and leadership.

Part II addresses the topics of monitoring and analyzing the media. Chapter 3 identifies questions that can be asked by the opinion analyst, usually engaged in monitoring the media. The following are the most common clusters of questions: Which publics have reacted to policies and announcements by the organization? What do people say about the organization? How do media depict the organization and its leaders? What catalysts drive media coverage and what are the spinoff issues? and Which trends have developed? Chapter 4 describes standard content analysis techniques that provide a means for analyzing data gathered from media sources, the Internet, correspondence, focus groups, and other communication content. The emphasis of the chapter is on media analysis, the most common organizational application.

Part III describes the basics of survey research, focus groups, Delphi techniques, stakeholder assemblies, and Q methodology. The intent of Chapters 5, 6, and 7 is to convey sufficient information to allow organizational researchers to frame research questions, construct and administer questionnaires, interpret the results of survey research, and critique research carried out on their behalf by survey research firms. The discussion is limited to topic areas that are most relevant to the work of organizational communicators, who rarely implement large-scale survey research projects without the help of outside firms. The emphasis of the chapters is on creating knowledgeable consumers and interpreters of survey research. This discussion also directs the reader to common errors in designing studies, sampling, framing and ordering questions, administering surveys, and interpreting results. Chapter 8 reviews the purposes, strengths, and weaknesses of focus groups, the stages through which the groups move, and common participant and moderator behaviors. Other topics include stakeholder assemblies, Q methodologies, and Delphi techniques, which are additional alternatives for gathering opinion data.

Finally, Part IV examines the impact of the media. Chapter 9 outlines the continuum of academic opinion on media effects and the ongoing academic debate on this topic. This debate brings into question the assumptions of organizational researchers who take for granted the powerful influence of media on audiences.

The book has many special features. The organization of public opinion theories in Chapter 1 is unique to this book, and although other books address the topic of public opinion theories, few seek to integrate the theoretical and the practical elements of this area of study. The menu of questions in Chapter 3 is an original contribution, which dates from the author's 1994 book on media monitoring. Graphs, tables, and sample analyses—uncharacteristic of other books on public opinion research—help the reader to understand applications described in the book.

Some omissions are deliberate. For example, this book does not discuss literature relevant to the psychology of audiences. The intent is to determine opinions and not the thinking processes behind the opinions. Also, even though many ideas are applicable to market researchers, this book does not explicitly reference the market research literature. Nor does the book purport to be a standard research methodology text. Similarly, the professional audience for this book will be communicators in business, government, nonprofit, and political organizations whose involvement with survey research design stops short of conducting the actual study.

The book has two audiences—academic and professional. Regarding the academic audience, this book is appropriate as a text in upper-level undergraduate or graduate courses that deal with public relations functions, the role of public relations in politics, corporate communication, issues management, political communication, and public opinion. Political science departments and government policy instructors will find the subject matter relevant to courses in political management and public opinion. The implications for issues management courses and strategic planning courses ensure the book's attractiveness to business schools. Professional communicators in corporations, policy analysts and communicators in government, political consultants and political managers, and training and development firms comprise the professional audience.

Acknowledgments

I acknowledge the contribution of many people who helped to bring this project to fruition. Those individuals made an invaluable contribution to the final "look" of this book. Reviewers Katie Theus and Christiane Pagé suggested many areas that required further development or clarification and took painstaking care in noting opportunities for stylistic improvement. I am sure that the readers will appreciate, as much as I, the many hours that they dedicated to this project. As editor of the series, Robert Heath made additional suggestions, which were often incorporated into the book.

I thank the team at Sage Publications for their advice and support. I particularly appreciated the insightful comments of Sage editor Margaret Seawell, who added balance and perspective to the editorial process. I also thank Sandra Krumbolz, editorial assistant to Margaret Seawell, who worked overtime to ensure that the book met production deadlines. I have appreciated the ongoing courtesies and professionalism of Astrid Virding, production coordinator at Sage, and Janelle LeMaster and Victoria Cheng of production. Dan Hays did a meticulous job of copyediting the book. The final product reflects the efforts of all these individuals.

I also owe a debt to some earlier contributors. Many individuals within the Canadian government community helped to shape and refine my thinking on the topic of public opinion. Mary Gusella, Nicole Henderson, and Peter Lantos deserve special note. Under the leadership of the late Don Rennie and Dennis Orchard, the Working Group on Public Environment Analysis guided my research in the late 1980s, and representatives from many government departments were members of this steering committee.

The Learning Advisory Panel on Communications, chaired by Assistant Secretary to Cabinet Ruth Cardinal and her senior adviser Toby Fyfe, provided a much appreciated opportunity for discussion and additional development of my thoughts in 1997 and 1998. I have enjoyed recent exchanges with Evan Potter of the Department of Foreign Affairs, who manages the department's public environment analysis function.

During the past 12 years, I have discussed the issues that make up the content of this book with hundreds of communication officers in dozens of workshops, and I have learned a great deal from their collective wisdom. Many of their suggestions have been integrated into this book.

I also pay tribute to my colleagues of many years at the University of Ottawa who have provided a supportive environment within which to work, in particular Hilary Horan and Marie-Nicole Cossette. I would like to thank France Dompierre for helping with the typing of the book.

Finally, I acknowledge the love and never-flagging support of my husband Stewart Ferguson and mother Maureen Devereaux. Others of great importance to me include Alexandra Hendriks, Cameron Velut, Eric Ferguson, Desiree Devereaux, Claire and George Smith, Barbara and Richard Champagne, and their extended families. Since I began this project, our collective family has celebrated two marriages, numerous child births, and the death of two much-loved pets, including my own dear Zachary. Such life events put the products of any career into a larger perspective. For me, grandchildren Erica, Emilie, and Solan have given new impetus to my resolution to take the time, after finishing this book, to undertake a computer search for water slides and children's parks and to extend my academic library to include glossy editions of Pooh's and Tigger's adventures.

To all mentioned or implied in these acknowledgments, thank you!

PART
I

Theory and Systems

1

Role of Public Opinion in Democratic Societies

The classical debate over whether the mass public has a role to play in the affairs of government continues unabated, even after centuries of discourse. At the same time, modern academic literature has added another theme to the debate: Assuming that there is a role to be played, is there any credibility to the manner in which leaders engage the public? While the scholarly debate continues, political leaders ponder the very pragmatic question: How can I cope with the consequences of yesterday's opinion poll and predict tomorrow's public opinion crisis?

The Classical Debate

Authors such as Plato, Hobbes, Hamilton, and Madison express serious reservations about the potential of the average citizen to make a meaningful contribution to the workings of government. Plato (427-347 B.C.) believes in a society governed by a philosopher king, whose wisdom far exceeds the knowledge and intellectual capabilities of the general population. In *The Republic,* Plato (trans. 1963) argues that the average person is not capable of comprehending the complexities of government. Thomas Hobbes (1588-1679) also questions the value of involving the masses of people in the workings of government. Although Hobbes (1963 version) believes that public consent is a prerequisite to the formation of government, he does not think that the role of the public extends much beyond this point. He says that once the people have committed to a social contract, forged to protect them against the "solitary, poor, nasty, brutish, and short" vagaries of life without government, they should acquiesce to the ruling powers (p. 143). In other words, they should "confer all their power and strength upon one man, or one assembly of men, that may reduce all their wills, by plurality of voices, unto one will" (p. 149).

Alexander Hamilton (1937 version) espouses a similar view in 1787 when he urges the Constitutional Convention not to trust the "many" to make judicious decisions on matters pertaining to government. He says that their decisions are too grounded in emotions and too often based on selfish motives. Hamilton further argues that the tendency of the masses to oppose groups with wealth can lead to unwarranted change and unstable and chaotic conditions. James Madison agrees with Hamilton that the people best able to govern are those who hold property. He says that conflicting interests and divided loyalties on the part of the masses create a lack of incentive to cooperate for the common good. For this reason, Madison (1961) takes a federalist stance that argues for separation of powers in government and a loose confederation of states.

In *Democracy in America*, French statesman Alexis de Toqueville (1805-1859) also expresses grave reservations about the wisdom of involving the public too heavily in the machinations of government. In coining the classic phrase "the tyranny of the majority," De Toqueville (1957 version, p. 115) articulates the fear that the majority may not always protect the interests of minorities. In the twentieth century, Walter Lippmann (1922) takes his place alongside these classical and later writers when he argues that citizens cannot understand the intricate workings of government. He says that any individual "lives and works on a small part of the earth's surface" and sees "at best only a phase and an aspect" (p. 53). The psychic affiliation of Lippmann with the views of some of the earlier elitists can be seen in his reference to Hamilton as the "most imaginative" of the founding fathers. Thus, this first group of philosophers and political scientists view citizens as having no role to play in the workings of government. In a modern twist, political theorists worry that the rapid pace of change in science and technology creates a situation in which the public is unable to keep abreast of the changes. They worry that this inability to keep up with change has "profound implications for democracy" (J. Kitzinger, personal communication, November 26, 1999). Many major funding bodies, as well as firms such as Leverhulme, have committed large sums of money to the study of this topic.

A second group of philosophers adhere to the view that even though the mass public has little to contribute to government, their elected leaders cannot afford to ignore their views. In other words, they view citizen engagement as a necessary evil. For example, in *The Prince,* Niccolo Machiavelli (1469-1527) writes that public opinion can either support individual ambition or, alternatively, the collective good. In *The Prince,* Machiavelli (trans. 1963) states that public opinion is fickle, driven by the fact that humans are "ungrateful, voluble, dissemblers, anxious to avoid danger, and covetous of gain; as long as you benefit them, they are yours" (p. 120). To remain in power, rulers must either manipulate or accommodate public opinion. To ignore its existence is to risk loss of power. British philosopher David Hume (1711-1776) agrees that even the most despotic or authoritarian of governments cannot disregard this public will. He notes that it is "on opinion only that government is founded" (as quoted in Yeric & Todd, 1989, p. 8). According to German philosopher G. W. F. Hegel (trans. 1952), public opinion is "the unorganized way in which a public's opinions and wishes are made known" (p. 149). Despite the fact that public opinion contains "all kinds of falsities," it wields "great power" (p. 149) that no leader can ignore. Even though Hegel does not believe that public opinion should guide political action, like Machiavelli and Hume, he argues that those in positions of power must be aware of public wants and needs. In summary, the second group of philosophers view citizens as uninformed but nonetheless strong in their potential to bring down an unpopular government. Thus, out of necessity, they have a role to play.

A third cluster of philosophers espouse the view that public opinion has a critical role to play in democratic societies. Plato's most renowned student, Aristotle (384-322 B.C.), departs from the views of his mentor when he speaks about the benefits of involving the "many" as opposed to the "few" (phrases that were later put to other uses by Hamilton). In Book III of *Politics* (trans. 1962), Aristotle recognizes the potential superiority of a collective intelligence: "They may surpass—collectively and as a body, although not individually—the quality of the few best" (p. 123). He is optimistic that public debate and discussion can be the vehicles for informed, intelligent decision making.

John Locke (1632-1704) makes a major contribution to the debate over the role of public opinion in democracy with his book, *Two Treatises of Government* (1690). Although recognizing (like Hobbes) that the legitimacy of government derives from a social contract with the people, Locke (1952 version) argues that those in power have a duty to protect the rights of the governed. He says that the community ultimately is the "supreme power," and that the law of public opinion is equal in importance to civil and divine law (p. 59). *The Social Contract* (trans. 1963), written by French philosopher Jean Jacques Rousseau (1712-1778), reflects the philosophies of Aristotle and Locke. Like Aristotle, he views the "organic" or "general" will of the community as more than the sum of individual opinions. He argues that this general will is "always right and tends always to the public advantage" (p. 123). Nonetheless, Rousseau warns,

> It does not follow that the deliberations of the people have always the same rectitude. Our will always seeks our own good, but we do not always perceive what it is. The people are never corrupted, but they are often deceived. (pp. 223-224)

As the first major philosopher to use the term *l'opinion publique,* Rousseau speaks of the importance of public opinion, its impact on rulers, and the necessity of being able to influence and control opinion. Writing in 1802, Jeremy Bentham (1748-1832) displays some of the same pragmatism. Bentham warns legislators that they must recognize and increase the moral force of public opinion as well as regulate its intensity. Thomas Jefferson (1743-1826) is one of the most articulate advocates for taking public views into account. Adamant that well-educated people can act with judgment and responsibility, Jefferson sees farmers as the most independent, virtuous, and loyal of the citizenry, by virtue of their ties to the land, and he believes that the abundance of land in the newly forged United States creates the right conditions for mass participation in government. The *Declaration of Independence* (trans. 1963) operationalizes Jefferson's strong faith in the ability of people to participate in government. Thus, this final group of philosophers and political scientists sees the potential for citizens to perform a critical and important role in the governing of a country.

In conclusion, the first school of philosophers (pessimists) views citizen engagement as undesirable and unnecessary. The second school of thought (pragmatists) views citizen involvement as undesirable but necessary. The third group of philosophers (optimists) views citizen engagement as both desirable and necessary.

This preamble establishes a backdrop against which many contemporary discussions are set. The fundamentals of the debate have not shifted, and many civic leaders believe that they face a no-win situation. They are damned if they "do" and damned if they "don't." If leaders follow public opinion, critics say that they have no leadership qualities—that they follow public whims, which change on a daily basis. If leaders ignore public opinion, however, critics attach labels of elitism and arrogance. The most cynical say that governments monitor public opinion to learn how best to influence and manipulate that opinion. Knowing the philosophical foundations of the debate cannot solve the problem that leaders face on the issue of how much priority to give to public opinion; it can help us to understand their dilemma, however.

The Modern Debate

Some claim that Lippmann's (1922) work, a bridge into the modern age, shifts the emphasis from philosophical treatises on public opinion to scientific studies of opinion. This statement is only partly true, however, because in fact the philosophical debate continues, with a twist. The current debate can be articulated as follows: Should organizations engage in public opinion research? Bauman and Herbst (1994) describe the evolution of the debate as follows: "Since the early Greek democracies, people have debated about the nature of public opinion. Only recently, however, has the debate over the character of public opinion been tied (at times almost exclusively) to polling data" (p. 142).

Lipari (1999) offers one of the most cogent accounts of this debate. She says that there are three schools of thought: the populist, social constructionist, and critical perspectives. Curran (1996a, 1996b) and Morley (1996) discuss a fourth perspective—the revisionist perspective. It is interesting to consider these four perspectives against the three-pronged classical debate (engaging optimists, pragmatists, and pessimists) over the role of public opinion in society.

Populist Perspective

The populist perspective (also characterized as a liberal functionalist approach) assumes that "communication in society flows from bottom to top; that an aggregation of individuals constitutes a public; and that these individuals have values, beliefs, and opinions separate from political institutions, which are capable of being measured" (Curran, 1996a, p. 138). According to the populist perspective, media facilitate a two-way flow of communication between governors and their constituencies. Thus, public opinion research has an important role to play in democratic societies because it provides a means for the mass public to participate in and influence government (Lipari, 1999).

The populist view reflects the optimism of Jefferson, Rousseau, and Aristotle. Adherents include individuals such as the "deliberative democratic theorists" (Cohen, 1989; Gastil & Dillard, 1999), who search for better ways to inform and engage citizens in the democratic process. Populists view citizen participation as credible because they view Western media as highly autonomous. They argue that market systems force the media to consider public needs, wants, and opinions (Curran, 1996a).

Social Constructionist Perspective

This perspective views public opinion as the product of symbolic interactions in society involving language, greatly influenced by political discourse. In the spirit of Machiavelli (the pragmatic perspective), the social constructionist approach views public opinion as malleable and subject to manipulation by those in power. The implication, however, is that people participate in the process: Lavine and Latane (1996) note, "We believe that public opinion is the complex result of nonlinear dynamic processes occurring within the minds of individuals and as a result of social interaction and communication" (p. 56). According to this view, the drive for cognitive consistency interacts with the process of social influence. The emphasis on the symbolic departs from the classical debate, which does not address intrapersonal or psychological dimensions of public opinion. Social constructionists believe that people create their own realities through interacting with others and through co-constructing and living stories. These processes of interaction are reciprocal, reflexive, binding, and long-term in their consequences. Social constructionists view persons in conversation as the raison d'etre for living (Pearce, 1995; Pearce & Cronen, 1980). They believe that the manner in which people communicate can be as important as what they say to each other and that communication has long-term effects that are reflexive in nature. Social constructionists do not believe that one truth exists. Pluralistic in their orientation, they honor the principle of multiple truths and the validity of many cultural traditions. Curious about the world, they believe in participating actively in a quest for greater understanding.

As noted previously, the origins of social constructionism are highly pragmatic, influenced by individuals such as John Dewey (Griffin, 2000), Mead (1934), and Blumler (1972). According to the constructionist perspective, public opinion research is a "mechanism of managed democracy" (Lipari, 1999, p. 86), and political will can become manifest only through political and social discourse. Through symbolic interaction with others, people form their political views and attitudes, which are flexible and sometimes contradictory. Therefore, polls and other opinion research instruments can only capture moments in time, not ultimate truths about what people believe and think. Thus, although public opinion research has a function, this function is limited by the nature of the communication process, which is ongoing, changing, and difficult to capture. The realities of individuals are shaped by their interactions with others in their social universes; thus, no one reality exists. Social constructionists would advocate the concept of multiple publics, each with valid concerns.

In comparing social constructionist theory with the views of the classical pragmatists, it can be stated that, like Machiavelli and Hegel, constructionists recognize the existence of many different publics with varying degrees of influence. These publics have distinct views that, although constantly changing and evolving through the social and political discourse of the day, have the potential to impact on positions of leadership at any given moment in time. This third school also reflects the philosophy of Lippman (1922), who said that we construct "pictures in our heads."

Critical Perspective

Highly pessimistic in its point of view, the critical perspective (also called the "radical functionalist" approach) states that what masquerades as mass opinion, in fact, is elite opinion because the elites (including those in government) manipulate the polls to achieve their own ends. Adherents include individuals such as Habermas (1962/1989), Herman and Chomsky (1988), and Ginsberg (1989). Critical theorists would not agree with Hamilton or Madison that elites should control society; nonetheless, they would argue that elites do exercise control. Curran (1996a) discusses the three strands of what he terms radical functionalism:

> One strand of radical functionalism holds that the political economy of the media—its ownership by corporate business, its links to the state, the socialization of media staff into organizational norms, and the constraints imposed by market distortions, advertising, and the pursuit of profit more generally—all predispose the media to serve dominant interests (Murdock and Golding, 1977; Curran, 1977). Another structuralist-culturalist strand of radical functionalism sees the media as shaped by the dominant culture and power structures of society (Hall, 1986; Hall, Critcher, Jefferson, & Roberts, 1978). A third, more mainstream tradition argues that the structures of control within media organizations intermesh

with those in society (Herman and Chomsky, 1988). But common to all three positions is the conviction that the media tend to sustain dominant social forces in
society. (p. 129)

Proponents of "political economy of the media" believe that monopolistic
control of media is happening on a global, not just national, level. Because
media serve commercial interests, they cannot be independent, they do not
act in the public interest, and they do not reflect the full range of public opinion. Instead of producing consensus, the media produce consent (Herman &
Chomsky, 1988).

Other critics charge that mainstream media tend to reflect the views of official sources and professional communicators while ignoring other sectors of
the population (Page & Tannenbaum, 1996). Philo (1995) claims that media
neglect "whole areas of opinion" while they upgrade or downgrade other areas. Moreover, he notes that broadcast media are undemocratic in their manner of choosing spokespersons, favoring senior civil servants. Finally, he argues that media often use the opinions of low-status individuals to "back up"
the dominant view, including only "brief unsubstantiated" comments from
minorities (p. 183). Carter, Branston, and Allan (1998) discuss the way in
which media tend to disregard the views of women. Others, such as Isaacs
(1998) and Yankelovich (1991), also speak cynically of the yawning gap between mass and elite opinion.

In summary, this school of thought views public opinion research as another manifestation of a drive to manipulate and control the mass public, to-
ken and negative in its implications. If these assertions are accurate, then obviously media monitoring would only illuminate the views of elites and not
those of the mass public. Some critics claim that the views of elites are already overrepresented in data acquired from public opinion polls. Elites, they
say, tend to be more affluent, better informed, and more conservative in their
ideological orientations. Faced with survey questions, they are able to offer
informed opinion on many of the questions compared with the less informed
masses who give "no opinion" or random responses. Thus, "numerically
small publics . . . can significantly influence the frequency marginals of infor-
mation-dependent questions" (Althaus, 1996, p. 3).

Many early adherents to critical traditions have modified their views in recent years. Feminists are among those who have questioned the critical or
radical functionalist philosophy. Recent trends in radical research include
"the reconceptualization of society in more pluralistic terms, the waning of
radical political economy, the stress on source competition, the emphasis on

ambiguity and 'tension' in media texts, the celebration of audience power" (Curran, 1996a, pp. 136-137). Thus, the radical position has moved closer to the populist liberal tradition.

Critical theorists accept some of the ideas embedded in social constructionist thought. For example, they believe that media construct alternate realities that depict the social order in ways that conform to dominant coalitions of power. By including some elements in media depictions and excluding other elements, they construct an erroneous sense of the whole, but audiences accept the depictions as physical and social reality.

Perceived Impact of the Media

The previous philosophical discourse presumes that civic and other leaders feel in control of their issue environments—that they have the power to influence and manipulate public opinion as they wish. In fact, a large body of popular evidence, including the statements of most political and corporate leaders, suggests otherwise. Most authority figures believe that, in reality, they are operating in an environment characterized by lack of control—an environment marked by staggering amounts of information generated by countless sources of questionable identity, increasingly representing global, multiracial, and multicultural constituencies. As early as 1976, Warren Bennis wrote about the unconscious conspiracy faced by leaders who have no time to lead because they are always putting out fires. In particular, authority figures feel threatened by characteristics of new media. The following characteristics draw their attention: its immediacy, its interactive potential, its availability to all levels of society at the same time, and the consequent compression of time available for decision making. Those who would like to be able to influence and control public opinion worry about the tendency of media (old and new) to be drawn to the bizarre, sensational, and dramatic and especially to celebrity figures. They fear the interpretative function of media and the diligence with which journalists act out their historical role as watchdogs of society (Ferguson, 1994).

The immediacy of new media means that the masses can receive information at the same time (or even earlier) than authorities, whereas historically such authority figures held tight control over the dissemination of information. For many centuries, the practices of the Roman Catholic Church exemplified this kind of control. Numerous examples of authoritarian governments (the Roman Empire, China, Russia, and Cuba) also illustrate their obsession with restricting access to information. In such situations, the people at the bottom of the social ladder are held prisoner due to their lack of information. In modern technological society, however, information flows freely, and those at the bottom of the pyramid have direct access to information at the same time as those at the top—sometimes sooner. They also have access to information that may conflict with (or offer an alternative explanation to) "official" statements. In contrast to the "traditional hierarchical model," the "simultaneous access" model holds that decision makers face dramatically reduced time for reflection and decision making (Ferguson & Ferguson, 1988). Constituencies may learn about legislative agendas before government officials have finalized them. Debates over mergers may move into the public arena before they are finalized in corporate boardrooms. Details of a free trade agreement or peace negotiations may become Internet or newspaper headlines before negotiators achieve consensus on wording for the agreements. Media professionals detect incipient issues and disseminate discourse on them; therefore, the public-media interaction sets the policy agenda. In a world characterized by massive information exchanges among corporations, political systems, governments, special publics, and the mass public, decision making becomes incredibly complicated.

Because collapsing of time is the most common characteristic of the new information environment, government leaders often perceive themselves to be in a perpetual state of crisis. Citizens expect their leaders to make almost instantaneous decisions on vital matters. The introduction of e-mail has exacerbated public expectations that responses to queries and concerns should be immediate and personal. Thrust into reactive positions, government leaders and politicians often appear more as "followers" than "leaders."

"Real-time" coverage of events on the Internet, television, and the radio has caused the "float" time between the occurrence of an event and the circulation of information on the event to virtually disappear. In today's environment, information is expandable, portable, leaky, and shareable—difficult to control (Cleveland, 1985). Cameras appear at violent crime scenes before SWAT teams arrive. In the case of the 1999 homicides at Columbine High School in Littleton, Colorado, cameras were in place in time to observe the maneuvering of police into strategic positions and the exodus of terrified teenagers from the school. The interactive potential in new media also generates a certain level of discomfort among authority figures. The possibility of communicating in real time with the president and top advisers creates the expectation that this communication should occur on a regular basis. The emergence of cable technology and the Internet has created the possibility for, and interest in, instantaneous referenda and a new dimension of participatory democracy. Those who have little faith in the wisdom of the masses believe that collective ignorance could soon govern the daily workings of government.

Another threatening characteristic of media is their tendency to be drawn to the outrageous, the bizarre, and the dramatic. Media organizations operate for a profit, and making that profit means garnering audiences. The unusual, the sensational, and the controversial sell newspapers and television programs. Ferguson (1994) notes,

> If pro-lifers position themselves before an abortion clinic and thrust baby gifts at women entering the clinic, the event will almost surely be televised. The picture of a young widow, at the grave side of her husband killed in military action, will receive preference over a less emotional depiction. Images of starving children in Somalia and the bleeding victims of an airline crash have the stark dramatic quality that television demands. (p. 351)

Visually interesting settings receive preference over uninteresting settings. In the same way as for television, the National Inquirer, USA Today, and the Daily Mirror encourage their reporters to cover the stories that will titillate the readers and expose the foibles of human nature. News and entertainment media like to tell stories; therefore, they are drawn to cover events that involve human drama, such as the bombing in Oklahoma City, the wrongful conviction of a man for rape or murder, or an event involving assisted suicide. The presence of a celebrity also increases the chances that media will cover an event or issue. Airplanes are rerouted thousands of times every day, but if the president of the United States is aboard an aircraft that has to vary its landing plans, the event is newsworthy. Sometimes, this ability to garner attention works to the advantage of those in power; at other times, leaders cringe at the thought that they will face the cameras once again.

Groups in positions of power also fear the interpretative power of media. Just as media set agendas, they act to package opinion on topics of interest. Immediately following a presidential debate, State of the Union address, or update on the war in Yugoslavia, media analysts assess the performance of spokespersons. They interpret the statements and repackage them for public consumption. Leaders, who would like to speak directly to key publics, are often frustrated by media's interventionist techniques. They complain that everything they say is restated, reworded, analyzed, and dissected by those who mediate and package public opinion. They argue that what remains of their words, in the end, is the journalist's interpretation. Their complaints are made more real by the tendency of television to use voice-overs to fit excerpts within time constraints and to compensate for technical problems such as poor audio.

The watchdog function of media also makes authority figures uneasy. Media professionals champion the public's right to know, whereas governments claim the right to withhold information for the public good and corporations argue for their right to guard trade secrets. Although some would argue that media are part of the establishment, a classical theory of the press puts journalists in the role of guardians of democratic society. In this role, they often perceive themselves to be in conflict with the establishment as they seek to expose fraud, scandal, and corruption. In this capacity, media tend to stress the negative.

Television also has other characteristics (the ability to bypass language filters, subjective camera, and perceived selling power) that create uneasiness in executive circles. The visual nature of television makes it difficult to control access to the medium. Whereas radio and newspapers require the translation of ideas into the local dialect or official language of the country (a situation that implies a certain level of control), television bypasses those cultural filters. The dominant characteristic of television is its visual property. Even without knowledge of the language, people can access the products of television. The international outcry in the early 1970s regarding the direct broadcast satellite had its roots in this ability of television to bypass local authority figures and to convey)information across cultural boundaries. The ongoing debate within Canada over issues of cultural sovereignty reflects this same sensitivity to the threat posed by American television and cable signals. English Canada is far more paranoid than French Canada regarding the transmission of signals from the United States to Canada.

At the same time that authority figures cannot control access to television or how people process the information, they cannot control the highly subjective and selective decisions made by camera operators, editors, and directors. Like the political cartoonist, television caricatures and demystifies authority figures by concentrating on some of their characteristics and ignoring others. Television portrayed former President Gerald Ford as bumbling and inept, falling down airplane steps or tripping over his own feet. Ford, however, was a trained athlete, a former college football player. Media depicted former Canadian Prime Minister Joe Clark as equally awkward and incompetent, losing his luggage when traveling abroad and having a near miss with a bayonet that had been unsheathed for a welcoming ceremony at a military event.

Those in positions of influence also worry about the perceived selling power of television. Legislators, for example, know that constituents "back home" will see and evaluate their performance, and they believe that television will set these standards for assessment. This impression can lead to an emphasis on "looking good" as opposed to performing their jobs well. Politicians perceive that television sells images in the same way that it sells soap, toothpaste, and deodorant. As Terkildsen, Schnell, and Ling (1998) noted,

> Successful political players must work within the known set of media-imposed constraints. They need to understand media's news criteria and tailor their messages accordingly. That means providing drama and good visuals, simplifying arguments, communicating through events, and generally fitting conventional news formats. (p. 57)

The fastest growing medium, the Internet, has other threatening characteristics, leading governments and many citizens to want to regulate it. The increasingly synchronous nature of communications over the Internet means that messages are sent and received almost instantaneously. Not only are speed and adaptability "of the essence," according to Juniper (1999), but also the medium is "shadowy, flexible and anarchistic" in its potential. Juniper argues that "the hierarchical structures of most bureaucratic entities place them at a disadvantage on the digital field." Many on-line campaigns, such as the Zapatista campaign (initiated by the natives of southeast Mexico), are composed of "like-minded activist cells across the net operating independently from each other."

For all the previously discussed reasons, governments and corporations monitor media (old and new) on an ongoing, often daily, basis. They do not believe that any modern institution can ignore the role of public opinion in society, and they hold an equally strong belief that media have the power to influence that opinion in direct and indirect ways. In an effort to cope, politicians and top executives often create pseudoenvironments that give the appearance of reality, whether in the form of town halls, television debates, or "infomercials" (Boorstin, 1961; Nimmo & Combs, 1990). They also engage in systematic and routine tracking of corporate issues that could pose a threat to the organization. They commission surveys and polls and track the latest discussions on the Internet. They attend association meetings and monitor newsletters and the community press. In other words, they spend much of their time—and more than a small part of their budgets—trying to "second-guess" public opinion. Chapter 2 discusses some of the specifics concerning how they accomplish this task.

Conclusion

The classical debate continues over whether the public has a role to play in affairs of state. In the spirit of philosophers such as Plato, Hobbes, and Hegel, some do not agree that the public is sufficiently informed or motivated to make a useful contribution to government. They certainly do not believe that governments should check daily public opinion polls or referenda to decide their agendas. To support this view, they cite studies that demonstrate the low levels of literacy and low levels of political knowledge. They say that members of the public are so ill informed that they cannot possibly know what is best for the country. They also argue that when leaders look to public opinion (as manifested in surveys, focus groups, the press, and Internet news groups), they become followers rather than leaders. These critics view government by polls as an inappropriate way to decide affairs of state. The advocates of full participation in matters of government, however, argue that decisions made without knowledge of public opinion will represent elite opinion, often influenced by lobby or special interest groups. They contend that a one-way flow of information, funneled from government to the people, is not appropriate. More appropriate, they believe, is an exchange of information that heeds feedback and seeks to accommodate public opinion. The latter view is more in line with the position of philosophers such as Aristotle, Locke, Rousseau, and Jefferson, who had a greater faith in the masses.

The modern debate has added another chorus. Populists believe that public opinion research makes a valuable contribution by ensuring the full participation of citizens in government. Critical theorists believe that public opinion research does not really reflect the "public" but rather the elites who govern. Therefore, the exercise is deceptive and useless. The social constructionists claim that manipulation does occur, and this manipulation occurs through symbolic discourse. In other words, the media build reality for their publics.

Government leaders (and their corporate peers) are not paying very much attention to the academic debate because they are too busy reacting to yesterday's crisis and trying to predict tomorrow's crisis. Public expectations have increased, whereas time available for decision making and responding has decreased. The ability of people at all levels of society to access information in real time, the interactive potential in new media, the routine interplay between media and public agendas, and other dominant characteristics of today's media environment can create the perception that leaders have been invited to a party that was planned without their involvement. Authority figures find that they have been thrust into the position of follower rather than leader, and they often blame media for this loss of control. In the current media environment, politicians, government executives, and chief executive officers can no longer depend on their traditional gatekeepers to filter and control information because new media bypass these gatekeepers. Whereas political and corporate advisers carefully plan and create the content of communication products intended for public consumption (speeches, press releases, etc.), they face enormous difficulties when they try to abridge information or restrict its flow.

In brief, modern government and corporate leaders would likely disagree that they have a high level of control over mass or elite opinion. Like the most diligent academics, top bureaucrats and corporation chiefs scan the current literature for panaceas to the current situation, even though they know that change is taking place at a pace that they cannot hope to shape in any definitive way. They understand that the top-heavy bureaucratic structures, designed at the time of Weber, cannot compete with the light, effortless movements of whole populations of people riding on the backs of new technologies. Many corporate leaders and boards of directors suspect that they are equally out of control as commerce saturates the Internet. Chapter 9 evaluates these fears against the academic debate over media effects.

2

Establishing Intelligence Systems to Capture Public Opinion

In the twentieth century, our society has moved toward the empowerment of many different groups that previously had no audible voice—women, seniors, and ethnic and racial minorities. Empowered groups expect to participate in decision making, and participation implies that organizations listen to, and understand, the opinions and needs of these diverse voices. Taking a populist approach, this chapter discusses the importance of listening to key publics, sources that feed an environmental intelligence system, three common components of such systems, and approaches to setting up the intelligence system. In the context of this chapter, the term *environmental intelligence systems* refers to systems established to gather data on the opinion environment.

Importance of Listening to Public Opinion

As early as the 1980s, surveys indicated that the CEOs of many large companies were spending as much as 40% to 50% of their time obtaining information from, and interacting with, the external environment (Buchholz, Evans, & Wagley, 1985). This trend has progressed decidedly since that time. A recognition of the need to become more client centered has led organizations to become more responsive to the demands of a broad range of constituencies (vendors, competitors, shareholders, employees, customers, and others) and to institutionalize opportunities for "continuous learning," a buzzword used in recent years to refer to the "learning" organization (Redding & Catalanello, 1994). This kind of organization strives to stay abreast of the latest political, economic, technological, and social developments as well as trends in public opinion. On the basis of such acquired intelligence, the organization responds to the needs of its constituencies.

Some claim, however, that governments and others are listening more to those with influence and power and less to members of the mass public (Entman & Rojecki, 1993). Yankelovich (1991) described the problem as follows:

> The fateful decisions are made in Washington, in corporate boardrooms, on Wall Street, in state legislatures, and in city halls. They are shaped by economic experts, military experts, scientific experts, trade experts, PR experts, media experts. Less and less are they shaped by the public. (p. 2)

Increasingly, government relies on these experts in its policy making. Different value sets, levels of knowledge, lifestyles, and modes of expression, however, separate experts in science, foreign policy, finance, civil service, business and industry, and other specialized areas from the mass public. For example, Isaacs (1998) discovered a notable discrepancy between elite and mass opinion in two different situations: the massacre of Chinese citizens at Tiananmen Square and the attempted coup against Gorbachev by anti-reform communists. Isaacs concluded that the mass public does not follow elite opinion on foreign policy questions.

Moreover, although governments argue that they conduct polls to determine the needs of their citizenry, most public opinion polls fail to differentiate between "top-of-the-mind, offhand views" (mass opinion) and "thoughtful, considered judgments" (public judgment) (Yankelovich, 1991, p. xii). A variety of tools—ranging from consultation to media analysis, focus groups, and surveys—must be used to reach valid conclusions on the public's "considered judgments." Making this distinction between "offhand" public views and "considered judgments" explains the seeming volatility of public opinion on many major societal issues.

Yankelovich (1991) argues that this gap between the leadership elite and the mass public is the "weak link" in the democratic system: "But history shows—a lesson that most public officials have to learn and relearn—that to move ahead on important national issues without public support is to invite being undermined in the long run" (p. 117). Effective intelligence-gathering systems can help to ensure that the government knows as much about the views of the mass public as it knows about the views of elite opinion leaders.

The same is true for business, in which the use of intelligence support systems constitutes a necessity, not a luxury (Gilad, 1991; Hamel & Prahalad, 1996). Organizations without an intelligence function tend to ignore the information needs of top management. In such situations, executives charged with writing the strategic plan make their decisions without the proper data. Alternatively, they undertake the gathering and analysis of information on their own initiative, without the specialized skills required to collect and collate the intelligence.

Sources That Feed the System

Many different information sources can provide intelligence on public opinion (Figure 2.1). The organization can consult media representatives, special interest groups, internal stakeholders, and others. Businesses study media trends to determine responses of key publics to policies, environmental practices, products, and services. Governments commission studies to identify relevant characteristics of the opinion climate into which a new policy will enter or attempt to anticipate responses to new legislation. Both business and government organizations track developments on contentious issues. By *issues*, I mean fundamental policy questions that confront an organization. Analysts study correspondence to isolate areas of client dissatisfaction. Large corporations, in turn, track shifts in government policies to identify threats and opportunities. The business of the organization determines which sources are consulted. Economic considerations and the will to know the full range of opinions on a topic or issue typically determine how many sources are consulted.

A survey that collected responses from 15 directors of public affairs, vice presidents, and CEOs from *Fortune* 500 companies (Ferguson, 1993) showed that virtually every organization monitored magazines and newspapers. Ongoing studies by Robinson and Levy (1996) suggest that newspapers remain "America's premier source of public affairs information" even though members of the public think that they get most of their news from television (p. 135). Therefore, this emphasis on monitoring the print news media may be well justified. At least 80% of the respondents in Ferguson's (1993) study also consulted business and financial reports, newsletters, television, and books. Seventy percent relied on conference proceedings and academic jour-

Business/Industry	Special Interest Groups	Elected Representatives
Academic journals & conferences Advertisements Annual financial reports Brochures Business & financial journals Corporate magazines Correspondence Employee newsletters Hotlines International data bases Internet (news groups, web pages) Interpersonal contacts (clients, consultants, competitors, suppliers, etc.) Newspapers Patent applications Press releases & press conferences Research reports Sales reports Speeches Technical journals & conferences Trade journals and shows TV & radio documentaries & news reports Wall Street trading reports	Access to information requests Advertising Consultations Correspondence Ethnic media Group profiles generated by commercial firms Internet (news groups, web pages) Interviews with spokespersons Letters to the editor News & feature articles News releases Newsletters originating with interest groups Position papers Presentations to House & Senate committees Records of lobbyist efforts Reports of conferences & meetings Speeches Surveys Talk shows (TV & radio)	Administrative decisions Comments in State legislatures Congressional representatives Court decisions Household newsletter Internet (web pages) Interviews Media Records of House & Senate debates Speeches Voting records of Senators & **Organized Labor** Correspondence Court cases Internet (web pages, news groups) Interviews Newsletters Print & electronic media Speeches Trade magazines
Mass Public	**Government**	**Elite Opinion Leaders**
Census reports Correspondence Court cases Customer & client service reports Evaluation & audit reports Focus groups Internet (news groups, web pages) Letters to the editor Print & electronic media Public consultation reports Public inquiry records Records of complaints Speakers' bureau reports Surveys & polls	Annual reports Background papers Briefing notes Cabinet records Employee survey reports Executive agenda Internet (web pages) Interviews News releases & press conferences Publications Requests for access to information Speeches State of the Union address Strategic plans	Association meetings Briefs to government committees Correspondence Internet (web pages, news groups) Interviews Journal articles Letters to the editor Print and electronic media Profiles generated by commercial firms Reports by think tanks Speeches Surveys Talk shows

Figure 2.1. Sources of Intelligence (Reproduced With Permission From Ferguson, 1994, pp. 34-35)

nals. Approximately 60% referred to records of House and Senate debates, trend-monitoring reports, radio, surveys, correspondence, and futurist journals. Approximately 50% consulted "think tank" reports, focus group reports, opinion leader reports, telephone inquiries, public consultation reports, and interest group profiles and interviews. Forty percent noted that they study records of complaints, court cases, and lobbyist reports. Twenty-five percent said that they examine records of Cabinet decisions. At 10%, films and theater ranked low on the list of sources consulted by *Fortune*

500 respondents. (A current version of this survey would include a question on monitoring of the Internet.)

An additional study of Canadian federal government communicators mirrored the results obtained in the United States (Ferguson, 1993), and an Australian study found that most public relations practitioners monitor their environments through a wide variety of means, including expert panels, consultative committees, industry associations and publications, and government bodies (Walker, 1994). International databases can also be an important source of intelligence for multinational corporations.

Some criticize the tendency of organizations, engaged in a search for environmental intelligence, to monitor mainstream media such as newspapers and magazines to the exclusion of other kinds of media. According to Nelson (1984), mass media "carefully and consistently monitor professional and scientific journals in search of new stories . . . and this symbiotic relationship is perhaps the most neglected factor contributing to ongoing media coverage of issues" (p. 57). A proactive approach to issues management would dictate that organizations monitor the same sources that media monitor. Important sources of information on emerging issues can be films, theater, fiction, scientific and professional journals, and alternative media. New ideas often surface in works of fiction and art. Throughout history, writers, filmmakers, and other creative artists have been subject to great restrictions when they operate in authoritarian states. Almost definitionally, artists invent new ways of "seeing." Thus, many issues surface in television movies and films before the mainstream news media cover them. From the time of Archie Bunker to the present day, filmmakers have pricked the social conscience of viewers by raising taboo topics, such as incest, rape, domestic violence, and youth suicides.

Another important medium, which has gained in popularity in recent years, is talk radio. Roth (1993) discusses the ways in which native Canadians used radio to garner public support in their standoff against authorities at Oka, Quebec, and Herbst (1995) and Jones (1998) describe the role of talk radio as a vehicle for public discourse in the United States. The number of talk radio stations increased from 200 in 1988 to more than 1,000 in 1998. Talk radio programs garner 15% of the radio audience, and talk radio "trails only country music as the nation's most pervasive format" (Barker, 1998, p. 83). Nine talk show hosts ran for local or state offices in the 1994 election (Davis, 1997). Rush Limbaugh's syndicated show is broadcast to more than 20 million people each week through a network of 700 stations. Barker describes the potential influence of this medium as follows:

> Mainstream media sources have given talk radio credit for the Republican land-
> slide in the 1994 midterm elections. Furthermore, the freshmen Republicans of
> the 104th Congress have dubbed themselves the "dittohead caucus." . . . The
> White House has even hinted that talk radio may have influenced the Oklahoma
> City bombing. (pp. 83-84)

President Clinton has both used and spoken against talk radio programs. Barker concludes that Limbaugh's assault on Clinton's health care reform package may have played a role in its failure.

Another study examines the role of talk radio in forcing nominee Zoe Baird to withdraw her name from consideration for the office of U.S. attorney general. Despite revelations that Baird hired illegal aliens and failed to comply with social security regulations, mainstream media predicted her confirmation. Members of key publics, who did not agree, expressed their point of view in angry calls to radio talk shows and senators. This "outpouring of public outrage . . . turned the tide against the nominee" (Page & Tannenbaum, 1996, p. 33). In this case, as in a growing number of other instances, members of affected publics found a voice in alternative, not mainstream, media.

Television talk shows such as CNN's *Larry King Live* and *Crossfire* have also gained in popularity. Early morning variety shows such as *Good Morning America* and *Today* and investigatory programs such as *20/20* and *Dateline* are other examples of television shows that combine treatment of political and popular topics. In 1995, presidential hopeful Bob Dole cohosted *Saturday Night Live. Oprah, Montel Williams,* and *Geraldo* also address many social and political issues within a predominantly entertainment format (Davis, 1997). One study found that the audiences of radio and television talk shows tend to be more conservative in their ideological orientations (Pan & Kosicki, 1997).

Many candidates in the 1992 presidential election chose to reach Americans through talk shows and tabloid programs, electronic town hall meetings, toll-free telephone numbers, and computer bulletin boards (Weaver, 1994). As the campaign progressed, it was clear that mainstream media, the candidates, their advisers, journalists, pollsters, academics, and other interested citizens were discussing the issues that had surfaced first in nontraditional media. The highest turnout of voters in a presidential election since 1968 (nearly 56% of the voting population) added credence to the possibility that new media had made a difference in levels of voter engagement. No other presidential election in the twentieth century had such a voter turnout. Of 142 participants in a 1992 panel, none said that they had learned about the candidates from news commentators, analysts, or pundits. Instead, they mentioned television talk shows, early morning shows, and shows sponsored by the candidates (Sandell, Mattley, Evarts, Lengel, & Ziyati, 1993).

Hayes (1985) said that poor monitoring can be "not acquiring information on significant subjects, getting incorrect information, or failing to update frequently enough" (p. 30). Poor monitoring can also imply not looking at the right sources of information. An Internet discussion cited J. Lynn Reed (1999), campaign consultant for Democratic hopeful Bill Bradley, as saying

> e-mail, chat groups, and web sites may not replace the coffee social in New Hampshire's presidential primary campaigns. But candidates increasingly look to reach voters through the Internet. Presidential hopefuls are using web sites to recruit and organize volunteers, solicit donations, and discuss issues more than they did during the 1996 campaign. (p. 4)

He noted that Republican Gary Bauer was the only 1996 candidate without a web site. Al Gore was the last candidate for the Year 2000 election to bring his campaign on-line (April 1999).

The publications of activist groups can offer insights into their motives, needs, and demands. In the case of environmental protests against an American firm that was trying to establish commercial operations in Belize (formerly British Honduras), activists bypassed mainstream media to communicate through newsletters and specialized communication networks (Anderson, 1992). According to Grunig (1977), highly involved publics do not depend on traditional mass media channels for information or communication purposes. Instead, they rely on "high-involvement" media, including "specialized business publications, published social reports, or dialogue sessions with members of active publics" (Anderson, 1992, p. 155). Many bypass media entirely, concentrating on direct mail campaigns, letter writing, personal visits, and telephone calls to members of "attentive" publics (McCombs, Einsiedel, & Weaver, 1991). Juniper (1999), who is currently studying the ways in which the native peoples in Canada and abroad have created "networks of resistance," found that "through information warfare, small, independent actors have created networks which enable them to circumvent traditional purveyors of news such as television and newspapers and reach hundreds, thousands, or even millions of people." Interestingly, however, a study of USENET communications (5,611 messages) found that liberal or left-wing political groups were, on the whole, less active and less organized than other groups (Hill & Hughes, 1997).

Internet communication illustrates the *strength of weak ties* (Granovetter, 1973; Liu & Duff, 1972; Rogers, 1973), which refers to the idea that information spreads through the larger population through weak, not strong, links. The term *links* refers to the ties that bind groups together. Interlocking personal networks (in which an individual interacts with friends who also interact with each other) involve strong linkages. Although strong links support effective communication within the group, they act as obstacles to the spread of information outside the group. More conducive to the spread of information is the radial personal network, in which "an individual interacts directly with friends who do not interact with each other" (Rogers & Agarwala-Rogers, 1976, p. 115). The radial networks established through the Internet are highly conducive to the spread of information because the ties are weak, with frequent changes of membership, anonymous participants who often hide their identity, and intermittent contact over varying periods of time. Although Internet buddies occasionally meet in person, the majority probably never have a face-to-face encounter with other network members. In this regard, the Internet is perfectly suited to a population that is highly mobile and transient. Monitoring such networks, however, poses great challenges to public opinion analysts, who are more accustomed to studying interlocking personal networks created by more traditional activist groups. It is much more possible, with interlocking networks, to know the source of critical comment, to consult, and to negotiate.

On-line databases provide important new sources of information for those who track the development of issues. Thomsen (1995) found that issues management groups relied on the databases more than any other group. Masterson (1992) describes several databases that are useful in monitoring, and Hauss (1995) discusses how to use the Internet to track news events. Research directors often complain that budgetary constraints make it necessary for organizations to rely on relatively inexpensive, easily available information (e.g., newspapers and magazine articles) rather than more costly information sources (e.g., surveys, consultation reports, focus groups, and monitoring of the Internet). Even when government officials realize that media do not accurately predict public opinion, they often give priority to these information sources because they know that it takes a great deal of time to construct and administer surveys and focus groups and to analyze Internet discourse. Typically, bureaucrats and government leaders want to know what is happening today, not yesterday (McCombs et al., 1991). Also, politicians and CEOs often ask communicators to concentrate their efforts on high-visibility media such as newspapers and television because they are concerned about image-related questions. Ironically, however, organizations that monitor only mainstream media will spend much of their time in reactive mode.

Some scholars (Walker, 1994) argue that our definition of *research* needs to be enlarged to include the day-to-day activities of calling colleagues in other organizations, reading newspapers and magazines, attending conferences and association meetings, visiting regional offices, and accessing corporate knowledge held in files and records. Important information sources reside within the organization (Robert, 1990). The president of one research and analysis firm said that more than half of the competitive intelligence required by companies already exists within organizations. Others place the figure between 75% and 90% (Day, 1992). Both employees who have been with the company for a long time and those who have worked with other companies are important internal sources. Senior managers and executives who are in frequent contact with government and industry leaders can be excellent sources of information. Consultants, who usually collect information from inside the organization before they go outside, recognize the value of these internal sources. After adding some information from the outside, they sell the package back to the organization (Roush, 1991).

How does one obtain this information? Some of the most valuable information comes from personal meetings and networking. CEOs say that they favor face-to-face meetings (Pavlik, Vastyan, & Maher, 1990). Ten of 15 respondents who participated in a survey of *Fortune* 500 companies said that they had found informal meetings to be on a par with surveys and formal interviews in generating useful information (Ferguson, 1993). An Australian study found that most survey respondents considered informal networking, interviews, and observation to be important sources of information (Walker, 1994). David Culver, then-president of Alcan Aluminum, Ltd., said that multinational corporations also depend on informal communication to convey major messages of the organization. Employees say that they value interpersonal compared to other sources, and they prefer their information to come from top managers and other official sources instead of from coworkers (Cameron & McCollum, 1993; Reddin, 1998). An information management review found that bureaucrats in the Privy Council Office, a central agency in the Canadian government, had deliberately avoided formalizing some of their communication channels in favor of the informal exchanges that occur on a daily basis.

Aguilar's (1967) benchmark study found that personal sources (whether located inside or outside the company) can provide up to 70% of the strategic information required by an organization. Important information can come from unexpected personal sources: a conversation on a plane, a chance meeting in the cafeteria, or a casual encounter with a friend or neighbor. Confirming this point, a survey of *Fortune* 500 companies found that approximately half of the respondents claimed to have received useful information from such chance encounters with people (Ferguson, 1993). Classical studies of informal communication have found that the most important source of unpublished information is rumors. Davis (1953) concludes that rumors are fast, highly discriminating in their patterns of movement, and often accurate. Corning's experience with setting up an environmental intelligence system confirms what many other studies have found: The percentage of rumors that are accurate may be more than 70% (Roush, 1991).

Cosmopolites serve an especially important information-gathering function in organizations. The term *cosmopolites* refers to people who act as boundary spanners. They stand at the periphery of the organization in positions that allow them to pass information between internal and external constituencies and to represent the "perceptions, expectations, and ideas of each side to the other" (Friedmann & Podolny, 1992, p. 29). Cosmopolites function at the top and at the bottom of most organizations. The receptionist in a medical office, a door-to-door salesperson, and the interoffice courier all act as cosmopolites, serving as the "open doors and windows of an organization, allowing for cross-ventilation of new ideas" (Rogers & Agarwala-Rogers, 1976, p. 140). The boundary-spanning nature of marketing and sales departments means that they are rich information sources (Cespedes, 1990). Likewise, the executive who joins a golf club, the politician who speaks at a banquet dinner, and the bureaucrat who attends a convention in a distant city act as cosmopolites. As boundary spanners, they not only give information on the organization to stakeholders but also obtain feedback from these groups and individuals on their organization's performance (Dozier, Grunig, & Grunig, 1995).

Scanning systems incorporate individuals such as salespersons, purchasing agents, and professionals who attend conferences (e.g., scientists and engineers) into their information networks. In the normal course of their work, these individuals acquire new and useful information (Martino, 1985). A consultant is another kind of cosmopolite, whose association with the organization allows for the entry of an outside viewpoint. Although most organizations value input from executives or consultants who act as cosmopolites, they rarely attach the same credibility to information derived from lower-level cosmopolites. Classical studies, however, confirm that the most important strategic information flow in organizations is bottom-up (Aguilar, 1967). Kanter (1997) provides an extensive discussion of the role of business cosmopolitans.

This finding suggests that organizations should rely more heavily on sources situated lower in the hierarchy. In this spirit, Frito-Lay management encourages service and salespeople "to pass information upwards, rather than just be recipients" (Day, 1992, p. 47). Honda, NEC, Sharp, Sony, and others have established elaborate formal and informal intelligence-gathering networks (Kodama, 1992). The marketing director at Banc One supervises an extensive network of employees who regularly scan the marketplace for signs of change (Fuld, 1991). In another system that took 4 years to construct, an individual in a major plastics manufacturing firm operates at the hub of a 500-member electronic mail network. This person receives up to 30 messages a week, which he summarizes and publishes in a monthly newsletter. He also maintains a data bank of responses (Fuld, 1991). Redding and Catalanello (1994) argue that organizations should encourage all employees to become boundary spanners who assist with environmental scanning and information-gathering tasks. Organizations should also promote direct contacts between customers and employees (especially employees who work behind the scenes), attendance of organization members at trade shows and conferences, and the establishment of strategic alliances with customers, suppliers, and competitors.

Organizations with little upward communication flow are at risk of losing vital environmental intelligence, gained at lower levels of the organization. In a properly organized system, one person (working part-time) can coordinate the collection of information from other people, and computers can assist in the task of recording information and identifying patterns (Martino, 1985).

The organization can learn the opinions of its members through a variety of techniques, including surveys, interviews, newsletters, corporate magazines, hotlines, suggestion boxes, and web sites (Redding & Catalanello, 1994). One interviewee in Walker's (1994) study noted that corporate files can tell a story "of budgets, successes, failures, cooperation, stonewalling, etc." (p. 153). Results achieved in previous communication campaigns can yield important insights regarding how internal and external stakeholders reacted.

Components to Environmental Intelligence Systems

Any useful environmental intelligence system includes three functions: scanning, monitoring, and trend analysis and forecasting. The term *scanning* refers to gathering of new signals from the environment (e.g., identifying emerging issues). *Monitoring* refers to tracking previously identified issues. Using the analogy of radar, scanning involves broad sweeps of the early warning radar, and monitoring entails a telescopic examination of whatever has been spotted on radar (Meng, 1992). Whereas scanning is future oriented, monitoring is present oriented (Forbes, 1992). In contrast, the term *forecasting* refers to an organization's attempt to project "a scenario of the terrain that lies beyond its monitoring and scanning capacities" (Gollner, 1983, p. 128).

Scanning and monitoring activities can be carried out in an irregular, periodic, or continuous way (Fahey & King, 1977). Reactive in nature, *irregular* systems respond to environmentally created crises. Focusing on specific short-term problems, individuals in such systems rarely identify or evaluate environmental trends. Environmental analyses carried out in irregular systems are often ad hoc, responding to some immediate situation. These analyses tend to be retrospective in nature, making them most useful for tactical rather than strategic planning. Organizations using these systems often lack strategic planning cultures. *Periodic* (regular) systems differ in degree, rather than in kind, from irregular systems. Although they draw on the past, they focus on the current situation. Participants in these scanning and monitoring systems often carry out annual reviews of the environment. They attempt to identify current issues and to delineate alternative choices of action. In this sense, periodic systems have a proactive element: They anticipate the near future. *Continuous* systems differ from both irregular and periodic systems. Their focus is broad. They shift from identifying possible problem areas in the environment to locating opportunities. Continuous systems draw on experts with eclectic backgrounds. Analysts monitor many different environments, including political, regulatory, and competitive. They do not restrict themselves to monitoring specific events. In other words, the approach is systems oriented. In a continuous system, the time span brought into consideration may vary from long to futuristic. Whereas issues management teams in periodic systems restrict themselves to issues likely to mature in the next 18 to 36 months, those working in continuous systems extend their focus of interest to 5 or more years.

Justification for this longer term approach can be found in studies that indicate it takes 8 to 15 years for a need or an idea to become law. Five steps intervene between the seeding of the idea and the passing of legislation: acquiring membership support, seeking media attention, gaining prominent endorsements, obtaining a government study or investigation, and introducing the idea to the legislative process. Scanning and monitoring teams in continuous systems track ideas from their seeding to their final development. Most experts agree that environmental analysis systems should not operate in spurts: "Data is [sic] like a shooting star: visible one moment, invisible the next. Corporations cannot assume that the competitor is going to reveal his hand during the strategic planning cycle, when an intensive research effort takes place" (Fuld, 1991, pp. 15-16). A survey of 15 *Fortune* 500 companies found that 2 had irregular systems, 8 had periodic systems, and 5 had continuous systems (Ferguson, 1993).

Scanning for Emerging Issues

Environmental intelligence systems pick up signals (sometimes "weak" signals) from the larger environment, analyze the signals' significance for the organization, track the most relevant of these signals, and forecast trends (Ansoff, 1975). Few changes in the environment occur spontaneously. They start as ideas, which eventually obtain public expression in the press, radio, television, university conferences, and scientific journals. Scanning involves a way of picking up early hints of change from media or other sources (Aguilar, 1967). The purpose of environmental scanning is "not to foretell accurately the future but to plot the issues which are most likely to have an impact on the company and be prepared to cope with them when they arise" (Preble, 1978, p. 14). For example, many single-issue groups, still in the early stages of organization, will be influential years from now. Divorced fathers, older Americans, grandparents who have been denied access to their grandchildren, and societies against genetic engineering currently have relatively little influence. Evidence suggests, however, that they will be powerful lobbies in the future. In the past, gay and lesbian groups had little credibility with legislators and employers when they argued for spousal benefits. Their voices have grown much louder and their demands more strident in recent years. Many employers and governments have begun to act on these demands. Millions of people now belong to thousands of activist organizations, and studies have documented significant growth in recent years in the numbers of groups aligned against business (Pattakos, 1992). Some caution that even the smallest activist group can threaten the viability of a major corporation (Mintzberg, 1983). The successful boycott against Nestle in the 1980s (a protest against the sale of infant formula to Third World countries) illustrates this power (Anderson, 1992). An increasing number of activist groups have demanded that corporate goals complement societal goals. Davis (1995) argues that "a group's real power should be measured by its skill at defining and redefining an evolving issue to its advantage as circumstances warrant" (p. 29).

Scanning systems concentrate on identifying, at an early stage in their development, issues with growth potential. Weiner, Edrich, and Brown, based in New York City, established one of the best known scanning systems. This Trend Analysis Program was designed for the insurance industry. The system depends on a network of scanners in the organization (Brown, 1979). These volunteer scanners assume responsibility for reading, on a regular basis, one or more publications. The relative ease of using print sources means that scanning typically relies most heavily on these sources. In reading the publications, which range from the *Wall Street Journal* to *Omni* or the *Futurist,* scanners search for articles that meet certain criteria. These criteria vary from organization to organization. Sometimes, the scanners also include conference proceedings, academic papers, books, television shows, films, and plays in their reading or viewing materials. Publications chosen for examination can include both trade and specialized magazines. An organization may scan as many as 100 or more sources. Typically, the publications represent four different areas: science and technology, social sciences, business and economics, and politics and government.

Scanners prepare abstracts of the articles, conference proceedings, books, or films. After adding their personal comments, they submit the abstracts to an analysis committee that is composed of middle managers. Committee members examine the abstracts for information that could affect future decisions of the organization. When they synthesize the material, they retain the most interesting, relevant, and novel information. They distribute summaries of their findings to the scanners, other organizational members who have a need for the information, and a steering committee of senior managers or executives. These upper-level managers have the authority to decide future organizational actions or policies related to specific programs or operations. From the point of view of issues management, these executives can decide to track some issues, request in-depth analysis of others, or put some issues on the back burner. Consulting firms (e.g., Weiner, Edrich, and Brown) provide other scanning services, which supplement the efforts of organizational scanners. Consultants generate monthly reports based on information gleaned from a core list of up to 50 publications. A survey of *Fortune* 500 companies found that one fifth of the respondents had hired outside firms to report on a standardized list of publications (Ferguson, 1993).

Dividing up the environment for purposes of scanning increases the likelihood that an organization will pick up and decode signals in the environment. When issues have more than one dimension (e.g., political, economic, or technological), specialists from different areas of an organization come together to understand their potential interaction. For example, in what way will current economic trends influence the political aspects of an issue? What will be the impact of the new digital technologies on social uses of television or buying habits? How will demographic trends influence the real estate industry? Scanning creates an opportunity for people to view issues from a broader organizational perspective, to look beyond the limits of individual responsibility. This engagement allows the scanner "momentary entry into the otherwise closed policy circles of the firm, and the opportunity to experience a breadth of perspective denied to all but a few peers" (Oxelheim & Wihlborg, 1991, p. 293). This expanded perspective can motivate participants to put aside the biases that come with membership in a business unit or government department.

A scanning unit dedicated to the gathering of environmental intelligence (including public opinion) should include communication specialists, economists, business and financial analysts, social scientists, environmental experts, and technologists. Some desirable characteristics include strong methodological skills and knowledge in content analysis, economic and financial analysis, trend analysis and extrapolation (including patent trend analysis, portfolio analysis, and competitor analysis), time series estimation, scenario generation and strategy simulations, paths and tree construction, technology assessment, market research methods, and techniques employed in interviews and group dynamics (Millett & Leppanen, 1991). Scanners must be able to recognize crossover relevance to developments in different areas. The requirements for functioning as a scanner include energy, flexibility, and openness to change.

Monitoring

Many people use the terms scanning and monitoring interchangeably. In fact, few organizations have institutionalized scanning systems. Many more have relatively well-developed monitoring systems whereby they track issues over time using methodologies such as public opinion surveys, content analysis of press coverage, and focus group testing. Organizations try to identify the responses of key publics to organizational initiatives or to new products, services, policies, legislative proposals, or "trial balloons" floated by governments. Sometimes, organizations want to know public reaction to a crisis event (e.g., a product recall, accusations of deceptive advertising, fraud charges, or other scandal). They want to know about threats and opportunities related to those on whom the organization depends (vendors, subcontractors, financiers, venture and alliance partners, etc.). The most progressive organizations also monitor public opinion within the organization. Notable changes in the internal environments of many firms, especially multinationals, reflect the glacial shifts occurring in the larger society. Sometimes, these attitudinal and value shifts result in a questioning of the mission, mandate, and objectives of the organization (Smart, 1985). Organizations also monitor image-related questions that could have an impact on operations and employee morale. Reputation management is a growing area of interest.

Chapter 3 deals in more depth with the questions frequently asked by monitors of public opinion. Ultimately, these opinion research efforts should enable the organization to respond to critics; improve policies, programs, and operations; engage in reputation management; and meet the expectations of internal and external publics. Managers who work in knowledge-based sectors of the organization expect that the communications function will have the same research underpinnings as the business units.

Monitoring teams have a more reactive function than scanners because they track issues already identified as priorities. They do not necessarily aim to identify new or emerging issues. For example, 13 of 15 respondents in a *Fortune* 500 survey indicated that their monitoring duties include the analysis of reactions to a policy or program announcement, legislation, or other event. Two thirds said that they analyze the historical development of an issue, positioning it in the current issue climate. More than half stated that they analyze the issue climate immediately prior to an event, policy or program announcement, or legislation. Issue monitoring reports in one third of the organizations take the form of a monthly trend report. Relatively few said that they analyze reactions to the general performance of the company or its officers. All the companies that responded to the survey said that they have in-house issue-monitoring functions, and 27% said that they sometimes contract out their monitoring activities (Ferguson, 1993).

Monitoring requires the ability to pay attention to detail, synthesize large amounts of information, and identify trends. Unlike scanners, monitors become experts in the specific policy areas that they track. Too often, however, monitoring practices tend to center on only one aspect of an organization's environment (e.g., technological, political, or financial). Although corporations may study the economic and regulatory environments, including the climate for mergers and acquisitions, they may fail to broaden their scope to include other relevant environments, such as technological and social. Governments, however, tend to concentrate on political variables and often ignore other dimensions. Stoffels (1982) noted that "the more strongly a company . . . identifies with a single dimension, the greater the risk of being blind-sided over time by the emergence of important issues from other dimensions" (p. 7). Most issues have many dimensions—social, technological, political, economic, and others. They are multidimensional because the environments in which they originate are multidimensional. At the beginning of a new millennium, these environments also tend to be "discontinuous, conflicting, and highly interdependent" (Smart, 1985, p. 14). Crises rarely result from changes occurring in one sector of an environment but stem from changes in many or all sectors. Structural and qualitative shifts in the whole of society account for many crises faced by business. For this reason, business and industry need to become more attuned to changes in other sectors. They need to monitor not only "visible" competitors (companies and industries in their own sector) but also "invisible" competitors (companies outside the industry with technological capabilities that could pose a threat if turned to new markets) (Hamel & Prahalad, 1996). Such companies may not show up on a company's "structural screen" because a competitor can be anything that takes customers' money (Reimann, 1992). Robert (1990) notes,

> Movie theatres now compete against home video rental centers and cable TV. The post office now competes against Federal Express, and both compete against electronic mail. Banks compete against Merrill Lynch and Sears Roebuck, all of them offering a variety of competing financial services. Greyhound and Trailways buses now compete against airlines, of all things, offering no-frills fares, and both compete against video games and computer games. Mail-order catalogs compete against shopping. Travel agents compete against direct, desktop computer reservations systems. (p. 24)

In the future, it is likely that movies will compete against virtual reality games, and modeling agencies will vie against the manufacturers of virtual reality fashion models.

Organizations also monitor events, groups, and issues with the potential for impact on other organizations on which they depend. One such group includes the suppliers of parts, services, and critical resources. Businesses monitor the legislative and regulatory agendas of local, state, and national governments. Researchers at Coors sort, file, and analyze news coverage on major competitors and monitor governmental developments. It is necessary to monitor government policies and actions because many government interventions aim to create new industries, to change competitive conditions for existing industries, and to create or protect industries perceived as critical to defense interests (Ring, Lenway, & Govekar, 1990). Strong interdependencies exist between firms and their political environment.

A 1992 survey of *Fortune* 500 companies found that only 3 of 15 firms said that they monitored reactions to performance of the organization or to individual officers of the firm (Ferguson, 1993). Nonetheless, firms such as Opinion Research Center, Inc., Louis Harris and Associates, and Yankelovich, Skelly, and White hire outside consultants to collect information on organizational image (Baskin & Aronoff, 1992). Also, politicians and bureaucrats keep a close watch on image.

Monitoring systems search for indicators that will provide early warnings of potential problems to the organization. According to Martino (1985), monitoring involves the following steps: (a) collecting the information (deciding which sources to monitor, how many, and in what depth), (b) screening the information (deciding what information should be retained), (c) evaluating the significance of the information (determining whether it could have an impact on products, services, suppliers, or processes), (d) classifying the information (categorizing and coding the information, retiring useful but historical items to inactive files, and eliminating items that have lost their usefulness), and (e) establishing a threshold (identifying a point at which it is appropriate to give a warning).

Forecasting and Trend Analysis

A discussion of forecasting and trend analysis can benefit from defining terms such as events, issues, and trends. The term *events* implies social, political, or technological "happenings," such as the recent takeover of Hong Kong by the People's Republic of China, a corporate acquisition, the signing of a trade agreement with Mexico, or a decision by insurance companies to exclude the cost of mammograms from the health coverage of women less than 40 years old. As previously defined, *issues* are fundamental policy questions that confront an organization. Issues are debatable, involving at least two sides or points of view, and unresolved. Although the term *trends* can be used in a generic way to refer to patterns that develop over time, trend analysts apply the term to changes in demographics, social conditions, regulations, and economic activities. Analysts use this kind of data to forecast the timing of future events and, by extrapolation, issues. In other words, a trend such as increasing numbers of older Americans can translate into an event such as a drain on the country's social security funds. The decreased amount of money in these funds generates the issue, or fundamental policy question: Should the government take measures to ensure that younger Americans contribute increased sums of money to the social security system?

Two of the most subjective methods used to forecast the timing of events are intuition and extrapolation. Intuitive insights may be described as "gut feelings," with the analyst relying on his or her collective experience and judgment. Extrapolation assumes that the analyst can use the past as a valid guide to the future. Obviously, sometimes this approach works better than at other times. More objective methods, such as quantitative forecasting models, try to reduce the impact of personal judgment and bias. Such models, however, are difficult to apply in areas involving values, human behavior, and new technologies, which respond better to sound judgment (based on highly educated instincts) (Enzer, 1989; Gollner, 1983). Some combine the qualitative and quantitative approaches. Jones and Chase (1979) argue that trends precede and coalesce into issues.

Although the planning literature discusses forecasting models in-depth, only 6 of 15 *Fortune* 500 companies reported sometimes using social forecasting or futures research techniques to decide the priority of issues. The remainder responded that they seldom or never rely on these techniques. None indicated that they rely extensively on the techniques (Ferguson, 1993). The current disillusionment with forecasting techniques may have resulted from a tendency to oversell these techniques in the 1950s. An emphasis on "questionable, long-range, pie-in-the-sky projections led the whole field of futures studies, except for a few major think tanks, to fall into disrepute" (Heath & Nelson, 1986, p. 161).

Despite the move away from formal forecasting models, organizations still rely on precursor analysis. Precursor analysis assumes that leaders establish trends that eventually "trickle down to the rest of society" (Wimmer &

Dominick, 1997, p. 332). Precursor analysts look to bellwether states and cities for early hints of change in public attitudes. For example, California tends to be a trendsetter in areas related to insurance and Florida in health care (Wimmer & Dominick, 1997). Many early studies paved the way for trend analysis. In a study of 200 daily American newspapers, Ewing (1980) identified California, Oregon, Washington, Connecticut, and Florida as bellwether states. The analysis of 100 years of historical data enabled Molitor (1979) to classify the following seven U.S. jurisdictions as "early innovators" and harbingers of sociopolitical change: two cities (Boston and New York City), one county (Dade County, Florida), and four states (California, Illinois, Massachusetts, and New York). Typically, Boston, New York City, and New York State were approximately 4 years ahead of the next category, "early adopters." Early adopters included Dade County, Florida, California, Illinois, and Massachusetts. Jurisdiction characteristics included the fact that the areas were highly urban, densely populated, affluent, highly educated, youthful, and progressive. "Early and late majorities" included many state and local jurisdictions, which followed the early adopters by approximately 4 to 8 years. Southern states, such as Mississippi, Louisiana, and Alabama, and rural areas such as Wyoming typically trailed by an additional 2 to 6 years. Characteristics of these jurisdictions included the fact that they were rural, tradition bound, and nonaffluent (Molitor, 1979).

Rogers (1995) uses similar terminology in discussing the spread of innovations through society. People do not adopt innovations at the same time. Rather, they fit into one of the following adopter categories: "innovators," "early adopters," "early majority," "late majority," and "laggards." As in the Molitor study, these terms suggest the rate at which people adopt new ideas. Engaged in a pursuit for new ventures, innovators tend to leave their circle of friends and move into more cosmopolite relationships. Innovators not only associate with other innovators but also help to "launch" new ideas by importing novel concepts from outside system boundaries. In the same way, they function as gatekeepers (Rogers, 1995).

Early adopters tend to act as opinion leaders. Other potential adopters seek advice from the early adopters. By adopting the innovations ahead of their peers, early adopters remove some of the uncertainty from the decisions of those who follow. Early adopters maintain their position at the center of local communication networks by making wise decisions. The early majority rarely occupy opinion leadership positions. By standing between the early adopters and the late majority, they offer connectedness to the system. In one of the two largest grouping of adopters, the early majority constitute one third of the members of a system. The time required to make a decision is longer than that of the innovator or the early adopter (Rogers, 1995).

The late majority represent another one third of the adopters. Increasing peer and economic pressures typically motivate the late majority to adopt an innovation. They adopt only after most of the uncertainty is removed from the situation, however. The last to adopt an innovation, laggards are the most provincial of all adopters in their outlook. They have little contact with others in the same social system. Laggards are traditionalists, suspicious of change and new ideas. They use the past as a benchmark for decisions. Partly because they have limited resources, laggards do not adopt innovations until virtually all risk has been removed from the situation (Rogers, 1995). Understanding the behavioral patterns of individuals suggests that, even within states or regions that tend to be trendsetters, some parts of the population will adopt earlier than others. The cosmopolite nature of many urban dwellers helps to explain the patterns that tend to manifest in centers such as New York City and Boston.

Other studies have identified trendsetting countries. Early innovators in the area of social and political change are Sweden, Norway, Denmark, The Netherlands, and Switzerland. Sweden is typically approximately 10 years ahead of countries such as Great Britain, Germany, the United States, and Canada. These second-cycle countries, in turn, are several decades ahead of many developing countries (Thomas, 1980). Evidence suggests that Canadian family law typically follows that of Sweden and The Netherlands. Constitutional law precedents are typically set by Great Britain, Germany, and France. Advances in criminal law most often come from the United States. These leading jurisdictions are 3, 5, or even 7 years ahead of Canada (Nicholson-O'Brien, 1989). By studying what is happening in trendsetting countries, a country can predict options on its legislative, media, and public agendas a few years in the future. Similar to governments, businesses also search for developing trends (Sonnenberg, 1992).

Analysis of trends in the international arena can give organizations a critical edge in both planning and positioning (Davidson, 1991). Recommendations on how to move organizations toward a global perspective on the management of public opinion include the following:

- Tailor reading programs for managers and executives.
- Substitute global information sources for some domestic information sources.

- Ensure a global component in information packages circulated to managers and executives.
- Include a global perspective in analyses of issues.
- Establish a global component in business plans.
- Commission special studies of the structure and dynamics of international events.

Despite the need for an international perspective, the Society of Competitive Intelligence Professionals concluded that many American organizations remain committed to domestic data sources and a focus on American competitors. A review of the intelligence-gathering function at Dow Corning, for example, found that approximately half of the company's competitors were foreign based; at that time, however, Dow Corning subscribed to a limited number of foreign publications. Upgrading the system implies a need to establish formal scanning and monitoring procedures with a global perspective, including mechanisms for synthesizing and analyzing the resulting data (Roush, 1991). To correct this kind of deficit at Kodak in the 1980s, CEO Colby Chandler hired the former director of the U.S. Census Bureau to establish an intelligence infrastructure (Herring, 1991).

Approaches to Organizing
the Intelligence Function

Formal intelligence-gathering systems vary greatly from organization to organization and even within the same industry. Some organizations monitor patent applications, and others establish tracking systems to identify innovative companies and technologies or to follow the organization's issues in media. They identify the issues and contribute to the definition of strategic options (Simpson, 1992). Informal intelligence-gathering operations often call on managers, employees, and research assistants to gather and disseminate information. The Japanese rely extensively on the latter approach (Kodama, 1992).

Organizations have taken different approaches to setting up the intelligence function. In some cases, marketing groups carry out this function. In other situations, public relations units gather opinion data. *Fortune* 500 corporations report that their scanners and monitors most frequently occupy positions in public affairs or public relations, although some also work in planning, personnel, legal, executive, finance, policy, service, sales, marketing, administrative and clerical, and specialized research units (Ferguson, 1993). In some situations, more than one unit (e.g., legal, finance, and marketing or policy and communication) cooperate on environmental analysis tasks.

In ideal circumstances, organizations create specialized research units with staff functions to support line management in researching and analyzing the company's opinion environment. In such a situation, the research unit may have a standing equal to human resources, marketing, finance, and other support functions. This specialized unit gathers and analyzes environmental intelligence and feeds the knowledge to strategic planners. The size of the research units varies according to the size of the organization and the scope of the unit's mandate. Two or three people carry out the function in many companies. A large government department or corporation, however, may require a staff of 12 or more analysts. The organization typically contracts out some of the work.

No matter which group is responsible for the function (human resources, marketing, finance, or other unit), most organizations agree that successful intelligence-gathering operations depend on the support of (and broad use by) upper management as well as cultural acceptance of the function within the organization (Herring, 1991). Some research units experience an initial credibility problem in getting decision makers to accept and use their products (Roush, 1991). Lack of acceptance of the analysis function in organizations often stems from a tendency to summarize rather than analyze data. As products become more sophisticated, management becomes more dependent on them. Research and analysis units with the highest credibility are those that "add value" to the original material: interpret the information, draw implications from the data, and extrapolate trends (Roush, 1991). Those units with the lowest credibility do no more than provide raw data, abstracts, and summaries of the results of their scanning and monitoring efforts. The process of analysis converts data into intelligence.

Indicators of the extent to which the intelligence function has gained credibility in the organization include the following:

Institutionalization of the function—the extent to which firms have made specific units responsible for the function (established a research and analysis unit, created special job categories for people who perform this function, or granted responsibility for the function to a specific unit such as public affairs)

Reporting accountability—whether or not the director of the intelligence unit reports directly to the highest level of management (e.g., the CEO), sits on executive committees, and attends board meetings

Integration with line management—the extent to which research and analysis specialists consult with line managers and policy experts on an ongoing basis to obtain their views and perspectives as well as to address managers' concerns in the scanning and monitoring processes

Regularity of committee meetings to discuss scanning and monitoring results—the extent to which the organization schedules regular and frequent meetings to discuss scanning and monitoring results, thus creating opportunities for a proactive rather than a reactive response to escalating or emerging issues

Circulation of research and analysis products—the extent to which the organization circulates trend reports, media analyses, survey results, and other materials generated by the research and analysis units

Resource allocation—the extent to which business units are given sufficient staff and money to carry out the function

Recommendations to those establishing an intelligence system include the following (Getz, 1991): (a) Assess the information needs of top management and identify potential organizational strengths and weaknesses that could come into play in implementing systems to meet these needs, (b) establish clear goals for the intelligence function, (c) determine clients to be served in order of priority (e.g., CEO, board, top-level executives, and policy committees), and (d) institutionalize the interface between top decision makers and intelligence professionals by making the function routine—a part of the ongoing operations of the organization.

Studies have found a relationship between the extent to which an organization has formalized its intelligence operations and the extent to which it depends on external institutionalized groups. A survey of 130 issues management specialists in the utilities industry found a significant correlation between interest group pressures on an organization and the allocation of human and financial resources for the intelligence-gathering function (Greening, 1991).

Governments appear to be setting the trend for intelligence models that work. Both the American and the Canadian governments have developed systems to gather and analyze public opinion. Some commercial organizations have followed suit. For example, a former Central Intelligence Agency officer assisted Motorola in establishing an intelligence unit at that company. In this system, the CEO and the director of intelligence services share responsibility for designating priority issues for the company. The director attends all executive committee and board meetings. In an ideal model, the director reports directly to the CEO. Gilad (1991) notes,

> The history of military intelligence activities has proved that placing layers between the commander-in-chief and the intelligence officer is tantamount to destroying the effectiveness of the function. . . . A good intelligence adviser presents the CEO with more than important facts or intelligence estimates: He or she attempts to increase the decision maker's understanding of how other players think (e.g., competitors, customers, regulators) as well as the pattern of logic behind events in the environment. As an independent observer with no stake in particular strategy options, the DOI (director of intelligence) is probably the only corporate player who can offer the CEO a relatively objective assessment of the consequences of adopted strategies. (pp. 24-25)

At Motorola, researchers and analysts work together with internal experts, who serve the function of account managers or account executives. They operate on task forces and project teams charged with understanding specific clientele. In such a system, experts track competitors, technology experts, government officers, particular technologies, and designated agencies. The researchers and analysts draw on this network of internal experts for help in acquiring and analyzing data. Some public sector organizations also assign account executives to different branches of the organization. When strategic or operational planning occurs, these account executives provide a communication perspective based on insights acquired through intimate contact with the client group. Those who have set up intelligence systems believe that the essence of any worthwhile system is its ability to coordinate internal expertise (Gilad, 1991).

Public relations staff members contribute to the intelligence function in many ways. Routine research and analysis services, performed by communication staff members, include tracking issues in media (old and new); analyzing correspondence; planning, conducting, and analyzing focus group sessions; designing and interpreting surveys; researching the views of elite opinion leaders; generating interest group profiles; providing information to planners; writing monthly trend analysis reports; and contributing to issues management and crisis management strategies. The first priority of opinion research officers is to respond to requests from the CEO and other executive officers. Research officers also consult regularly with business managers regarding their information needs, and their analyses feed into strategic and operational planning systems. Some units create libraries to organize and store the products of their research (e.g., survey and focus group results, trend reports, media analyses, competitor profiles, market data, special studies, and database directories).

An increasing number of organizations make use of electronic mail networks to establish news clippings folders. At the beginning or end of each workday, research analysts place items that are relevant to different organizational members in their respective clippings folders. In other cases, analysts flag important or emerging issues. Regular meetings of opinion research analysts facilitate coordination of this function. Some organizations hold biweekly meetings to discuss and prioritize issues. Figure 2.2 illustrates a typical format for reporting issue developments.[1] Six of 15 *Fortune* 500 companies indicated that they hold monthly meetings to discuss the results of their monitoring efforts; another company holds semiannual meetings. Participants include executives, senior managers, middle managers, and staff. The most frequent attendees are middle and senior managers (Ferguson, 1993). Figure 2.3 illustrates a media inquiry report, which also feeds into the environmental analysis systems of the organization.

What is the role of communicators in these systems? By the 1950s, academics had modified their communication models, placing greater emphasis on the concept of feedback and reciprocity of exchange. This trend was fed by the increasing popularity of systems theory, espoused by authors such as Bertalanffy (1937/1968) and Katz and Kahn (1966), who wrote about organizations as "open systems" that functioned on the basis of outputs and inputs from the larger environment. The 1990s have witnessed an increasing emphasis on the idea of consulting with publics to learn their points of view. Governments, in particular, have initiated massive consultative processes to learn more about public views and perceived needs. Consultative models can range from those that elicit a high level of engagement from publics to those that call for minimum levels of involvement (Ferguson, 1998, 1999). Whereas policy officers have customarily conducted consultations for governments, communicators are becoming increasingly involved in this function. Related duties include public opinion research (conducting surveys and focus groups and tracking issues on the Internet and in media) and strategic planning based on this opinion research (Ferguson, 1993, 1994, 1999). Thus, communicators have an active and valued role to play in the establishment and operation of intelligence systems that call on internal and external publics for input (Lauzen, 1995, 1997; Lauzen & Dozier, 1994).

Issue:
Proximity Based on Strategic Objectives:

Trends in Issue Development:	Events Influencing:

Opportunities for Organization:	Threats to Organization:

Action Required:
Responsible Party:

Figure 2.2. Sample issue tracking report format. This chart is a variation on formats developed by Sharon Hanna and the issues management team at Employment and Immigration Canada (now Human Resources Development Canada).

Conclusion

Some companies have expressed the fear that intelligence units could be misunderstood by the general public, media representatives, customers, and even their own employees. Such systems, however, shield organizations from the

---

Media Inquiry Report

Name of
requestor:_____

Organization:_____

Subject of request: _____

Question(s):
_____
_____
_____

Response:
_____
_____
_____
_____

Request handled by: _____

Date:_____

Figure 2.3. Example of a form for recording media requests. This form is used by some of the Canadian government departments.

unexpected and contribute to informed decision making. Organizations most in need of intelligence programs are those with large external constituencies and a global focus. The more open the organization, the more uncertain its environment and the greater the need to be alert to change. For many organizations, scanning, monitoring, and forecasting (especially trend analysis) precede strategic planning. The situational audit draws on information acquired through these techniques. Almost half of the *Fortune* 500 companies that participated in the 1992 Ferguson survey said that they have a formal strategic planning framework into which their scanning and monitoring functions feed (Ferguson, 1993). This is a good indicator of the extent to which the environmental intelligence functions have gathered more than rhetorical commitment from some decision makers. In the past, scanning units were not integrated into the organization, and when their advocates (executives who established the function) left the organization the scanning units disappeared (Russell & Prince, 1992).

The superiority of some environmental intelligence systems compared to others will relate to the organization's investment in human resources (knowledge, skills, and time), financial resources, support systems (clerical, storage, and retrieval), quality of networks in place (face-to-face and mediated), and the long-term commitment of upper management. In setting up intelligence systems, the organization will need to ascertain the existing gap between its information needs and its information sources (people, money, and support systems). Some believe that what is required, in many organizations, is not additional people or more resources but a better organized effort and a new "architecture" molded to the existing corporate culture and decision-making processes (Hamel & Prahalad, 1996). To support this view, some scholars argue that most organizations engage in research on an ongoing basis. They do not always identify these efforts as research, however. They do not view reading a newspaper, speaking to someone on the telephone, attending a convention or an association meeting, or studying past transactions with the public as research. They tend to view research as more formal and structured. In reality, however, all these kinds of data-gathering efforts should be incorporated into the organization's scanning, monitoring, and forecasting systems.

PART
II

Monitoring and Analyzing the Media

3

Monitoring the Media

Asking Questions

A cademics spend a great deal of time debating whether media have a direct effect, an indirect effect, or no effect at all on audiences. Paradigms of thought have evolved to accommodate these debates. Presidents, prime ministers, and corporations, however, rarely ponder such questions. They hold an unwavering belief that media have powerful effects of an indirect and direct nature. Adhering to this conviction, governments and corporations pay hundreds of thousands of dollars to survey research firms, they commission focus groups, and they establish sophisticated media monitoring systems designed to track and analyze media response to the organization's issues. Whereas *governments* monitor the media to obtain feedback on their policies and programs, *corporations* monitor the media to learn more about the pressures exerted on top-level government officials and to project the likely consequences of these pressures.

Pressure on corporate leaders can originate with activist groups or the larger public. Because American CEOs believe that their greatest challenge in the twenty-first century will be the threat from increased government regulation, they search for indicators of where government is headed (Herring, 1991). They also seek to document perceptions of the organization to learn more about corporate reputation. In addition, corporations monitor the media to evaluate the success of their communication strategies. Have mass media

51

or specialized media carried the organization's messages? Does media coverage suggest that the public understands and supports the corporate position on contentious issues? How do key publics perceive corporate leadership?

To answer these questions, government and corporate leaders establish media monitoring units such as the ones described in Chapter 2 that are populated by communication and policy specialists. Typically, these media analysts respond to a menu of questions. First, they want to know which publics have reacted to policies and announcements by the organization. Who are the stakeholders in a particular issue? The elite opinion leaders? Which groups appear to be in control of the media agenda? Second, they want to understand what people know and say about the organization. What arguments have surfaced in support of, or opposed to, particular policy positions? Third, media analysts study the ways in which media treat issues of interest to key publics or advocacy groups. Fourth, analysts also want to know the catalysts that are driving the coverage. Finally, analysts search for trends in media coverage of issues in newspapers, popular magazines, specialized media, or other sources. (Refer to the list of information sources in Figure 2.1 for the range of sources that can be monitored.)

In brief, interest in studying the development of issues in media (new and old) derives from the assumption that media reflect, or possess the power to shape, public opinion. Chapter 9 addresses the question of limits, which is often debated in the academic sector.

Which Publics Have Reacted?

Decision makers want to know which key publics or stakeholders have expressed a viewpoint on an issue. I use the term *key publics* to refer to the multiple publics of organizations—publics who "attach themselves to issues in quite different ways" (McLeod, Kosicki, & McLeod, 1994, p. 150). A similar term, *stakeholders,* refers to those who are "affected by an organization" (Grunig & Repper, 1992, p. 127). Carma International, a consulting firm that specializes in media analysis for corporate clients, defines a stakeholder as "any individual, group, or organization that has an interest and/or influence, either direct or indirect, on your corporation" (ICM presentation, 1999). Stakeholders may include customers, employees, managers, owners, stockholders, vendors, regulatory bodies, trade unions, distributors, competitors, journalists, and public officials.

Corporate leaders, policymakers, and politicians are interested in the views of these key publics. They want to know who supports or opposes the organization's position on specific issues or who offers an alternative explanation of events.

Appropriate questions include the following: Whose attitudes dominated the coverage? From whose point of view were arguments presented? A lobby group? A foreign government? Industry? Government? A political party? What time or space was allocated by media to the views of different stakeholders? With what frequency were the views of different groups reported in print and broadcast media? At what points did shifts in coverage occur?

Activist Publics

If organized, stakeholders may surface in the form of unions or interest or lobby groups. Highly critical coverage of an organization's stance on issues often results from capture of the media agenda by special interest groups or even foreign governments. Anderson (1992) discussed the case of environmental groups that lobbied against a U.S. company's plans to grow and export oranges from Belize, Central America (formerly British Honduras). The situation was diffused only after the public relations director of the firm made personal contact with environmental groups such as Friends of the Earth. The director later commented (as quoted in Anderson, 1992), "We should have spent much more time understanding . . . who the players were and the network. We would have gone to meet with them if we had known that they were there. The hard part is knowing that they are there" (p. 161).

Groups with sufficient resources to prepare background materials, factual reports, and analyses have the best chance of having their views represented in media coverage. For the "resource-poor" groups to achieve coverage, they must be defined as "newsworthy." Group members must take some extraordinary, imaginative, or radical action, or a prominent personality must adopt their cause. For example, Calvin Klein captures media attention for AIDS activists when he hosts an outdoor fashion extravaganza that involves top models. Melanie Griffith achieves prominent news coverage when she gives out supplies at a food bank. The cameras swivel to Whoopi Goldberg when she refuses to cross the picket lines at a major film studio that has locked out striking technicians. Media analysts not only identify stakeholders in issues but also comment on their levels of activism and potential to propel issues to a higher plane of prominence. As noted previously, on-line campaigns such as the one initiated by the natives of Zapatista, Mexico, have demonstrated the tremendous potential in new media to raise the profile of issues supported by activist publics (Juniper, 1999). Similar "information war" campaigns have been conducted by the Mohawks, who operate from reservations that straddle Canada and the United States. Given the right conditions, campaign, or support, even the smallest activist groups have the capability to topple giant corporations, as evidenced in the case of Nestlé when activist groups successfully lobbied against the sale of infant formula to developing countries (Mintzberg, 1983). The ability of these groups to secure media attention is often enhanced by the tendency of media to give a disproportionate amount of attention to issues with highly emotional content, such as abortion, gun control, animal rights, capital offenses, and many environmental issues such as the destruction of the rain forests.

Foreign Governments

Sometimes, foreign governments exercise a significant influence on domestic media agendas. For example, former South African President Pieter W. Botha regularly created diversions to capture international press attention at times when he faced criticism by the United States and Commonwealth countries. On one occasion, Botha invited two Canadian native leaders to visit South Africa, precisely at the moment that Canadian Foreign Affairs Minister Joe Clark was in caucus with representatives of southern Africa considering ways to increase the pressure on the Nationalist government. Botha encouraged the Aboriginal leaders, on their arrival, to compare the conditions of South African blacks with the living conditions of Canadian Aboriginals. Despite the obvious nature of the ploy, the international press corps gave Botha the coverage that he sought and, at the same time, diverted attention from the foreign minister's tour.

In a second case, the Canadian press gave extensive coverage to a U.S. lobby against a Canadian film distribution bill. When Jack Valenti traveled from Hollywood to Canada to meet with Communications Minister Flora MacDonald, the Canadian press corps was eager to cover his visit. American views dominated the headlines of Canadian newspapers for the duration of Valenti's visit. Even when interest groups do not reflect the more general perception of issues, they can be a potent force. Figure 3.1 illustrates a protocol for collecting information on points of view. Figure 3.2 illustrates the application of this protocol to the coverage of crime stories.

	Stakeholder	Space/Time
1		
2		
3		
4		
5		
6		
7		
8		

Figure 3.1. Stakeholder Perspective: Control of the Media Agenda

	Stakeholder	Space/Time
1	Victims of crime	50 minutes
2	Perpetrators	23 minutes
3	Law enforcement agencies	20 minutes
4	Families of victims	65 minutes
5	Families of perpetrators	15 minutes
6		
7		
8		

Figure 3.2. Stakeholder Perspective: Control of the Media Agenda

Opinion Leaders

Pack journalism has become a much discussed phenomenon in recent years (Crouse, 1972; Nimmo & Combs, 1990). This term refers to the phenomenon whereby some journalists and commentators act as opinion leaders on specific topics. Media analysts often seek to identify how media pundits (those who comment on political and social issues of the day) "line up" on issues. Which pundits espouse similar points of view or occupy similar stances on a particular topic? Sometimes, media analysis reports include graphic depictions of pundit positions. Such graphs typically reveal clusters of opinion on specific issues. In the same way, analysts can search for clustering of journalists on issues. For example, some journalists may favor increasing the level of monetary support for United Nations actions in East Timor, others will support the status quo, and a third group will probably argue to decrease the level of financial assistance. The media analyst seeks to identify these opinion clusters.

Sometimes, newspapers assume the role of opinion leader. For example, the *Washington Post* was an opinion leader on the topic of Watergate. The *New York Times* often acts as an opinion leader on foreign affairs. Other opinion leaders may be important members of the community or celebrity figures. Opinion leaders vary from topic to topic. If the organization can identify opinion leaders on organizational issues, it can consult with them, gain useful information and insights, negotiate differences in viewpoint, clarify points of misunderstanding, and present the organization's point of view. The Allensbach Survey Center in Germany developed a Strength of Personality scale to identify opinion leaders (Wiemann, 1991). Some commercial firms also compile profiles of opinion leaders and other elites.

Summary

In the previously discussed instances involving domestic and international media, the media analyst attempts to discover who is in control of the media agenda (i.e., dominating the agenda or exercising the greatest influence) at given points in time. The analyst logs the amount of air time or newspaper space devoted to different points of view. The tabulation of this kind of information allows the researcher to draw conclusions about dominant influences on the media agenda. The analyst also tracks shifts in opinion over extended periods of time.

What Do People Say About the Organization?

When representatives of key publics speak out in newspapers, radio, television, or on the Internet, they often make recommendations on how to resolve problem areas. Sometimes, they urge government or other groups to exercise caution in specific areas. Other times, they assign blame. The media analyst seeks to identify acceptable solutions to problem areas—that is, acceptable in the eyes of stakeholders. Sometimes, the media analyst seeks to establish the limits of acceptability of policies and platforms. Is there an invisible line at which point stakeholders will balk? Do key publics have confidence in the organization? Other questions asked by media analysts relate to levels of public awareness and understanding. Do the comments by affected publics and their representatives indicate that they understand the issues?

An organization, whether government or business, can best answer its critics if it knows the grounds on which issues are being argued. Decision makers want to know what people say about the organization, its leaders, and its issues, including the following:

- Key concerns related to emerging and current issues
- Major criticisms of the organization's policies, programs, and representatives
- Assignment of blame—who is responsible for the problem(s)
- Perceived loopholes in regulations, laws, and policies
- Key arguments in support of the organization's policies, programs, and representatives
- Birth of arguments—where and with whom they originated
- Shifts over time in argumentation and reasoning
- Cautions and warnings about proceeding with some initiative or activity
- Recommendations for action or conditions for engagement (e.g., stated conditions for engagement in a United Nations peacekeeping mission in East Timor)
- Anticipated effects of the policies, programs, or executive actions on different stakeholders
- Perceived legitimacy or illegitimacy of operations or processes
- Expressions of confidence in leaders, business organizations, or governments

Targeted and strategic communications require an understanding of the beliefs and opinions of key stakeholders. Therefore, media monitors search for evidence of how these key publics stand on issues, as manifested in press interviews with spokespersons, letters to the editor, news group interactions on the Internet, and other avenues of public and interest group expression. Do some groups lack understanding of key points of policy or legislation? Do key publics know about a recent merger or acquisition or about the restructuring of a government department? Do they know where to go for information that they may require for health, business, social, or other purposes? Do they know what the organization is contributing to the community? Are key publics aware of research activities with implications for their communities? In the most extreme cases, do key publics even know that the agency or organization exists? Some organizations have little visibility in the public eye. For example, more Canadians know about NASA than about the CSA (Canadian Space Agency). When astronauts Julie Payette or Marc Garneau embark on a new space venture, the media and public turn their attention to the skies but not necessarily to the space agency based in St. Hubert, Quebec. Some groups, however, such as intelligence agencies, prefer low visibility because high visibility almost always implies controversy. Therefore, the desired (or required) levels of visibility may vary by organization.

Governments also monitor press coverage to determine which aspects of legislation or policies have been accepted by mass or key publics, which elements appear to be the most controversial, key concerns expressed by stakeholders, the perceived effects of legislation on different stakeholder groups, cautions urged in implementing new policies, conditions specified for engagement in some proposed action, recommendations for modifications in legislation, perceived loopholes in proposed legislation, major arguments against legislation, the nature of argumentation in favor of new policies, or the perceived legitimacy of proceedings or policies. The following discussion develops some of these less obvious points in more depth.

In the case of impeachment proceedings against Bill Clinton, some U.S. citizens perceived the process to be illegitimate—an inappropriate exercise of power by Republicans who dominated the Senate. A question related to the perceived legitimacy of the process could have been "Did media coverage suggest that Americans perceive the impeachment proceedings to be a legitimate exercise of Senate power?" Analysts can also examine the extent to which an interest group has achieved legitimacy in the eyes of key publics or media. Cobb and Elder (1983) claim that groups seek to create an aura of legitimacy that makes their messages more acceptable. The best questions are derived from an understanding of specific issues.

Computer programs can be useful in tracking the origin of arguments. For example, keywords can be used to identify the first appearance of an argument, the newspaper in which the argument appeared, the spokesperson who first raised the argument, and the journalist and newspaper that published the argument. Computer programs can also track the development of argumentation on an issue, noting those who picked up the discussion and where permutations in argumentation and reasoning occurred (Fan, 1988; Jasperson, Shah, Watts, Faber, & Fan, 1998). Clients can suggest key names, topics, or words to be tracked: "organization's name, staff names, products or services, and even similar or competing organizations" (Cutlip, Center, & Broom, 1994, p. 421). Wimmer and Dominick (1997) noted, "Many documents and publications in on-line databases such as Vu/Text or Nexis can be searched for key topics and phrases in a matter of seconds" (p. 126). Nonetheless, some studies have found that results from a computer analysis of data differ from those of human-scored analyses (Kaufman, Dykers, & Caldwell, 1993). Unlike computers, media analysts can evaluate the validity of arguments by the different stakeholders (e.g., Are the arguments substantiated by reliable evidence? To what extent are the arguments based on emotion rather than logic?). Ultimately, the organization uses such analysis products to determine whether to clarify and argue its position to stakeholders or to change its position.

Organizations can learn from their critics. Sometimes, experts in specific areas will speak out, offering concrete and valuable recommendations. Consumer groups, for example, may urge companies to undertake more research in certain areas, to create needed products, or to correct problems. Lawyers may point to loopholes in legislation. Health care practitioners may suggest solutions to the problem of overcrowding in hospitals. The organization may want to know how many critics offered specific direction for change. How many agreed on priorities or strategies for change? At other times, experts may accept the organization's intended course of action but urge caution in proceeding or set conditions for engagement. In the weeks following the reunification of Germany, many foreign policy experts accepted the reunification of Germany as a political priority but urged that the American government obtain clarification on certain points related to NATO commitments. Some publics may have accepted the air war against the Serbs but warned that they would not accept an escalation of the conflict into a ground war. An analyst may want to examine the perceived legitimacy of NATO operations or the expressed level of confidence in the ability of NATO to secure the safety of ethnic Albanians in Yugoslavia.

Analysts can search for levels of expressed confidence in government or leaders. Does media coverage suggest that confidence in the U.S. presidency has diminished since independent counsel Kenneth Starr's investigation of President Bill Clinton? Does the coverage suggest that the Iraqi people have lost any of their confidence in Saddam Hussein with the renewed outbreak of hostilities? The media analyst should make conclusive statements that contrast the spirit of the coverage with the realities of the situation.

The media analyst can also search for assignment of blame. Key publics and journalists typically assign blame to some parties and exonerate others. If Mohawk Warriors (members of the Mohawk Indian community who assume the traditional role of "warrior") establish a roadblock to protest the municipal government's appropriation of traditional burial grounds, media spokespersons will find someone to blame for the problem—the Warriors, the municipal government, politicians, the federal land agency, or factions within the Mohawk government. When the Republicans lost five seats to Democrats in the past congressional elections, journalists searched for the reasons. They had the option of placing blame on Kenneth Starr, Newt Gingrich, or others who were investigating President Clinton. In the recent school killings in Kentucky, Colorado, and Georgia, media assigned blame to many different parties, including legislators, Internet providers, commercial companies that sell video games, establishments that sponsor video games, school administrators, teachers, parents, and even other students for not recognizing or dealing with the problems at an earlier stage in their development. The analyst can attempt to identify the parties on whom blame has been placed. Sometimes, the assignment of blame shifts, over time, from one party to another. Analysts can track these shifts as they occur. Figure 3.3 provides examples of ways to organize discussions related to the question "What do key publics say about the organization?"

How Do Media Frame the Story?

This question asks how media "frame" the story. *Framing* refers to a "central organizing idea or story line that provides meaning" (Gamson & Modigliani, 1987, p. 143; see also Rhee [1997] and Tuchman [1978]). Many different concepts fit under framing of news stories, including plot lines and characters, color and tone of coverage, focus and parameters of media attention, place on the media agenda, depth and sophistication of coverage, and messages carried by media.

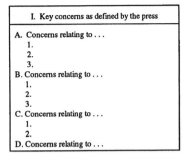
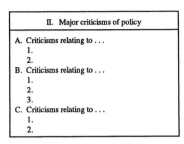

Figure 3.3. Protocol for Analysis of Arguments and Reasoning

What is the ranking of the issue on the media agenda? What is the focus of media coverage? Do journalists demonstrate a knowledge and understanding of the issues? Is the coverage in-depth and sophisticated? Is the tone of discussion favorable or unfavorable to the organization? Is the coverage neutral or balanced? Do media carry the organization's preferred messages? To what extent do media depict the organization and its representatives as having a particular situation under control? To what extent is the coverage optimistic or pessimistic in tone?

Plot Lines and Characters

Olson (1995) defines frames as "presentational formats" applied to the discussion of issues, such as whether a news story employs a dramatic or mythic theme. He states that news stories draw their plots from literary origins and

```
┌─────────────────────────────────┐   ┌─────────────────────────────────┐
│        V.  Cautions urged        │   │ VII.  Recommendations for action │
│                                  │   │   explicit or implicit in press  │
│ A. Cautions in area of . . .     │   │              accounts            │
│     1.                           │   │                                  │
│     2.                           │   │ A. Recommendations relating to . │
│     3.                           │   │     1.                           │
│ B. Cautions in area of . . .     │   │     2.                           │
│     1.                           │   │ B. Recommendations relating to . │
│     2.                           │   │     1.                           │
│     3.                           │   │     2.                           │
│ C.  Cautions in area of . . .    │   │     3.                           │
│     1.                           │   │     4.                           │
│     2.                           │   │ C. Recommendations relating to . │
│                                  │   │     1.                           │
└─────────────────────────────────┘   │     2.                           │
                                       │ D. Recommendations relating to . │
┌─────────────────────────────────┐   │     1.                           │
│ VII.  Trends evidenced in        │   │     2.                           │
│       argumentation              │   └─────────────────────────────────┘
│                                  │
│ A. In area of . . .              │
│     1.                           │
│     2.                           │
│                                  │
│ B. In area of . . .              │
│     1.                           │
│     2.                           │
│     3.                           │
│ C.  In area of . . .             │
│     1.                           │
│     2.                           │
│ D.  In area of . . .             │
│     1.                           │
│     2.                           │
│     3.                           │
│ E.  In area of . . .             │
│     1.                           │
│     2.                           │
│     3.                           │
└─────────────────────────────────┘
```

Figure 3.3. Continued

that these same literary plots appear in stories by all major media—newspapers, television, and news magazines (McCartney, 1987; McCombs, Einsiedel, & Weaver, 1991). In other words, journalists work within a genre that includes a limited variety of story formats, and they choose from this inventory when they write their news stories. Many studies have confirmed that media coverage of terrorist and other hostage incidents draws heavily on these dramatic formats (Lule, 1991; Picard, 1991). The media analyst may find it useful to identify the formats employed in coverage of specific issues and to examine the extent to which parties were depicted as victims, heroes, or in other roles.

Do media portray key players as confident and in control of their issue environments? Does the story depict the organization as having an agenda and direction or as reacting in a knee-jerk fashion to developments outside its control? Even when decision makers sprint to keep abreast of current developments, they often lag behind the news makers. A president or head of state may learn about some event that has transpired on another continent at the same time that his or her constituents hear the news. A CEO for a public corporation may acquire vital information after his or her shareholders obtain the same information. These situations can be frightening to those who want to remain in control of their organization's issues. Therefore, analysts frequently ask the question, "To what extent do journalists present the organization as being in control of its issues environment?" One of the most frequent criticisms of government is that leaders fail to act when action is required. Corporations are also often accused of dealing, in an apathetic or disinterested way, with critical issues related to safety or environmental concerns. Key publics, however, may view evidence of too much control as manipulation.

From whose perspective is the story told? Identifying stakeholder perspective can be important. The perspective can shift over time from one group to another. For example, many groups speak out on the issue of gun control, including parents, students, spokespersons for the National Rifle Association, legislators, and school authorities. From whose perspective is the story framed? Shifts in perspective over time can reveal a great deal about the development of the issue. (See Figures 3.1 and 3.2.)

Color and Tone of Coverage

Other concepts, associated with the framing of news stories, relate to color and tone of coverage. The analyst asks, "Does the coverage suggest that a bad situation is likely to improve?" Can Company X stave off bankruptcy? Does coverage suggest that the NATO air missions will succeed in their efforts to bring an end to the Serbian attacks against ethnic Albanians? In other words, the analyst judges the level of optimism or pessimism that is present in the telling of the story.

Judgments on tone involve classifying a news item as positive (favorable to the organization's stance on an issue), negative (unfavorable to the organization's position), mixed (representing a balanced view), or neutral (lacking a point of view). Governments want to know citizens' opinions about their administration and policies. Business and industry want to know consumers' and communities' opinions about their products, services, and operations. Analysis of tone can also indicate the intensity of feeling evidenced in the

```
Positive ___  ___  ___  ___  ___  ___  ___  Negative
Strong  ___  ___  ___  ___  ___  ___  ___  Weak
Active  ___  ___  ___  ___  ___  ___  ___  Passive
```

Figure 3.4. Level of Intensity in Tone of Coverage

news coverage. To obtain a measure of intensity, researchers use a 7-point Likert scale or a semantic differential scale such as that shown in Figure 3.4.

In assessing the directionality or tone of coverage (positive vs. negative), analysts must be very clear about what they are measuring. They must frame a specific research question to which they will respond in assessing tone of coverage. For example, analysts can assess the tone of news articles in regard to policy direction. They could ask, "Does media coverage suggest that key publics favor the concept of free trade?" Alternatively, analysts can assess how key publics feel about the implementation of the policy. In the first instance, the research question would be "Does media coverage suggest that Americans support free trade as a concept?" In the second case, the research question would be "Does media coverage suggest that key publics agree with the way in which the free trade policy has been implemented?" Assessment of tone may vary according to the question that is asked.

A second example illustrates this same point. Americans may agree with a policy concept (drug searches at the U.S. borders) but disagree with the approach taken in implementing the policy (random strip searches). Classifying a news article in some generic way, without reference to a specific research question, makes little sense. In the case of the previous example, the research question could be "How do Americans feel about the right of customs officials to conduct searches for illegal drugs?" or "How do Americans feel about random strip searches at U.S. borders?"

A department of foreign affairs monitoring media coverage in the summer of 1999 could have asked the following kinds of questions about media coverage of the NATO war in Yugoslavia: What is the tone of coverage toward the concept of continued air bombings of Belgrade and Kosovo? What is the tone of coverage toward ground intervention? What is the tone of coverage toward continued membership in NATO? What is the tone of coverage toward a Russian peace proposal? As noted for the case of free trade and drug searches, an organization will learn little from an overall assessment of tone that makes no reference to a research question. At best, the organization will obtain some imprecise impression concerning its corporate reputation; at worst, top bureaucrats and business leaders will receive a distorted impression of the coverage they are receiving.

Unfortunately, attractive graphs and charts can mask the futility of the exercise to the uninitiated. Translated into numbers, the highly subjective and qualitative judgments behind the numbers may achieve a respectability that they do not merit. Problems also occur when different analysts use different questions.

In addition, different analysts use different criteria to assess tone. Common manifestations of bias in a news story occur in the form of editorial, language, attribution, graphic, and contextual bias.

Editorial or *column bias* is the most obvious kind of bias in a newspaper article. Both editors and columnists generally state or argue a point of view in quite explicit terms. The reader can choose to agree or not to agree with the statement of opinion expressed by the journalist.

Language bias, however, derives from choice of words and use of "loaded" language. In 1991, the following headline appeared in the Toronto *Globe and Mail:* "Canada Shackling Some Deportees: Banning of Forcible Sedation Results in Gagging of Unwilling Passengers." Terms such as "shackling," "gagging," and "forcible sedation" carry heavy negative connotations. Others vary in their levels of intensity. For example, the headline "Company Hedges on Environmental Policy" is quite different in intensity from "Company Pauses to Consider Alternatives." The headline "Lobby Group Warns President That Problems Lie Ahead" carries a different connotation from "President Meets With Lobby Groups to Discuss Areas of Concern." Some analyses view headlines as one way of assessing the tone of media coverage. News stories can also have different intensity ratings based on their use of strong or weak language.

Attribution bias refers to bias that derives from the sources cited in any news story. Were the spokespersons (chosen for comment) favorable or unfavorable toward the organization and its policies? Were some spokespersons given a more prominent place than others on the agenda? Did some have more space or time to express their points of view? Many believe that the space allocated to different spokespersons in terms of air time or lines of print in newspapers can bias the coverage. That is, whether a point of view appears at the beginning, middle, or end of a news story can have an impact on how one reads the article. The number of sources that are quoted in support of, or in opposition to, a specific point of view can contribute to a perception of bias in the coverage. Television demonstrates attribution bias when it chooses to televise an interview with one person in preference to an interview with another. The bias can originate at the time that the individuals are selected for the interview or at the time of editing. Person-in-the-street interviews, for example, will be edited before broadcast. A talk show will invite some people to appear on the program and will not invite others. In these latter instances, the bias is built into the show. Newspapers and magazines demonstrate bias in the same kinds of ways.

Graphic bias refers to bias that may be present in photographs or other visuals. The visuals may appear in a newspaper or magazine, on television, or on an Internet site. At the time of Argentina's invasion of the Falklands, for example, a poignant picture of a young Argentine widow, bowed in grief over her husband's casket, achieved international news coverage. The picture appeared in the British and American press as well as in other newspapers throughout the world. Some Britons believed it was inappropriate for the press to convey images that generated sympathy for the Argentinians. Negative political campaigns often contain graphic bias. One U.S. public relations firm edited a speech in a way that depicted the opposing candidate as nodding his head as he spoke. The head nodding transmitted the nonverbal message that the candidate was a "yes" man, an individual without strength of conviction. A photograph of a Canadian prime minister that appeared in newspapers throughout the country during an election campaign gave the distinct impression that he had horns. On television, the graphics that appear in the upper corner of the television screen or that serve as a backdrop for commentators can carry nonverbal information that biases the viewer's perception of the verbal message. Prominent American journalist Leslie Stall lamented that audiences paid little attention to her critiques of President Reagan's administration when attractive visuals of the smiling president appeared as "wallpaper" or background for the commentary. Communication theory tells us that when such inconsistencies exist, audiences will favor the nonverbal over the verbal message (Ekman, 1985).

Contextual bias refers to the relationships between items carried in the news. For example, an article on war and famine in Yugoslavia will be read against the glamorous women and men who populate the perfume and liquor advertisements in the same news magazine (Berger, 1972). The announcement of strike action by a union will be read against the visual images of unruly union members shoving police officers (Fiske, 1982; Hartley, 1982). A television address by a repentant presidential hopeful will be interpreted against the dog food commercial that precedes the address and the soap commercial that follows it (Ferguson, 1976). Television stations carried live coverage of the O. J. Simpson trial in time slots normally occupied by daytime soap operas, establishing a nonverbal linkage between the two media events. Many of the viewers of *Days of Our Lives* would have been audiences for the court proceedings involving O. J. Simpson. Semiotic theory suggests that the significance of one item is tempered by the import of an adjacent or linked item. The congruence or lack of congruence of the two will carry meaning to the reader. A university newspaper carried a banner on its Christmas edition that read "Season's Greetings." Beneath the banner, the headline read "Government Cuts Funds to Universities." Beside the article was the smiling portrait of the responsible government official. The inconsistencies in these three adjacent items created a grim and not so pleasant irony. Semioticians tell us that nothing can be viewed in isolation from all that surrounds it (Barthes, 1988; Eco, 1976; Saussure, 1966). Figure 3.5 summarizes the elements that influence judgments of tone, including editorial, language, attribution, graphic, and contextual bias. Figure 3.6 displays an example of a protocol sheet for correspondence. This protocol includes space for evaluation of tone.

Focus and Parameters of Media Attention

Identifying the focus of media attention (in regard to specific issues) can be important. For example, issues related to seniors include housing, transportation, health, safety, pensions, recreation, and desire for independence and autonomy. Because media and public interest in these topic areas varies over time, the media analyst can track and predict upcoming shifts in the focus of coverage. Shifts in focus will call for the modification of strategies for dealing with the issues. For example, a rupture of pressure tubes occurred at a plant in Pickering, Ontario. This rupture allowed radioactive material to move from one area of the reactor to another. Shutting down the plant and replacing major components in the nuclear reactor cost approximately $1 billion. The events at Pickering received extensive press coverage, and government departments with a stake in the crisis issues tracked their development. In the process, Peggy Binns (personal communication, 1989), a government analyst, made the following discovery:

A review of clippings on the nuclear industry over the past 6 months indicated there was frequent mention of things such as the cost of nuclear power when

Source Bias	Newspaper or Media Outlet	Journalist
Perceived as positive		
Perceived as neutral		
Perceived as negative		

Attribution Bias (Sources quoted or cited)	In space allocated to sources	In numbers of sources cited	In placement of comment by sources
Predominantly positive			
Balanced			
Predominantly negative			

Language Bias	Choice of words	Explicit opinion expressed
Slanted positive		
Neutral		
Slanted negative		

Graphic Bias (Photographic, cartoon, etc.)	
Slanted positive	
Neutral	
Slanted negative	

Setting or Contextual Bias (congruency of adjacent materials with content of article)
__ Congruent   __ with positive tone __ Incongruent   __ with neutral tone __ with negative tone

Figure 3.5. Protocol for Analysis of Bias in Print or Electronic Media Coverage

compared to coal-generated power, the cost of replacement power for the Pickering shutdowns, the cost of repairs for the Pickering plants, etc. These references to costs were labeled as *concern about the economics of nuclear power* [italics added]. When this coverage was compared to coverage in the 6 weeks before the Pickering incidents, it was found that in the earlier period, there was a greater concern with topics such as arms, war, bombs, disarmament. These concerns were labeled *armament/disarmament* [italics added]. These findings provided a basis for the conclusion that one of the impacts of the Pickering incident was to change the focus of media coverage on the nuclear industry from one on armament/disarmament to one on the economics of nuclear power.

	For	Against	Balanced	Date of Letter	Sex of Writer		Writer's State of Residence
	F	A	B		M	F	
1							
2							
3							
4							
5							
6							
7							
8							
9							
10							
11							
12							
13							
14							
15							

Figure 3.6. Protocol for Logging of Correspondence

Recent coverage of the nuclear power plant at Pickering has displayed a concern with safety issues. Thus, discussions have focused on three different areas of concern during the past decade: armament and disarmament, economics, and safety. If the organization is to answer its critics, it must know the dominant concerns of stakeholders at a particular point in time. Shifts in the focus of coverage or shifts in argumentation and reasoning can necessitate the revamping of strategic approaches. If the press, for example, is arguing for greater regulation of nuclear industry on grounds of public safety and the government is responding with arguments based on economic concerns, then adjustments in strategies will be required.

Some of the discussions on news frames also refer to the focus of news coverage. For example, Durham (1998) found that three "frames" were used to explain the explosion of TWA Flight 800: the presence of a bomb aboard the flight, a missile fired from the ground, and mechanical malfunctioning of the aircraft. In other words, he talked about the development of a social narrative about causes of the crash. When the plane of John Kennedy, Jr., crashed off

Nantucket Island, journalists used the following four frames to explain the crash: the curse of the Kennedy family, sabotage, structural failure of the aircraft, and pilot error resulting from heavy fog and inadequate training. The coverage began with speculation about the Kennedy curse, linking the event to earlier tragedies in the Kennedy family. As the story unfolded, journalists moved to other frames, with most journalists talking about pilot error in the days leading to the funeral. The following was a fifth frame developed at the time of the funeral: Would Caroline Kennedy carry the Kennedy banner in future years? Sometimes, analysts will also want to examine cause-effect relationships. See Figure 3.3 for an example of this point.

Cobb and Elder (1983) argue that some issues have greater ability to attract attention because they can shrink or expand in focus to appeal to different groups. Debates related to the Siskiyou National Forest illustrate this concept very well. The focus in these debates expanded from a narrow emphasis on "roads and timber sales in a limited area" to "family and free enterprise, bureaucratic accountability and reform, or the prevention of global environmental upheaval" (Davis, 1995, p. 31). As national environmental groups became involved and local groups jumped on the bandwagon, "the lines between local Siskiyou issues and regional and national old growth, spotted owl, and timber management issues began to blur" (p. 30). Eventually, the very pregnant issue portfolio included "old growth, salmon streams, water quality, erosion, the spotted owl, the Siskiyou National Park proposal, rights to judicial review of Forest Service timber sales, Forest Service reform, forest resource economics, biodiversity, and global warming" (p. 31). A media analyst could examine the extent to which issues shrink and expand from a limited to a broader focus over periods of time. Figure 3.7 illustrates a format for recording the focus of news coverage on Siskiyou National Forest issues.

Place on the Media Agenda

The term *agenda setting* refers to the capacity of mass media to direct attention to specific issues and to ignore other issues. Identifying the place of a particular news item on the media agenda enables the organization to assess the prominence of the item (Walker, 1994). Some studies suggest that lead stories in newscasts have more influence than other stories. For this reason, many analysts record the placement of a story. Does the story appear on page 1 of the newspaper? First, middle, or final third of the broadcast? Was the placement of the story significant?

___ Old growth
___ Salmon streams
___ Water quality
___ Erosion
___ Spotted owl
___ National park proposal
___ Right to judicial review of timber sales
___ Forest service reform
___ Forest resource economics
___ Biodiversity
___ Global warming

Figure 3.7. Focus of Coverage, Siskiyou National Forest

Some analysts believe that almost as many readers read the last page of the newspaper as the first page because people flip from front to back while reading. Others believe that the first page of the financial section is a more significant location than the front page for some articles (e.g., the stock market or the U.S. budget deficit). Moreover, any conclusions concerning the prominence of a story must take competing items into account. For example, a scandal involving a company official can receive headline coverage or be relegated to page 8 depending on what else happens on that particular day. If Jesse Jackson negotiates the release of U.S. airmen captured by the Serbian forces on the same day that a scandal breaks, the story about the misadventures of a corporate head will receive little press attention. An airplane crash off the coast of Long Island, a bombing in Oklahoma, a mudslide in California, or an avalanche in Colorado can bury other news stories. At the other extreme, a slow news day can result in extensive coverage of a cultural debate regarding whether audiences will accept a maverick version of the classic ballet *Swan Lake*. Assessing the news values of other items that appear on the same news day or tracking the placement of a news item, over time, can suggest the long-term priority of the item. In this fashion, analysts can also ascertain the issue's survival time (how long has it occupied first, second, third, or other position on the news agenda?). Sometimes, the researcher is interested in knowing how different media rank the story—that is, the relative space or time granted to the issue by different media. The resources invested in covering the story give further indication of the perceived importance of the story. For example, are location shots, on-the-spot interviews, or interstation hookups used to record and distribute the event? (For more detailed consideration of the theoretical framework for this question, refer to the discussion on agenda setting and priming in Chapter 9.)

Depth and Sophistication of Coverage

Analysts can seek to assess the extent to which media cover issues in an in-depth and sophisticated manner. Although no direct relationship exists between exposure to information and acquisition of information, mass media can "raise the information level about a topic significantly—especially if people can find a use for the information or if it is in line with their existing attitudes" (Scanlon, 1990), and most communication specialists believe that awareness precedes the development of attitudes on a particular issue (Atkin & Freimuth, 1989; Backer, Rogers, & Sopory, 1992). Journalists, however, often face a situation in which they must cover issues to which they have had little exposure. The case of Oka, Quebec, illustrates this point well. When the Mohawk Indians erected their barricades in a small Quebec town, near the U.S. border, few journalists understood the history or origin of a dispute that spanned two centuries. As a consequence, early coverage of the dispute over land claims contained many inaccuracies, as reflected in the "myth versus fact" sheet (Table 3.1). Myth versus fact sheets enable an analyst to identify misconceptions in public perception or media coverage of a particular issue. (See also Table 3.2.)

In the case of the confrontation between Mohawks and French Canadians at Oka, the journalists also showed little appreciation of the complexities of the situation. Media coverage tended to be simplistic and geared toward the sensational elements in the case as Warriors enhanced their media status by assuming code names such as "Lasagna." With the exception of the army, most stakeholders in the dispute (the natives, the Quebec police, and the federal government ministers) received uniformly bad press. Media depicted federal political figures as shirking responsibility for the conflict and Quebec police as "bad guys" who kept food and medical supplies from everyone who was, willingly or unwillingly, behind the barricade. The Warriors also received extensive negative press coverage. Television cameras zoomed in on tattoos of "Mother" written on Warrior arms, and an evening news broadcast showed a native woman shoving a young Canadian soldier into a barbed wire fence. Other shots showed Warriors cleaning their guns.

At the other extreme, journalists who stayed behind the barricades with the Warriors tended to give highly sympathetic coverage; a colleague later accused them of succumbing to "Stockholm syndrome," a reference to the tendency of hostages to identify with their captors (Scanlon, 1990). In short, a perceptive analysis of media coverage of the face-off at Oka would have pinpointed media ignorance of the issues as a primary characteristic of the situa-

TABLE 3.1 Myth Versus Fact in Media Coverage of the Oka Crisis

Myth	Fact
Natives were united in their support of the barricade at Oka, Quebec.	There was dissension in the native camp, with many people opposing the barricade.
The Warriors were the accepted leaders of the natives.	There were two groups, traditionally opposed to each other, competing for leadership.
The Warriors were a group of American natives with no right to be involved at Oka.	The situation was much less clear-cut, with both Canadian and American natives involved. Neither recognized the Canadian-U.S. border as a legal designation affecting native territory.
The land claim dispute concerned only Mohawks.	A second native tribe had a conflicting claim to the disputed land and opposed a government settlement with the Mohawks.

TABLE 3.2 Myth Versus Fact in Media References to BR 126 Aircraft

Myth	Fact
There is inherent weakness in the design of the engine mountings on the BR 126 medium-range turbo jet.	Two cases of failure to fix bolts on BR 126 flight frames involved gross disregard of flight time replacement specifications.
There are more accidents involving BR 126 aircraft than any other medium-range aircraft.	BR 126s account for more than the total of all other types of aircraft flown by medium-range operators. The percentage of accidents among BR 126s is one of the lowest in the industry.
Deregulation of airlines will result in corner-cutting in maintenance.	Failure to comply with manufacturer-specified inspection maintenance and replacement schedules can result in an operator's license being withdrawn.
A spate of structural failures and crashes can be expected in the near future as a consequence of an aging fleet of aircraft.	Schedules of aircraft inspection and maintenance are drawn up by manufacturers and are enforced by international airline authorities.

tion (Post-Oka symposium, 1990). The fact that the journalists were largely unschooled in the history of the native land claim dispute led to superficial coverage and contributed to the volatility of an already bad situation. In other cases, however, media cover issues with a clarity and sophistication that is commendable. The analysis in Box 3.1 on Central America illustrates a situation in which journalists demonstrated a sophisticated understanding of the issue about which they wrote.

Box 3.1

Example of Media Analysis (Executive Summary; Fictitious) Press Coverage of Central American Issues, August 1, 1987-November 11, 1987

In the period under consideration, the press showed a sustained interest in Central America, publishing numerous editorials and commentaries, even when no news events were being reported. Press response to the idea of U.S. support for the Arias Plan was unabashedly positive, with fewer than 10% of the editorialists and columnists opposing U.S. involvement.

Arguments in favor of U.S. participation in the peace plan were as follows: (a) The United States could make a valid and important contribution to peace, (b) the United States could answer critics who accuse the government of continuing to pursue the role of aggressor in world politics, (c) the United States could gain further friendships in the international community, and (d) the United States could reaffirm its position of leadership in the foreign policy area.

The domestic press appears to recognize that the role of the U.S. military is changing, and the large majority of journalists express approval for the shift from a more individualistic posture to an emphasis on acting with other international players.

Journalists did not appear to underestimate the complexity of the Central American issues or the influence of economics on the politics of these countries. For example, they saw Nicaragua as the key country that could influence a sequence of events in other countries; and they saw upcoming decisions in the U.S. Congress as critical to future developments in Central America. The press did not reach consensus on which countries had the best chance of experiencing success with the Arias Plan; however, El Salvador probably received fewer votes of confidence than did the other countries.

Recent accusations that the U.S. government has behaved inconsistently in its treatment of human rights violators did not influence the coverage of Central American issues. Although human rights abuses were mentioned, as was suspension of personal freedoms in other countries, no journalist suggested that these practices should influence the U.S. decision to give support to the Arias Peace Plan.

A dissenting point of view on the question of financial aid to Central America came from a Guatemalan organization whose representative was visiting the United States. The group expressed the view that the United States should encourage dialogue rather than offer financial aid to the Guatemalan government. Few interest groups were represented in the news coverage in the August to November period.

Relatively few references to the government's Central American refugee and immigration policy appeared in the August to November press; journalists writing on the topic championed a more open policy and argued against closing U.S. borders to Central Americans.

Newspapers in the southwestern United States were by far the most active on Central American issues. To date, the journalists who have been most critical of the U.S. position on other current foreign affairs issues, such as the U.S. stance on sanctions against South Africa, have been silent on Central America. If, however, these writers choose to become active on Central America, it is anticipated that their arguments could be drawn from a stock selection including references to (a) the political motives of the government, (b) Communist/Marxist affiliations of countries we are aiding, (c) human rights records of countries to whom we are giving assistance, (d) the risk of military involvement, (e) shirking responsibilities at home in favor of engagement abroad, and (f) the economic burden of helping Third World countries.

Messages Carried by Media

In the process of strategic planning, the organization decides on the messages that it wants stakeholders and other key publics to receive. Most organizations use "free" advertising techniques (public service announcements, press conferences, interviews, speeches, press releases, backgrounders, and pseudoevents) to carry these messages. Because even these free techniques are costly to orchestrate, organizations search for ways to evaluate the cost-effectiveness of such efforts. One way is to track the extent to which media have picked up and transmitted the organization's "preferred messages." In other words, organizations perform usage counts to determine which messages appeared in magazines, association newsletters, newspapers, television news casts, or other media (Dozier & Ehling, 1992; Dozier & Repper, 1992; Nakra, 1991).

What Are the Catalysts and Spin-Off Issues?

Analysts seek to identify critical events, triggers, or catalysts with the potential to drive news coverage. An Australian study (Walker, 1994) found that most practitioners try to identify trigger events that could have an impact on their companies. Pride (1995) talks about "redefining" critical events that alter perceptions of reality (p. 6). For example, a torrent of news coverage followed the revelation that Swiss banks hold large sums of money deposited by Holocaust victims in the years preceding and during World War II. The loss of five House seats to Democrats in the 1998 congressional elections acted as a catalyst for the forced retirement of Republican Newt Gingrich as Speaker of the House.

Identifying spin-off issues can also be important. Spin-off issues result from the expansion of issues discussed in the section on framing. The revelation of wrongful imprisonment of a man for rape or murder can provoke renewed discussion of the relative merits of capital punishment. Such seemingly unrelated events as the abduction of a young woman by an Internet acquaintance and the inexplicable acts of violence at Colorado and Georgia high schools have the power to stimulate a heated debate regarding the larger issue of freedom to disseminate potentially dangerous information via common carriers such as the Internet. Should information on how to make a bomb be accessible? Should controls be set in place to guard against Internet "predators"? Could movies or video games have been responsible for the youths' decision to shoot their peers and for their shooting prowess? Should governments censor the content of video games?

All of the previously mentioned issues provoke further expressions of concern about parental supervision, the role of school administrators in identifying problem youths, and the role of government in achieving a workable balance between the rights of individuals versus the rights of the collective. Should parents be held accountable when their children commit acts of violence with restricted firearms? Should school administrators be held responsible when youths bring weapons into schools? How should society seek to address such serious problems? Should local school boards pass legislation requiring that students wear uniforms to school? How can teachers, administrators, and students help to ensure that such antisocial acts are not repeated in schools throughout the country?

One event or issue can have a ripple effect felt across large spans of space and time. On May 20, 1999, a young man in Conyers, Georgia, celebrated the

1-month anniversary of the Littleton massacre by opening fire on classmates chatting in a school cafeteria. Media coverage of this copycat event gave energy to the debate. The coverage of one environmental issue, such as transportation of hazardous materials across state lines, can lead to an examination of more systemic issues related to corporate social responsibility and the role of government in protecting the public. Analysts sometimes seek to identify spin-off issues that may piggyback on other issues.

What Are the Trends in Media Coverage?

The quest for insights into the future is probably as old as humanity. Justified on the basis of offering metaphors or models that improve understanding of the present, the study of history enables societies to anticipate and (sometimes) to influence the future. Modern soothsayers, however, have a much more impressive array of tools to assist them than did their ancient counterparts. A massive amount of data are available to the media analyst in the form of print, sound and video recording, and computer memory. Although such a large compilation of information has its obvious benefits, it also has its liabilities. Information overload can blur the lines between the significant and the trivial, and the usefulness of the data will depend on the researcher's ability to detect significant patterns. In the search for an understanding of public opinion, media analysts can look for the kinds of patterns discussed in this section.

The analyst can compare coverage of an individual, concept, or institution at various points in time. For example, a study could compare Hillary Clinton's image during her husband's first term in office with her image during her husband's second term in office. Alternatively, the study could examine depictions of Hillary Clinton in the period before, during, and after the sex scandals involving her husband. The analyst can compare coverage of an individual, concept, or institution in different media. For example, a study could compare the ways in which print media and broadcast media cover Hillary Clinton. Alternatively, a study could compare coverage of Hillary Clinton in the *New York Times,* the *Washington Post,* the *Indianapolis Star,* and the *New Orleans Times-Picayune.* The analyst can compare coverage of an individual, concept, or institution in differing situations. For example, a study can compare press coverage of Hillary Clinton in situations in which she is accompanied by her husband with press coverage when she is on her own. The analyst can compare perceptions of an individual, concept, or institution in different regions of the country or world. For example, a study can examine public reaction to Hillary Clinton as she travels throughout the United States. A study can compare international and domestic perceptions of Hillary Clinton.

Meaningful interpretation of content data often involves comparison against a performance standard or benchmark (Holsti, 1969). For example, to note that 175 references to U.S. human rights policies appeared in press coverage between September 1999 and January 2000 is meaningless unless one compares this information with past trends. Are news media increasing their coverage of human rights issues? How does the coverage compare with last year's coverage in the same time frame? Knowledge of a performance standard enables the researcher to judge the significance of the 175 press items. In the same way, a researcher can compare typical media coverage of the pharmaceutical industry with coverage after a significant increase in the price of prescription drugs. To set a benchmark for analysis of media coverage of a corporation, the researcher must examine typical coverage of similar firms in the same sector. Similarly, in a political context, to reach valid conclusions on Bill Clinton's media image in his second term in office requires comparing media coverage with typical media coverage of presidents in their second terms of office.

Sometimes, the analyst must construct these standards or benchmarks for comparison (Wimmer & Dominick, 1997). For example, a researcher who wants to know the relative emphasis in California papers on gang violence must construct an index that will allow this comparison. In other words, the analyst codes sample coverage of gang violence in various states (e.g., New York, Illinois, Louisiana, Florida, and Texas) to use as a reference point or standard for gauging coverage in California. The analyst can compare the average amount of space devoted to the issue of gang violence in California with the average amount of space given to the issue in other states. He or she can also compare frequency of coverage during a designated period of time in California with frequency of coverage during the same period in other states. The same process can be followed in constructing standards for judging the coverage of other issues.

Finally, the analyst can compare content data with expert opinion or other aggregate data measures (Wimmer & Dominick, 1992). For example, the researcher can compare President Clinton's performance against some standard established by reference to expert opinion. A group of political scientists may point out that Democrats typically receive less support in their second term in office than in their first term. Some theories suggest, for example, that presidents experience a "honeymoon period" in their first term—a period of alliance with media (Grossman & Kumar, 1981). A competitive phase follows, which is characterized by media criticism. Relations become more formal and routine as the president enters a final phase called detachment. These phases can serve as benchmarks to help researchers to interpret data on media coverage of presidential terms. In other situations, as in research concerned with seniors, youth, or minority groups, aggregate data (such as census data) can help researchers to interpret their findings. For example, if researchers want to understand the trend toward greater activism among seniors, as evidenced in media coverage of their issues, they can examine lifestyle measures that suggest that seniors are more physically active, travel more frequently than in the past, have a larger disposable income, participate more in community affairs, remain in their own homes for longer periods of time than in the past, and comprise a large percentage of those who work in the voluntary sector. In other words, seniors are not behaving in a stereotypical fashion. There is a trend toward greater independence, higher levels of involvement in community affairs, and a greater tendency to behave in the same way as middle-aged Americans. Gerontologists now view aging as a continuum on which people move gradually into old age. Thus, the media analyst can better understand the trend toward greater activism, more organized lobbying efforts on behalf of retired Americans, and more vocal airing of their causes in mass and specialized media.

Although modern computer technology greatly enhances pattern recognition, the technology cannot suggest the meaning of the patterns for the organization. Deciding on the meaning of patterns remains a matter of judgment. Thus, the judgment of the analyst remains the critical factor in determining the quality of an analysis. Good research involves an "analytical edge—an appreciation not only of technique but also of how social and psychological forces lead to behavioral and attitudinal changes and the implications of these for the practice of public affairs" (Reid, 1988b, pp. 135-136).

Box 3.2 on the refugee determination legislation and Box 3.3 on pornography legislation are examples of analyses that respond to some of the questions asked in this chapter. See Appendix A for an example of a monthly trend analysis report.

Box 3.2

Example of a Media Analysis (Executive Summary; Fictitious) Media Response to Bill X, Refugee Determination Legislation

This analysis is based on a sample of 187 articles published in the print media between January 1, 1998, and January 15, 1998. Newspapers and magazines included in the sample are the *Wall Street Journal*, the *Baltimore Sun*, the *Los Angeles Times*, the *Washington Post*, the *New York Times*, the *Richmond Times-Dispatch*, *Newsweek*, and *U.S. News and World Report*.

Commentaries

Fifty opinion articles were published between January 1 and January 15, 1998; half originated in the Northeast, especially in New York City, Boston, and Washington, D.C. Many were published in the first 3 days after Bill X came into effect; journalists continued to comment on the legislation, however, throughout the first 2 weeks in January.

Arguments in Favor of Legislation

1. The processing of applications will be speedier.
2. The new procedures are less complicated, with fewer steps.
3. The new legislation ensures admission of genuine refugees while stemming the flow of bogus refugees.
4. The legislation has constitutional validity.
5. The new legislation meets both physical and emotional needs of claimants.

Arguments Against Legislation

1. The new legislation imposes unduly strict regulations.
2. The new legislation is costly to implement.
3. The legislation will eventually generate its own backlog, as did the earlier legislation.
4. The legislation ignores the emotional and human dimension of refugee claims.
5. The legislation violates constitutional rights (right to appeal, right to full and impartial hearing, right to legal counsel, guarantee against arbitrary search and seizure, and right to fundamental justice).
6. The legislation puts the physical safety of refugee claimants at risk.

7. The legislation prevents external agencies from legally helping claimants.

Additional Actions and Cautions Urged

1. Regulate immigration consultants.
2. Refute portrayal of United States as an easy haven for bogus refugee claimants.
3. Reconsider issue of safe Third World countries.
4. Apply the same regulations to all refugee claimants—no matter what the claimant's position in the public realm.

Interest Groups

Those opposing Bill X included church organizations such as the Inter-Denominational Committee for Refugees, immigration lawyers, immigration consultants, Citizens Against Violence, and the World Amnesty Organization.

Those supporting Bill X included some refugee claimants and various refugee aid organizations.

Trends

During the 2-week period, comments by the press became increasingly positive toward the new legislation. Although journalists tended to give sympathetic coverage to those refugees being sent home, they also praised the government for taking a firm stance. Some interest groups that had initially voiced the strongest opposition to the bill began to comment on positive aspects of the bill as well.

Box 3.3

Example of a Media and Correspondence Analysis
(Executive Summary; Fictitious)
Analysis of Reaction to Pornography Legislation

Press interest in the newly announced pornography legislation declined markedly after August 1, 1999, although there was a flurry of interest again in October with extensive coverage of the Welman report. An Associated Press article on the report was reprinted in at least 40 different large-circulation newspapers. Although media coverage of the pornography legislation continued to be predominantly negative, the first positive editorial appeared in September and writers began more often noting the difficult task faced by those who must frame such social legislation and the problems associated with our current reliance on community standards. Some editorial writers claimed that critics have exaggerated the weaknesses of the proposed pornography legislation. In other words, there seemed to be a certain "softening" in the press compared with the more uniformly cynical mood in the first week after tabling. Published letters to the editor most often reflected the popular position of the press, with critical letters outnumbering those supportive of the government's stance.

Arguments most frequently used by those opposed to the legislation related to the broadness and vagueness of the legislation; the failure of the government to make appropriate distinctions between hard-core pornography and erotica and to clarify the phrase "other sexual activity"; questioning of the credibility of the government in such matters as ignoring the Welman report, being inconsistent in banning sex but not violence on television and banning videos but not books; and accusing the government of threatening our basic freedoms, such as freedom of choice and expression. Critics of the bill often claimed that although many Americans believe there is a link between pornography and violence, these beliefs are founded in emotionalism and not based on research results, which they claim do not support a causal link. Occasional references were made to influential lobbies, such as the women's lobby and the religious lobby. Although potential interpretation and enforcement problems received much emphasis in earlier media coverage, these points were seldom mentioned after August 15th.

Arguments supporting the pornography legislation included the claim that legitimate filmmakers and artists have nothing to fear, pornographers' right to sell material is no more sacred than the public's right to be free of it, access to pornography may not be a lightning rod for sexual deviants, middle ground will be found, the scattergun approach adopted will ensure that some of the legislation gets through, and the new legislation pushes the onus back on the courts where it belongs.

Many references to potential loss of the bill and a suggestion on the part of two writers that parts of the bill deserve saving express a certain ongoing press interest in the pornography bill. A recent poll revealed contradictory findings regarding the views of Americans on pornography issues.

To date, more than 15,000 persons have written in to the Justice Department, stating their views on the proposed legislation; the large majority of these letter writers have been strongly supportive of the legislation. They say that the government is offering strong leadership and should not weaken the bill. Sometimes supporters write just to say "thank you for the legislation." Others state their belief in a relationship between crime and violence and pornography or their conviction that pornography perverts and degrades people and destroys relationships. Critics, however, say that the legislation threatens basic freedoms and that it is puritanical. Some claim that the government has failed to distinguish between hard-core pornography and erotica. They say that the government should be addressing more serious problems, such as violence on the television and serious social and economic concerns. It is important to note that a notable discrepancy exists between the dominant opinions expressed in correspondence to the Justice Department and newspaper articles and letters to the editor.

Conclusion

A word of caution is in order. Although the questions to which an analyst seeks answers may be reasonable and appropriate, the researcher may find that content data do not answer all or most of the questions or support assumptions or hypotheses. Sometimes, the questions that the researcher chooses in advance to answer will be far less appropriate than questions that become apparent in the gathering or analyzing of the data. Although it may be useful to identify a preliminary format or approach to data analysis, the analyst should be sufficiently flexible to accept the possibility that the analysis planned will not always be compatible with the data once collected.

Discovering the hidden structure of argumentation and reasoning can be much more rewarding than trying to plug round holes with square pegs. Answering questions that the data do not address and sorting extremely complex developments of arguments into simple categories such as positive, negative, and neutral can sometimes yield worthless information. Sometimes, what is most important in a body of data is what has been left out. An organization's intended messages to its publics may never emerge from a set of data, whereas other messages may surface. If the analyst either feels bound by a preconceived research protocol or, alternatively, is unable or incompetent to tap the significance of the data, the result may be a useless or, worse, misleading report.

Moreover, analysis of print or electronic media will not provide insights into some questions. Newspapers, radio, and television provide readers with a filtered view of reality. Because print and electronic media have limited news space and editors make choices on what should appear in that "news hole," the coverage is selective. The analyst can never know the extent to which the views represent the larger population. The biases of a free press can inflate the coverage of some issues, such as violence on the Internet or pornography on television, because these issues concern censorship and freedom of access to information. Other journalistic norms also intervene to bias newspaper coverage of issues. For example, newspapers try to balance opposing points of view in publishing "letters to the editor." Even if a newspaper receives 15 letters against a policy and 5 letters in favor, the newspaper will probably publish 3 letters against and 3 in favor of the policy. Another uncontrolled variable is the headline writer, an individual who has no connection with the story prior to generating the headline.

In short, media analysts judge final edited products. These products might or might not accurately reflect the knowledge, awareness, or attitudes of key publics toward the event, person, or concept being studied. For this reason, organizations should combine public opinion surveys, focus groups, correspondence analysis, and other measures with the results of media analysis.

Noelle-Neumann (1993) offers an additional caution. She discusses the "spiral of silence," a phenomenon whereby some people (often isolates or those with low self-esteem or low self-confidence) remain silent or express the majority viewpoint even when they do not share that point of view. Studies have found that the most vocal individuals are those who perceive that they will experience victory or those who hold the popular point of view; losers and those with deviant points of view remain silent or misrepresent their opinions on the topic (p. 21). By extrapolation, it appears obvious that media would reflect the loudest, but not necessarily the most representative, voices.

4

Content Analysis Techniques

Chapter 3 addressed questions asked by those who track opinion in the media, and this chapter and Chapters 5, 6, and 7 describe popular research tools used to answer the questions. This chapter describes techniques that can be applied to the analysis of data acquired through various means, including surveys, focus groups, media and Internet monitoring, and correspondence. Although a variety of applications are possible, organizations tend to use content analysis techniques in a fairly limited way. The most frequent application is media analysis. Organizations pay large sums of money to media monitoring and consulting firms to track and analyze media coverage of their issues. Within organizations, media monitoring teams assume the same kinds of job duties, and media analysts prepare reports that summarize and interpret the coverage.

History and Definition of the Methodology

Content analysis is not a novel methodology. Some of the earliest examples can be found in the Payne Fund film studies, which were carried out between 1929 and 1932. Edgar Dale reviewed, classified, and analyzed the content of 1,500 films (DeFleur & Dennis, 1981). Content analysis research continued into the 1930s and 1940s with the work of Becker (1930, 1932), Bruner (1941), and Lasswell, Leites, and Associates (1949). Bruner and others used these techniques to understand and learn how to counter propaganda techniques employed by the Nazi press in World War II.

Just as academic interest in content analysis was beginning to falter, Berelson (1952) and Stempel (1952) wrote well-publicized works on content analysis. The National Conference on Content Analysis (held in 1967) gave further impetus to the revival of this methodology, and Holsti joined with Gerbner, Krippendorff, Paisley, and Stone (1969) to edit a book on scientific and computer applications of content analysis. Krippendorff (1980) and Stempel (1989) continued this trend, and the early cultivation research by Gerbner (1977) stimulated a proliferation of studies in the 1980s and 1990s.

Although content analysis has been applied for many years to the study of numerous forms of communication, including the study of political campaigns, it has only recently become popular as a research tool within organizations. American Telephone and Telegraph Company was one of the first commercial firms to recognize the value of this analysis technique (Dozier & Repper, 1992), and Naisbitt and Aburdene's *Megatrends* (1991) and Naisbitt's monthly newsletter, *The Trend Report,* brought visibility to business applications in the 1980s. Like business and an increasing number of governments, Naisbitt saw content analysis as a viable technique for analyzing and forecasting issue development. Another pioneer in the area was Yankelovich (1991), who developed similar services to meet the needs of business and government. In the 1990s, many media monitoring and trend analysis firms set up business to meet the increasing demand for this kind of service. Later authors who have argued for the application of content analysis techniques to the study of public opinion include Merriam and Makower (1988) and Ferguson (1994). Others have described computer applications and mathematical models for predicting public opinion from mass media (Fan, 1988; Jasperson, Shah, Watts, Faber, & Fan, 1998). An increasing number of academic presses sell computer programs with content analysis applications (e.g., NUD•IST, Sage). These programs enable users to input and analyze data from all kinds of communication products, including public opinion research.

The classical question asked in most communication research is "Who says what, to whom, how, and with what effect?" (Lasswell, 1948). Content analysis involves asking the additional question, "Why?" Researchers study messages to make inferences about characteristics of a message or text, to understand the ideology espoused by the source, to suggest the conditions that could have generated the need for the message, and to speculate on the possible effects of the message. Those engaging in content analysis assume that messages have an effect. They also assume that an issue's place on the media agenda and how media cover a story can influence audience perceptions of the issue, the organization, and its chief executives. In brief, content analysis involves examining the message component of the communication process using as precise, objective, and systematic measures as possible (Berelson, 1952). This chapter details the steps most commonly followed in content analysis of messages. The examples are specific to the analysis of public opinion.

Steps in Conducting Content Analysis

Limiting the Study: Deciding What to Include and Exclude

Questions to be answered in deciding the limits of a study can relate to sources and scope. The answers to these questions derive from the purposes of the research. Sample questions related to sources include the following: Which sources should be consulted? Newspapers? The Internet? Electronic media? News magazines? Correspondence from experts or the general public? Activist publications? Trade and professional publications? Consumer complaints? Court cases? Ethnic or community media? Only the largest and most established presses?

A related question is the following: What criteria should be applied to selecting these sources? In referring to a Canadian newspaper chain with a reputation for a highly conservative bias and sensationalist coverage of news stories, a client once said to me, "Disregard those newspapers. We already know their opinion, and we don't care what they think." I wondered at the logic behind the statement because this particular newspaper chain had a very large readership. I asked the client whether any study that ignored such a large cachement of readers could reach valid conclusions. The same is true in the United States. If hundreds of thousands of Americans did not read the *National Inquirer,* the newspaper would not have the money to hire journalists with elite backgrounds and to invest huge sums of money in researching stories such as the trial of O. J. Simpson. It was rumored that the *New York Times* purchased much of its coverage of this trial from the *National Enquirer.*

Where should the analyst go to compile a data bank of source materials? The index to the *New York Times*? A media monitoring service? Internet monitoring service? The press clipping files of members of Congress or senators? The answer to this question is critical to the quality of the study. How representative is the sample of material?

If one uses Internet or media monitoring firms, will employees of media or Internet monitoring services understand the issues sufficiently well to enter the right keywords into the computer? The organization can provide the keywords that reflect what they already know, but can they provide key words for emerging dimensions of an issue that they have not anticipated? Will the omission of smaller newspapers or the ethnic press, publications that tend not to be accessible on the Internet, pose a problem for the analyst who wants to understand grassroots opinion and regional perceptions of issues?

Will other factors such as the budget of the organization restrict the potential of the monitoring firm to generate a representative number of media articles or Internet communications? Should multiple copies of the same wire story be included in the data sample? Many organizations (for budgetary reasons) request that monitoring services include only one copy of each wire story in their clipping packages. Although local newspapers sometimes publish an entire wire story, often they cut, paste, and rewrite the story for local consumption. Should the analyst be interested in changes and omissions in the accounts of local newspapers, television, and radio stations? If so, then the organization may need to ask the monitoring firm to include multiple versions of the same wire service articles in its clippings folders. In brief, what criteria will be applied to the selection of sources? If the organization is interested in learning the views of special target populations, as opposed to the general population, the choice of sources will reflect this interest. Directories of American newspapers include the *Ayer Directory of Publications* and the *Gale Directory of Publications and Broadcast Media* (Weber, 1990).

The following are examples of questions related to scope:

- Will the researcher restrict the analysis to certain kinds of materials? News clippings or editorials? Front-page stories or the business section of newspapers? Afternoon talk shows or all television talk shows? News or chat groups on the Internet?
- What is the geographical scope of the study? International? National? Regional? Local?
- What is the time scope for the study? The last 3 weeks? Three months? Two years?
- What is the scope of the topic? All types of violence? Family violence? Spousal or elder abuse? Random acts of violence? Violence stemming from Internet relationships?

The study of consumer reaction to a product recall could entail examining the coverage preceding, during, and following the recall. A researcher who tracks the development of the euthanasia issue may want to place the issue in historical perspective by examining a longer than average time frame to ascertain the extent to which the issue has escalated in perceived importance since the beginning of Kevorkian's crusade. Understanding the public's reaction to a new tax policy may necessitate examining reactions to earlier announcements of a similar nature to put the public response to this legislation into perspective. Analyzing public reaction to the president's visit to China, however, may only require the study of audience response in the days leading up to, during, and immediately after the trip. The event is short lived, although the decisions made at the meeting could be long term in their consequences. The study of crisis events can require tracking an event over a lengthy period of time to determine when the crisis has ended in the eyes of the public and media. At other times, the analyst may be interested only in learning when the crisis event (e.g., scandal involving a company official) drops from its place as front-page news.

Extensive experience with tracking public opinion on government issues in Canada reveals a 5- to 7-day lag between a newspaper's first articles on an event ("hard" news coverage) and editorial comment on the event. Thus, to gain a full understanding of how newspapers have covered the event, the organization may need to study the press coverage for a period of at least 2 weeks. Different patterns are present with television, in which agendas change rapidly, and the Internet, in which discussions may continue for months or years, with participants entering and leaving the group.

In addition to purposes of the study, other factors that govern the response to source and scope questions are time restraints and the willingness of the organization to invest in public opinion research. The more in-depth the analysis, the more time required to read and assimilate the information into meaningful patterns. The time spent on crisis management often detracts from the resources available for public opinion research and analysis, and contracting out the work can be expensive. Assigning "beats" to public opinion researchers can decrease the costs because new researchers must spend time in background reading. In deciding the parameters of a study, all these points are important, and in the end the analyst may make a statement such as "This study considers the news content on the front pages of the *Washington Post* and the *New York Times,* excluding Sundays, from January 1 to December 31 of the past year" (Wimmer & Dominick, 1992, p. 162).

Picking a Sample

Having decided the sources to be examined and the scope of the study, the researcher selects a representative sample of material from the available choices. The term *random sample* implies that every source has an equal or known chance of being selected. To ensure that every item has an equal chance of being selected, the researcher assigns numbers to all items (e.g., all press clippings, news group comment, correspondence, or other communications) in the sampling frame. Then the researcher relies on a table of random numbers to select the sample or picks randomly from the list of numbered items until he or she reaches the desired sample size (see Chapter 5). Sampling eliminates the necessity to examine every item.

To ensure distribution across a period of time, the analyst can limit the sample to several items each week or month that are picked randomly—for example, every fifth issue of a newspaper or every third broadcast day. Alternatively, for a shorter term study, the researcher can select several items per day during a 2-week period or can draw the sample from different days of the week (one Monday, one Tuesday, one Wednesday, one Thursday, one Friday, and one Saturday). To choose the specific Monday, the analyst selects randomly from all items that represent Monday and follows the same procedures for other days of the week.

Most people assume that large samples are more likely to be representative than smaller samples. There are points beyond which increasing sample size makes little difference, however. One study analyzed samples of 6, 12, 18, 24, and 48 issues of a newspaper. The researcher found each of the sample sizes to be adequate. He also found that increasing the sample size beyond 12 did not improve the accuracy of the results (Stempel, 1952). A study of television programming, conducted for purposes of producing a violence index, found that 1 week of fall programming produced results similar to that of a larger sample drawn throughout the year (Gerbner, Gross, Jackson-Beeck, Jeffries-Fox, & Signorielli, 1977). Another study compared the results from four different types of samples: odd-day samples, every-fifth-day samples, weekly samples, and every-tenth-day samples. The researchers found no noticeable differences between the results from data representing all days of the month and those representing odd-day and every-fifth-day samples. They did, however, discover that weekly samples and every-tenth-day samples were inferior (Mintz as cited in Lasswell, 1948). Riffe, Aust, and Lacy (1993) found that putting together a sample based on a composite week (one Monday, one Tuesday, one Wednesday, etc.) was superior to random samples and consecutive-day samples. In carrying out a series of content analyses on a single topic, a researcher may want to determine these optimum sample size cutoff points.

Sometimes, other variables can be more important than sample size. For example, a researcher who analyzes every seventh day's coverage could be examining only Sunday newspapers, which are a different variety from those of other days of the week. Other kinds of content vary by season. Election years will generate a different type of media coverage compared to that of other years. Christmas, Easter, Human Rights Day, and the Fourth of July produce coverage different from that of other days of the year. To avoid bias in results, the analyst needs to consider these kinds of factors.

At other times, researchers need to weight their samples in favor of certain categories of information. For example, assume that an organization wants to conduct a study of public opinion on gun control based on media coverage of this issue. A sample of articles, picked randomly from a general index of newspaper articles, would not necessarily yield a representative sample because newspapers with widely varying circulations would have an equal chance of being selected. By dividing the newspapers according to circulation figures (a technique called *stratified* sampling), the analyst could subsequently place a greater weight on high-circulation newspapers or, alternatively, over sample from that population. Other situations also justify the use of stratified samples. For example, to analyze differences in media coverage across regions, the researcher can sort the items by region before picking randomly from each regional group. To analyze the views of subgroups within the population, he or she can subdivide the responses into demographic or other clusters before picking randomly from each cluster. Therefore, sampling can involve several stages.

In conclusion, the researcher should consider the preceding factors when deciding which and how many materials to analyze. It is useful to note, however, that rigid conformity to sampling procedures can be impractical in an organizational context. *Purposive sampling* (drawing on a small sample of carefully selected media sources) sometimes makes more sense than using probability sampling procedures. The researcher, for example, can learn more about investment opportunities in Asia by examining a carefully selected sample of newspapers that subscribe to international wire services than by drawing a random sample from an index of newspapers (Stempel, 1989).

In other contexts, it may not be possible to ignore any item of information. Any staff member censured for not informing the CEO or political representative of some relatively obscure news item or editorial comment will appreciate this particular point. The culture of some organizations demands that all items of information be given at least cursory examination. Further complicating the situation is the fact that organizations often work with samples selected by media or Internet monitoring services, individuals over whom they have little control on a day-to-day basis. The most that can be done, in most cases, is to give the monitoring firm a list of criteria to use in making their selections. A more systematic and detailed description of the steps to be followed in sampling is provided in Chapter 5.

Deciding What to Count

Content analysis involves counting: the number of stories that refer to successful space missions, the number of times that NATO has been criticized for its bombing missions, or the number of times editorials have argued against a government policy to subsidize day care for working parents. Knowing what to count involves deciding on a unit of analysis. The unit of analysis in written content (a newspaper article, magazine story, or discussion thread on the Internet) might be a "single word or symbol, a theme . . . or an entire article or story" (Wimmer & Dominick, 1997, p. 119). Units of analysis in film can be "characters, acts, or entire programs" (p. 119).

An analyst, charged with documenting public opinion on an issue (e.g., whether or not to publish the names of convicted sexual offenders), has two options. The person can record every reference in every article to the issue, or the person can limit the count to a maximum of one reference per article, no matter the frequency of mentions within individual articles. In the latter instance, the analyst codes for the presence or absence of the attribute within a single document (Osgood & Walker, 1959; see also Budd, Thorp, & Donohew, 1967).

The unit of analysis, however, could be the paragraph, the sentence, the theme, the speaker, headlines, or a period of time (e.g., every 30 seconds of the broadcast or every time a new person begins speaking). If references to a product defect appear in 15 sentences of an article, and the unit of analysis is the sentence, the frequency count will be 15. If references to a product defect appear in 5 paragraphs of the article and the unit of analysis is the paragraph, however, the frequency count will be 5. If the unit of analysis is the article, the analyst records a count of 1 or 0, which signals whether the article contained a reference to the idea, person, or issue. (If the unit of analysis is the article, the same count of "1" would apply whether 1, 4, 9, 10, 12, or more references appeared within the article.)

Another possible unit of analysis is the theme. A theme is a "single asser-tion about one subject" (Wimmer & Dominick, 1997, p. 119). Multiple themes can appear in a single sentence, paragraph, or article. Consider the following sentence: "Rumors suggest that the CEO of Company X may be re-signing, and some say the company may be in financial trouble." Two themes appear in this sentence: the CEO's resignation and the company's financial difficulties. Many different themes tend to appear in a State of the Union ad-dress. One such address included references to social justice, economic re-newal, and constructive internationalism. An analysis of issues pertaining to the mentally challenged could find themes such as human rights, safety, housing, and employment. A theme may appear in only one sentence or may span several paragraphs of a news article. One theme ends when another be-gins. Themes are a good unit of analysis to use in analyzing discussion groups on the Internet. A study by Hill and Hughes (1997) illustrated the way in which researchers can conduct content analysis of Internet communications by identifying discussion "threads," a technique first applied to the analysis of computer conferencing.

Another possible unit of analysis is the speaker. If panelists discuss the topic of child abuse, each speaker's statements can be regarded as a separate speaking unit, to be analyzed for appearance of arguments or appeals. If a panelist speaks at three different times, the analyst can consider each of the three speaking occasions as separate units. If a second panelist speaks at five different times, the analyst can consider each one of the five monologues as separate units.

Some studies consider individual words or phrases as units of analysis. A study of political campaign rhetoric, for example, could include an analysis of adjectives used to describe the various contenders for political office. The analyst could search for the appearance of "appreciative" or "depreciative" adjectives. Examples of appreciative adjectives are "down-to-earth," "con-cerned," "capable," and "charismatic," whereas examples of depreciative ad-jectives are "irrational," "patronizing," "dishonest," and "inexperienced." Similarly, research into an organization's image could search for adjectives used to describe the organization, with the possibilities ranging from "inno-vative" and "committed" to "outdated" and "financially overextended." In the Siskiyou National Forest debates, loggers attempted to stereotype envi-ronmentalists as hippies; meddlesome outsiders; lawyers from the city; small, wealthy, and elite; and urban, white-collared, and eastern. They also attempted to link activist leaders with socialist causes (Davis, 1995, p. 37).

An analysis could have identified the frequency with which different labels were attached to stakeholders in the dispute.

Computerized versions of content analysis programs have reduced the financial cost and time to undertake this kind of analysis. Although the task would appear overwhelming, in fact computer programs perform this task more easily than they perform other kinds of analysis. The computer analyst enters a list of adjectives that would fall into the categories of appreciative and depreciative. Then he or she programs the computer to identify and count the number of times that the adjectives appear in the communications that are being analyzed. Whereas the identification of words does not require the judgment of the analyst, the identification of themes requires fine levels of discrimination, performed better by the analyst than by the computer. Sometimes, the two operate in conjunction with each other. For example, some consulting firms track the appearance of a concept or argument from its first mention in media. They note where and with whom the argument originated. Having identified the first mention of an argument through the use of a computer program, they can study the communication for additional information.

Contingency analyses enable researchers to identify how often two arguments appear in conjunction with each other. For example, an analyst could have tracked the appearance of concurrent references to Paula Jones and Monica Lewinsky to ascertain the ways in which journalists linked the two cases. In another situation, an analyst could examine the number of occasions on which journalists compared calls for a referendum on national sovereignty in Scotland to the ongoing debate over sovereignty in Quebec, Canada.

In the context of the debate over medical research ethics, an analyst could search for the connections between expressed support for genetic engineering and the cloning of Dolly the sheep. Sometimes, a political analyst will want to track the development of an issue in terms of how it is framed against other issues on the political landscape. Environmentalists in the Siskiyou National Forest debates attempted to link deforestation arguments to the production of the cancer-fighting drug Taxol, which is made from the bark of a tree indigenous to one of the threatened areas (Davis, 1995). An analyst could have examined the number of times that media referred to Taxol in conjunction with the issue of deforestation. Contingency analyses do not reveal cause-effect relationships; they do reveal patterns, however.

Some units of analysis are easier than others to count. For example, it is more difficult to define the boundaries of themes in print news media than to identify the boundaries of sentences, paragraphs, and articles. The same kinds of considerations apply to broadcast media. Wimmer and Dominick (1997) note,

> It is easier to determine the number of stories on the *CBS Evening News* that deal with international news than the number of acts of violence in a week of network television because a "story" is a more readily distinguishable unit of analysis than an "act." The beginning and end of a news story are fairly easy to see but suppose that a researcher trying to catalog content was faced with a long fistfight between three characters? Is the whole sequence one act of violence, or is every blow considered an act? What if a fourth character joins in? Does it then become a different act? (p. 119)

It is important to note that the analyst can obtain quite different results when using different units of analysis. Studies have demonstrated, for example, that the longer the coding unit (articles are longer than paragraphs, paragraphs are longer than sentences, and sentences are longer than words), the more likely the unit will be rated as biased (either favorable or unfavorable in tone) (Geller, Kaplan, & Lasswell, 1942). Agreement between coders (intercoder reliability) tends to suffer when smaller units of analysis are used.

Assume that the best way to assess the impact of an editorial is to count the number of favorable and unfavorable assertions in the comment. In this case, the sentence could be the unit of analysis. Using this technique, the content of one editorial could receive a rating of 41% favorable, 19% neutral, and 40% unfavorable. If the analyst makes a judgment on the entire article (not individual sentences within the article), however, he or she must place the entire article in one of the three categories: positive, neutral, or negative. Perhaps, if the greatest part of the content seems to be balanced between the positive and negative (41% favorable and 40% unfavorable), the analyst will choose to put the article in the neutral category. Alternatively, the analyst could decide that the beginning of the story led the reader in a negative direction, even if favorable remarks appeared later in the story. Using this reasoning, he or she could place the story in the negative category. Finally, if a highly credible spokesperson (perhaps the state governor) speaks in favor of the idea being championed in the article, and a highly incredible person (a maker of pornographic films) speaks against the idea, perhaps the analyst will think that the article falls into the positive category, regardless of other impressions received from reading the article. The point is that many different variables can influence assessments of tone.

The variations in rating derive from placing a weight on different points, judging the comparative importance of different aspects of the article, which does not happen as often when the sentence or individual assertion is the unit of analysis. Obviously, at the end of the whole process, the totals would vary for different units of analysis (sentences versus paragraphs versus articles). Which is correct? It depends: "The first view is that the effect of the whole is equal to the sum of its parts, the second position is that the impact of the whole is different from the sum of its parts" (Holsti, 1969, p. 120).

Morris (1994), using ZyIndex software, compared the results from human and computer coding of data. She found that the computer program agrees with human coders when the unit of analysis is the sentence or paragraph but disagrees when it is the entire document. That is, the program fails when it becomes necessary to draw implications from the cumulative mass of data, unlike humans, who achieve a higher level of agreement when they must reach an overall judgment. Table 4.1 provides operational examples of the vocabulary used in content analysis (universe, sample, and unit of analysis).

Generating Subject Categories, or Pigeonholes, for Data

The first three steps in completing a content analysis involved (a) limiting the study, (b) picking a sample, and (c) deciding on a unit of analysis. The researcher now begins the process of generating categories. The task of generating categories begins with a review of the material. A cursory skimming of the material, followed by a more in-depth consideration of content, is the takeoff point for creating useful, appropriate subject categories. Subject categories are similar to the major and subheadings in an outline. To create the subject categories, an analyst can begin by creating an outline of the content. This bullet point or keyword outline will contain the major subject categories. The examples in Tables 4.2 to 4.7 provide a better understanding of this point.

An analysis of press reaction to an impending plant shutdown could generate subject categories such as impact on Management, Community, Alliance Partners, Investors, and Financial Institutions. Relevant categories in the analysis of women's issues could be Housing, Child Care, Employment, Domestic Violence, and Pension Sharing. Argumentation on the topic of gun control could fall under subject headings such as Health and Safety Issues, Legal and Constitutional Issues, and Enforcement Issues. A foreign affairs

(text continues on page 102)

TABLE 4.1 Introduction to Vocabulary of Content Analysis: Universe, Sample, and Unit of Analysis[a]

Topic	Purpose of Analysis	Universe	Sample	Unit of Analysis
Doomsday cults	To learn more about cult groups that could pose a risk to themselves or others in the Year 2000	All web sites dedicated to the topic of the occult or abnormal	Random sample of materials appearing on web sites in the 3 months before the Year 2000	Web site
Food and Drug Administration (FDA) test results on new potency pill	To learn the response of U.S. consumer groups to announcement of FDA test results	All Associated Press stories appearing in top-10 daily circulation newspapers, January 2000	70 randomly selected stories that discuss FDA announcement	Headline
Air bombings of Yugoslavia	To examine the reaction of the international press to NATO air bombings	Front-page articles appearing in all major international newspapers, June to August 1999	50 randomly selected articles from the New York Times, Le Monde, London Times, and Globe and Mail	Article
Elder abuse	To learn the frequency with which references to elder abuse appear in newspapers published by senior organizations	All 1999 stories on elder abuse appearing in newsletters published by senior organizations	Random sample of 100 newsletters published by seniors groups	Newsletter
Gun control	To determine which gun control themes received the most frequent mentions in TV news coverage	All early evening TV news coverage in 10 large-population cities during spring 1999	Randomly selected news stories from three 1-week periods (also randomly selected) in March, April, and May	Themes within news stories

97

TABLE 4.1 Continued

Topic	Purpose of Analysis	Universe	Sample	Unit of Analysis
Homelessness	To gain information on popular media interest in issue	All TV talk shows on national networks from May to August 1999	Random sample of talk shows (daily or nightly broadcast)	Individual speakers on talk shows
Impaired-driving campaign	To ascertain the level of visibility given to the state government's impaired-driving campaign	All public service announcements aired on local stations between 8:00 P.M. and 12:00 A.M. during December 1999	Random sample of 3 weeks TV coverage	Public service announcement
Hostage taking	To learn whether local live TV coverage compromises the police's handling of hostage incidents	All local TV coverage of hostage incidents in 1998 and 1999	All footage showing activity at hostage site	Any news segment depicting incident

a. This example is based on a format created by Wimmer and Dominick (1997, p. 120).

TABLE 4.2 Common Patterns of Organization, by Stakeholder

Subsidized child care

I. Perspective of parents providing in-home care for children
   A. Proposed policy places unfair additional tax responsibility on Americans.
   B. Government should give better tax breaks to homemakers.
   C. Government should give the same tax allowances to parents of children receiving in-home care as to parents of children receiving out-of-home care.
   D. Government should not be using public funds for private purposes.
   E. Day care subsidies contribute to the economic, political, or moral decline of the country or all of these.

II. Perspective of parents requiring out-of-home care for children
   A. Government should give more financial support to parents requiring out-of-home care for children.
   B. Government must ensure the availability of more spaces for children in nonprofit centers.
   C. Government should ensure access to better quality out-of-home care.
   D. Government must ensure continuing subsidies for low-income families.

III. Perspective of profit day care centers
   A. Government must not abandon profit centers.
   B. When business does well, the community does well.

IV. Perspective of state government
   A. Government has a responsibility to subsidize out-of-home care for children.
   B. Government does not have a responsibility to subsidize out-of-home care for children.

TABLE 4.3 Common Patterns of Organization, by Region

Reaction to telephone rate increases

I. Reaction in Louisiana to rate increases
   A. Pro-corporation perspective
   B. Anti-corporation perspective

II. Reaction in Arkansas to rate increases
   A. Pro-corporation perspective
   B. Anti-corporation perspective

III. Reaction in Alabama to rate increases
   A. Pro-corporation perspective
   B. Anti-corporation perspective

IV. Reaction in Mississippi to rate increases
   A. Pro-corporation perspective
   B. Anti-corporation perspective

V. Reaction in Texas to rate increases
   A. Pro-corporation perspective
   B. Anti-corporation perspective

TABLE 4.4   Common Patterns of Organization, by Dimension

Drug testing in the workplace

I. Legal
   A. Arguments in favor of testing
   B. Arguments against testing

II. Social
   A. Arguments in favor of testing
   B. Arguments against testing

III. Moral
   A. Arguments in favor of testing
   B. Arguments against testing

IV. Economic
   A. Arguments in favor of testing
   B. Arguments against testing

TABLE 4.5   Common Patterns of Organization, by Chronological Order

Changing attitudes of consumers toward energy-efficient products

I. Attitudes of consumers in 1979
   A. Priority given to fuel consumption as a criterion for purchasing an automobile
   B. Priority given to home energy efficiency by buyers
   C. Priority given to energy guide rating by buyers of home appliances

II. Attitudes of consumers in 1989
   A. Priority given to fuel consumption as a criterion for purchasing an automobile
   B. Priority given to home energy efficiency by buyers
   C. Priority given to energy guide rating by buyers of home appliances

III. Attitudes of consumers in 1999
   A. Priority given to fuel consumption as a criterion for purchasing an automobile
   B. Priority given to home energy efficiency by buyers
   C. Priority given to energy guide rating by buyers of home appliances

TABLE 4.6   Common Patterns of Organization, by Cause/Effect/Solution

Air safety

I. Speculation regarding causes of present air safety problems
    A. Aging planes
    B. Inadequate maintenance
    C. Inadequate regulation
    D. Inadequate enforcement of regulations

II. Effects
    A. Pan-Am crash
    B. Gander crash
    C. TWA crash

III. Recommendations or solutions suggested
    A. New planes required
    B. Better maintenance
    C. Better regulation
    D. Better enforcement of regulations

TABLE 4.7   Common Patterns of Organization, by Issue or Theme

Seniors issues

I. Housing
    A. High rent costs
    B. Lack of availability of services
    C. High taxes
    D. High property maintenance costs

II. Transportation
    A. Air costs and services
    B. Rail costs and services
    C. Bus costs and services
    D. Cost of maintaining an automobile

III. Income
    A. Pension reform
    B. Retirement planning
    C. Grants for seniors
    D. Impact of free trade

IV. Health
    A. Diseases
    B. Fitness
    C. Abuse
    D. Euthanasia

V. Leisure

analyst could search for public attitudes toward various kinds of aid to Somalia: Economic, Technical, and Military. The major subject categories in all the previously mentioned examples can be divided into more specific subheadings. For example, Employment can be subdivided into concerns related to Hiring Practices, Salary, and Training Opportunities. If it seems useful, the analyst can subdivide Training Opportunities into On-the-Job Training, Workshops and Seminars, Mentoring, Conferences, and Enrollment in Educational Institutions of Higher Learning. In other words, as deemed appropriate, the analyst can make increasingly finer levels of discrimination on content characteristics.

The appropriateness of broad or narrow categories depends on the purposes of the study. If the categories are too broad, the researcher may not be able to answer critical questions. At the other extreme, the generation of too many subcategories can hinder interpretation of the data. The most important function of content analysis is the organization of data into meaningful categories. Generating scores of categories, many of which contain single items, confuses interpretation and reduces the reliability of the analysis. Reliability derives from the ability to get the same results from repeated measurements of the same material. Reliability suffers when coders must make fine distinctions among large numbers of categories. How does the analyst know how many subject categories to establish? Wimmer and Dominick (1997) provide one answer to this question:

> Common sense, pretesting, and practice with the coding system are valuable guides to aid the researcher in steering between the two extremes of developing a system with too few categories (so that the essential differences are obscured) or defining too many categories (so that only a small percentage falls into each, thus limiting generalizations). (p. 121)

Several rules govern the definition of subject categories (Holsti, 1969). The first rule states that categories should reflect the purposes of the research. In other words, the analyst asks, "Do the categories respond to the questions asked in this analysis?" Assume that the Justice Department wants to address the following question: "How does the public regard legislation that would require police departments to reveal the names of repeat sexual offenders?" Relevant categories for the analysis could be the following: Feelings Toward the Legislation (strongly favorable, favorable, unsure, unfavorable, or strongly unfavorable), Catalysts Driving Public Opinion on the Topic (recent events that have stimulated the public debate), Reservations Expressed (a list of specific concerns), and Conditions That Must Be Met (a list of conditions that must be met to ensure public support for the legislation). Less relevant categories (in the light of the purpose of the study) are the following: Historical Precedents for the New Legislation, Constitutional Rights of Sexual Offenders, and Recent Changes in State Laws on Early Release of Offenders. These latter categories do not respond directly to the research question.

A second rule states that categories must be exhaustive. That is, there must be a slot into which every relevant unit of analysis can fit. If some units do not fit, the analyst redefines the categories to accommodate the ideas that do not have a home. Categories titled Other or Miscellaneous are designed to capture units of content that do not fit into the other more specific categories. If 10% or more of the content is placed in the Miscellaneous category, however, the analyst should rethink the initial set of categories to capture more of the miscellaneous content. Whenever subject categories change, the researcher must reanalyze every individual communication to ensure that the results reflect the changes. For this reason, pretesting the categories can save time and money.

A third rule states that categories should be mutually exclusive. For example, in an analysis of seniors' issues, the category of Economic Concerns can overlap with Housing, Pensions, Health, and Transportation. To deal with this problem, the analyst can eliminate the more general category of Economic Concerns. An analysis of barriers to healthy lifestyles, however, could include headings such as Economic, Political, Social, and Cultural. In the latter instance, an additional category, Dietary Practices of Different Ethnic Groups, would overlap with the Cultural category. To correct this problem, the analyst can eliminate the overlapping category (Dietary Practices of Different Ethnic Groups) or can change it into a subcategory under Cultural. Many overlapping categories result from a failure to find the appropriate level for a category. As noted previously, the creation of a simple outline format can help to ensure that categories appear at the correct level.

The fourth rule states that categories (which appear together at the same level or under the same heading) should be derived from a single classification principle. For example, the analyst would not list Male, Female, Youth, Middle-Aged Adults, and Seniors under the same heading. Male and Female relate to a gender-based classification system, whereas Youth, Middle-Aged Adults, and Seniors relate to an age-based classification system. To solve the problem, the analyst can create two major headings, Male and Female, with subheadings that relate to age. Alternatively, the analyst can create major headings related to Age, with gender groupings under each, or the two ideas can be classified into totally separate category types. The research question determines the appropriateness of choices. In the same way, an analysis of public opinion on the question of making parents responsible for the criminal actions of their children could generate the following categories: Support the Legislation, Reject the Legislation, Arguments of Parents, Arguments of Teachers, and Arguments of Rifle Associations. The first two categories, however, address the question of support for the legislation, and the last three categories respond to the question of argumentation and reasoning on the topic. Therefore, the analyst must decide which categories should appear as main headings and which should appear as subheadings or, alternatively, whether they should appear as completely different groupings.

A final, easy to understand example relates to garbage. The contents of garbage cans often include the remains of frozen foods, candy wrappers, Coke bottles, leftover vegetables, stale bread, tissue paper, aluminum foil, tin cans, milk cartons, wine bottles, beer cans, grocery store receipts, apple cores, used razor blades, discarded paper products, and the remains of personal hygiene supplies. Many different classification principles can be applied to the analysis of these materials. For example, one analyst could classify the materials according to those that can be recycled and those that cannot be recycled. Another analyst could categorize the waste according to the material from which it is constructed—for example, glass, plastic, paper, wax, steel, aluminum, and natural fibers. Yet another researcher could classify the materials according to the principle of "natural" versus "human-made" products. The Natural category could then be subdivided into Food, Fiber, and so on. The Human-Made category could be subdivided according to some other classification principle.

Similarly, an analysis that seeks to answer the question of environmental uses of garbage could logically employ categories that relate to recyclable versus nonrecyclable goods or waste that can be used for compost versus waste that cannot be used for compost. A study of food patterns could divide the waste according to meats, vegetables, fruit, seafood, and others. A study of the extent to which Americans prefer hard alcohol to wine and beer could examine types of drinks consumed: wine, beer, vodka, bourbon, gin, and so on. A study of lifestyles could examine the extent to which consumers prefer prepared foods versus those that require preparation. It is easy to see that some of the materials that appear as waste products would be discarded from some studies and included in others. To warrant inclusion in the content analysis, the items should respond to the research question (the first classification rule).

Some attempts have been made to construct standard categories for analyzing newspaper content, especially in areas such as values and attitudes. Copyright issues evoke discussion of values, such as the right to own property, social responsibility, individual freedom, and protection of the individual. The debate over euthanasia, aggravated by the actions of Jack Kevorkian ("Dr. Death"), entails a search for the presence of values such as sanctity of life, self-determination, quality of life, dignity of the individual, rights of the individual versus the collective, and autonomy. Many researchers caution against relying on standard categories (i.e., categories that do not emerge from the specific material being analyzed). They believe that the most interesting studies involve the development of categories customized to the data being analyzed, and the quality of any analysis depends on the quality of the categories: "Content analysis stands or falls by its categories . . . [which must be] clearly formulated and well adapted to the problem and to the content" (Berelson, 1952, p. 147).

Coding the Data

The term *coding* refers to the process of classifying data, or units of analysis, into content categories. Coding is the most tedious part of content analysis. First, the coder (the person who is analyzing the content of the communication) records basic data on each unit of content. For example, the coder logs the following kinds of information for a newspaper article: source (e.g., name of newspaper or television station), date of appearance of the news item, type of article (news, feature, editorial, letter to the editor, column, interview, or other), and name of the journalist or columnist. Figure 4.1 shows a sample coding sheet that can be used to record source information for newspapers, and see Table 4.8 for definitions of different kinds of articles.

Other kinds of information are relevant to the analysis of correspondence. For example, the coder will probably want to record the geographic and demographic characteristics of correspondents, including their gender, place of residence, region of the country from which the correspondence originated, dates on which the correspondence was written or received or both, and whether the correspondence represents an organized lobby effort. In the case of correspondence from experts, the name could be important. In the case of Internet communications, the nature of the news group, time of communication, any identifying information on participants, sponsoring organization (where applicable), and so on could be recorded. Refer to Figure 3.6 for a

Type of Article:
☐ News
☐ Feature

☐ Editorial
☐ Column

Placement:
☐ Prominent
☐ Not Prominent

Newspaper:
☐ Wall Street Journal
☐ USA Today
☐ Daily News (New York)
☐ Los Angeles Times
☐ New York Times
☐ Chicago Tribune
☐ Newsday (Long Island)

☐ San Francisco Chronicle
☐ Philadelphia Inquirer
☐ Boston Globe
☐ Newark Star-Ledger
☐ Cleveland Plain Dealer
☐ Baltimore Sun
☐ Houston Chronicle

☐ Washington Post
☐ New York Post
☐ Detroit News
☐ Detroit Free Press
☐ Chicago Sun-Times
☐ Miami Herald

Wire Service:
☐ AP
☐ New York Times

☐ Los Angeles Times
☐ Chicago Tribune

☐ Knight-Ridder

Month in which Article Appeared:
☐ January
☐ February
☐ March
☐ April

☐ May
☐ June
☐ July
☐ August

☐ September
☐ October
☐ November
☐ December

Journalists:
☐ R.W. Apple Jr.
☐ Maureen Dowd
☐ Aaron Epstein
☐ David Hess

☐ Susan Moffatt
☐ Clarence Page
☐ Anna Quindlen
☐ James Rowley

☐ William Safire
☐ Jenny Scott
☐ Roberto Suro
☐ Calvin Woodward

Figure 4.1. Sample Date Sheet for Recording Demographic Information on Newspaper Articles

106

TABLE 4.8 Types of Newspaper Articles

Genre	Description	Examples
News story	Article that chronicles the who, what, where, why, and how of timely occurrences "Hard" news or "straight" news Designed to inform Often based on information drawn from wire services (e.g., AP or Knight-Ridder) May or may not include name of journalist Ostensibly impersonal, presenting unopinionated facts Bias enters through selection of quotations, details, or headlines	Reports of a speech by a ranking official Announcement of a new economic policy The initial revelation of an airplane crash Reports of an oil spill
Editorial	An article that analyzes an event, public question, or current issue Appears on editorial page Contains no specific reference to writer in most cases Assumed to have originated with editor of newspaper or at least to reflect management's views	Comment on recent layoffs by local plant Statement of newspaper position on political candidacy Comment on government's monetary policies Reaction to embezzlement charges against industry official
Column	An opinion article, usually written continuously by one person Appears in one or more newspapers Set apart from editorial by the fact that it is the opinion of one individual as opposed to the opinion of the newspaper management Name, and often a photograph, of the columnist appears	Comments on inappropriate behavior by union workers Comments on implementation of equity policies in local university Comment on spending policies of municipal government
Feature	An umbrella term that refers to many different types of stories Analyzes the news; entertains an audience; or describes people, places, or things in or out of the news Not governed by the same rules of formal objectivity that govern news story Often adds personal comment to basic news content Uses more graphic language than is the case with straight news stories	Human interest stories Personality profiles Stories that add interpretative comment to news events

(continued)

TABLE 4.8 Continued

Genre	Description	Examples
Letter to the editor	Expression of individual point of view, often a stakeholder in an issue May reveal institutional or other affiliation of writer Number of letters received may, or may not, reflect general public opinion on topic (For example, a newspaper may publish equal number of articles from opposing camps, but they may have received more letters from people who oppose policies than from people who support them.)	Letter on education funding issue written by university professor Letter on violence in the media written by father of a victim Letter on plant hiring policies written by president of a minority rights group

sample data sheet that can be used to record demographic information on correspondents.

The second step is to read or view each individual item of data (press clipping, television program, Internet discussion thread, or other unit of content). Then the coder undertakes a separate analysis for each unit of content. He or she seeks to ascertain how many of the subject categories appeared in the communication. Before computers facilitated the process of data entry, analysts filled out coding or protocol sheets by hand. They put an "X" or check mark before each relevant subject matter category for each unit of content that they analyzed. Analyzing 50 press clippings required the analyst to fill out 50 data sheets. Each data sheet contained the same list of subject categories. Although the basic process has not changed, analysts now enter their data into computer software, which is programed to tabulate totals, frequencies, correlations, and other comparisons. Figures 4.2 and 4.3 show completed data sheets documenting the appearance of arguments or ideas. Whether manual or computer assisted, the qualitative nature of coding remains the same. That is, the coder must make an individual, qualitative judgment on what has appeared in each press clipping, television news clip, or other communication. He or she must decide which subject categories appeared in the coverage and which did not.

Long-Term Positive Effects of Resignation

On general visibility of parent company	
On product sales	
On strategic direction of company	
On shareholder value	X
On employee well-being	X
Total	2

Short-Term Positive Effects of Resignation

On general visibility of parent company	X
On product sales	
On strategic direction of company	
On shareholder value	X
On employee well-being	X
Total	3

Long-Term Negative Effects of Resignation

On general visibility of parent company	X
On product sales	
On strategic direction of company	X
On shareholder value	
On employee well-being	X
Total	3

Short-Term Negative Effects of Resignation

On general visibility of parent company	X
On product sales	
On strategic direction of company	X
On shareholder value	
On employee well-being	X
Total	3

Figure 4.2. Example of Individual Data Sheet

I. KEY CONCERNS AS DEFINED BY THE PRESS

A. Concerns relating to specific exemptions that restrict the public's ability to access government documents.	Broad use of provision totally exempting Cabinet information.	X
	Broad use of provision allowing government officials to conceal records containing policy advice.	—
	Broad application of exemption to any meeting attended by government officials.	X
	Discretionary exemptions allowing information blackout on records affecting international and federal/state affairs and police investigations.	—
	Inability of courts to intervene when a document is described as Cabinet confidence or falls into an exempt category under the Act (becomes subject to the discretion of head of government institution).	X
	Practice of identifying person requesting government documents.	—
	Issue of whether quasi-government organizations should be exempt from legislation.	X
	Inadequate record keeping by government departments.	X
	Too many records destroyed too soon.	X
	Issue of lobbyist relationship with client.	—
B. Concerns related to personal data that is protected (relating to inadequate safeguards or inadequate ability of individual to access his or her own records).	Increasing size of government data banks; general threat to personal privacy.	X
	Cross-indexing of government records.	—
	Lack of deadlines for destruction of government records.	X
	Failure of exempt banks to meet the criteria of containing predominantly personal information or cases, or persons questioning the validity of exempt banks.	X
	Provisions in earlier acts that permit a federal court judge to order evidence withheld from trial court process on national security grounds.	—
	Inability of public to determine, in the case of exempt banks, whether a file exists.	X
	Inability of courts to order release of government files on individuals when exempt banks are involved.	X
	Inability to access criminal record files.	—
	Lack of internal safety checks in dealing with outside contractors and with files containing personal information on Americans.	—
	Threat posed by growth of microcomputers.	—
C. General concerns.	High costs for users.	X
	Limited knowledge of legislation provisions, lack of use by public, skepticism.	X
	Long delays and excessive red tape.	X
	Lack of aggressiveness on the part of the government officials in publicizing provisions of legislation.	—
	Lack of cooperation on part of civil servants.	—
	High costs and excessive time for government to process requests.	—

	II. RECOMMENDATIONS EXPLICIT OR IMPLICIT IN PRESS ACCOUNTS.	
A.	Recommendations relating to specific exemptions that restrict the public's ability to access government documents.	Need to narrow range of exemptions, making them specific, necessary, and limited. — X Need to empower courts to make decisions and to weigh injury against likely benefits of release of information. — __ Need better record management/preservation of records. — __ Need to bring Cabinet documents under legislation, subject to court review. — X
B.	Recommendations relating to personal data that is protected (related to inadequate safeguards or inadequate ability of individual to access his or her own records).	Need new guidelines for all government projects that collect, use, and destroy personal information. — X Need safeguards to ensure respondents to surveys are told why they have been selected. — __ Need specific clauses in all contracts with outside firms to govern protection of personal information on Americans. — X Need new process to ensure approval for release of personal information by government departments. — __ Need better safeguards to protect against improper release of personal information by government departments. — __ Need to empower courts to make decisions and to weigh injury against likely benefits of releasing information. — __ Need to "stay" trial proceedings until a judge can hold a hearing to identify evidence that can be released to the defense without damaging national security. — X
C.	Recommendations relating to general concerns.	Need to educate public regarding rights and procedures in using legislation. — X Need to eliminate complex wording. — __ Need to eliminate excessive fees. — X Need to eliminate delays and excessive red tape. — X Need to eliminate cumbersome appeal procedures. — __

Figure 4.3. Sample subject category sheet (completed by coder). The analyst uses one set of these category sheets for each news item analyzed. He or she places a check mark beside all categories that appear in the article. There may be many items checked. This example is fictitious.

111

Calculating Frequencies and Space and Time Measures

After completing the coding of information on individual news items, correspondence, or other research materials, the analyst calculates the frequency with which the different subject categories have appeared in the information that was subjected to analysis. When researchers count the number of times that an item appears in news coverage, they are operating at the level of nominal measurement. (See Chapter 6 for a discussion of the restrictions that apply in interpreting nominal data.) The cumulative data sheet in Figure 4.4 illustrates such tabulations of frequency. Computer programs can translate frequency counts into percentages or into bar and line graphs or other visual displays. The summaries of quantitative data typically appear in the appendix to a media analysis report.

Some researchers argue that frequent appearance of an idea does not necessarily denote concern, value, intensity, or focus of attention. Others say that not all units of content should be given equal weight because some themes, characters, articles, and words are more important than others. Therefore, analysts sometimes differentiate items appearing on the front page from those printed elsewhere in a newspaper either by coding the articles separately or by giving front-page items a greater weight.

Others use similar techniques to differentiate the position of items on a page or to give greater weight to larger print headlines. Some have advocated the usefulness of distinguishing between different typefaces and identifying column placement (Klein & Maccoby, 1954). Other studies adjust ratings to reflect the circulation of the newspaper in which they appear. These same kinds of adjustments can be made in analysis of broadcast or other media. Items that appear early in a broadcast (or receive an early announcement) may be judged to have greater prominence or potential for impact than those appearing later.

Some researchers measure column inches as an alternative to computing frequency. Because the news hole remains constant, this technique allows organizations to get a sense of the relative importance of a news item over time and in relation to other issues (Merriam & Makower, 1988). Many of the early content analyses used this technique, and researchers became interested in comparing the results obtained from frequency measures versus space measures. One study found that three different measures (column inches, frequency, and size of headlines) yielded similar results, but the fastest and easiest method involved measuring space (Markham & Stempel, 1957). The equivalent unit of measurement for film, radio, and television is time. The

Long-Term Positive Effects of Resignation

On general visibility of parent company	0
On product sales	0
On strategic direction of company	0
On shareholder value	20
On employee well-being	9
Total	**29**

Short-Term Positive Effects of Resignation

On general visibility of parent company	3
On product sales	0
On strategic direction of company	0
On shareholder value	4
On employee well-being	1
Total	**8**

Long-Term Negative Effects of Resignation

On general visibility of parent company	69
On product sales	1
On strategic direction of company	11
On shareholder value	2
On employee well-being	5
Total	**88**

Short-Term Negative Effects of Resignation

On general visibility of parent company	11
On product sales	2
On strategic direction of company	6
On shareholder value	1
On employee well-being	15
Total	**35**

Figure 4.4. Example of a data sheet with category totals. This spreadsheet reflects the total number of times that the content categories appeared in the sample of articles selected for analysis. Subtotals appear to the right of each subcategory. Each number represents an article. The number 20, for example, indicates that this topic category appeared in 20 articles.

continuing popularity of space and time measures is a result of the ease in applying them. Others have cautioned, however, that the measurement of space and time does not allow researchers to answer the most sophisticated questions. When analysts use these techniques on their own, they are able to assess the space or time given to a topic but not to evaluate the treatment. Some believe that space and time measures are most suited to analyses of mass media; even so, they are too crude to be adequate indexes of attitudes, values, or style. Figure 4.5 illustrates a protocol sheet that allows the analyst to record the time devoted to supportive or critical comment on a particular issue.

The purpose of frequency and space and time measures is to enable the researcher to make the following kinds of statements in an issue analysis report:[1]

Frequency counts to determine the newspapers or journalists who covered a particular issue enable the researcher to make statements such as "The newspaper showing the highest level of interest in health insurance issues is the *Washington Post*. The journalists who most often speak out on the issue are . . ." (Table 4.9).

Frequency counts of the number of articles appearing on a given topic over a period of time enable the researcher to make statements such as "Coverage of issues related to elder abuse declined in volume between September and November but increased in volume again in the new year." Frequency counts of types of articles enable the researcher to make a statement such as "Although most major newspapers carried news accounts of plant shutdowns in the month of March, editorial comment on these issues was relatively limited in the same period of time." Table 4.10 provides an example of data that would give rise to this kind of statement.

Frequency counts of major arguments or criticisms enable the researcher to make statements such as "The three major arguments raised in support of continued air bombing of Belgrade and Kosovo were . . ." or "The most frequent criticisms of Internal Revenue appearing in the press over the past 6 months have been . . ." Figure 4.6 provides an example of a category sheet that contains frequency counts on arguments raised in press coverage of access to information and privacy issues.

Frequency counts of major themes enable the researcher to make statements such as "Recent coverage of the issue of road rage reveals several major themes such as . . ." (Figure 4.7).

Frequency counts of major issues appearing in the press in a given time period allow the researcher to observe, "Issues receiving the greatest amount of press attention over the past 6 months included the Yugoslavian conflict (number one), youth violence (number two), and the economy (number three)."

	Supportive Comment	Time/Space Allocation
1		
2		
3		
4		
5		

Dominant supportive argument(s) from list above:

	Critical Comment	Time/Space Allocation
1		
2		
3		
4		
5		

Figure 4.5. Example of Space and Time Measures Applied to Analysis of Tone

Frequency counts of statements defending an organization's actions or position enable the researcher to say, "The numbers of newscasts that expressed a pro-interventionist point of view on the question of engagement in Yugoslavia fell significantly below those that criticized U.S. involvement. Nonetheless, the number of those who adopted a 'wait-and-see' attitude outnumbered the 'committed' by more than three to one" (Table 4.11).

TABLE 4.9   Media Response to Proposed Changes to Health Insurance
(December 19, 1998-December 26, 1999)

Source	Total
USA Today	14
Philadelphia Inquirer	21
Los Angeles Times	28
Boston Globe	14
Chicago Tribune	49
Washington Post	70
New York Post	7
Detroit Free Press	63
San Francisco Chronicle	5
Total	271

NOTE: The total number of articles with references to the proposed changes in health insurance appear in the last column.

TABLE 4.10 Media Coverage of Plant Shutdowns, March 1998[a]

	Number and Type of Articles, by Newspaper				
Source	News	Column	Feature	Editorial	Total
Chicago Sun-Times	8	2	4	2	16
San Francisco Chronicle	2	0	1	0	3
Philadelphia Inquirer	3	1	2	0	6
Boston Globe	0	1	0	0	1
Newark Star-Ledger	4	2	0	1	7
Cleveland Plain Dealer	1	1	1	1	4
Baltimore Sun	0	2	4	0	6
Houston Chronicle	2	5	1	2	10
Miami Herald	7	1	3	1	12
Total	27	15	16	7	65

a. This is a fictitious example.

Frequency counts to determine who controlled the media agenda in a particular period enable the researcher to make a statement such as "The perspective of the gun lobby was taken in two thirds of the broadcast news coverage of issues involving school violence" (Table 4.12).

Frequency counts of references to major stakeholders enable the researcher to make statements such as "The key players in the long-range missile testing controversy appear to be . . . ," "The key players in the controversy surrounding the company's refusal to withdraw product X from the market are . . . ," and "Leading critics of industry's position are . . ."

	I. KEY CONCERNS AS DEFINED BY THE PRESS	
A.	Concerns relating to specific exemptions that restrict the public's ability to access government documents.	Broad use of provision totally exempting Cabinet information.	27
		Broad use of provision allowing government officials to conceal records containing policy advice.	9
		Broad application of exemption to any meeting attended by government officials.	0
		Discretionary exemptions allowing information blackout on records affecting international and federal/state affairs and police investigations.	40
		Inability of courts to intervene when a document is described as Cabinet confidence or falls into an exempt category under the Act (becomes subject to the discretion of head of government institution).	6
		Practice of identifying person requesting government documents.	33
		Issue of whether quasi-government organizations should be exempt from legislation.	18
		Inadequate record keeping by government departments.	14
		Too many records destroyed too soon.	35
		Issue of lobbyist relationship with client.	0
B.	Concerns related to personal data that is protected (relating to inadequate safeguards or inadequate ability of individual to access his or her own records).	Increasing size of government data banks; general threat to personal privacy.	24
		Cross-indexing of government records.	5
		Lack of deadlines for destruction of government records.	40
		Failure of exempt banks to meet the criteria of containing predominantly personal information or cases, or persons questioning the validity of exempt banks.	18
		Provisions in earlier acts that permit a federal court judge to order evidence withheld from trial court process on national security grounds.	3
		Inability of public to determine, in the case of exempt banks, whether a file exists.	19
		Inability of courts to order release of government files on individuals when exempt banks are involved.	31
		Inability to access criminal record files.	0
		Lack of internal safety checks in dealing with outside contractors and with files containing personal information on Americans.	22
		Threat posed by growth of microcomputers.	13
C.	General concerns.	High costs for users.	39
		Limited knowledge of legislation provisions, lack of use by public, skepticism.	11
		Long delays and excessive red tape.	24
		Lack of aggressiveness on the part of the government officials in publicizing provisions of legislation.	2
		Lack of cooperation on part of civil servants.	0
		High costs and excessive time for government to process requests.	6

Figure 4.6. Example of Subject Category Totals for a Media Analysis

117

	II. RECOMMENDATIONS EXPLICIT OR IMPLICIT IN PRESS ACCOUNTS.	
A. Recommendations relating to specific exemptions that restrict the public's ability to access government documents.	20 5 0 12	Need to narrow range of exemptions, making them specific, necessary, and limited. Need to empower courts to make decisions and to weigh injury against likely benefits to release of information. Need better record management/preservation of records. Need to bring Cabinet documents under legislation, subject to court review.
B. Recommendations relating to personal data that is protected (related to inadequate safeguards or inadequate ability of individual to access his or her own records).	10 3 21 0 31 8 13	Need new guidelines for all government projects that collect, use, and destroy personal information. Need safeguards to ensure respondents to surveys are told why they have been selected. Need specific clauses in all contracts with outside firms to govern protection of personal information on Americans. Need new process to ensure approval for release of personal information by government departments. Need better safeguards to protect against improper release of personal information by government departments. Need to empower courts to make decisions and to weigh injury against likely benefits of releasing information. Need to "stay" trial proceedings until a judge can hold a hearing to identify evidence that can be released to the defense without damaging national security.
D. Recommendations relating to general concerns.	15 0 38 21 0	Need to educate public regarding rights and procedures in using legislation. Need to eliminate complex wording. Need to eliminate excessive fees. Need to eliminate delays and excessive red tape. Need to eliminate cumbersome appeal procedures.

Figure 4.6. Continued

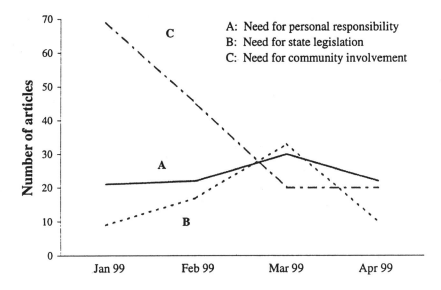

Figure 4.7. Dominant Themes Appearing in Media Coverage of the Road Rage Issue

Frequency counts of references to key concerns or reservations expressed by stakeholders could lead to statements such as "Key concerns over the release of a new diet pill include . . ." or "More than one third of the articles reporting on the potency pill Viagra have raised some reservations about long-term use of the drug."

Frequency counts related to tone of coverage (the numbers of positive, negative, neutral, and balanced articles) enable the researcher to state "Fifty-eight percent of the articles opposed testing for AIDS in the workplace, 14% supported the idea, and 26% expressed neutrality or ambivalence on the matter" (Table 4.13).

Frequency counts of the origin of arguments could lead to the observation, "When new arguments appeared on the topic of legalization of marijuana, they most often originated in the western part of the United States with spokespersons such as . . ." (Table 4.14).

Frequency counts of the regions from which communications originated could lead to statements such as "Issues related to gang violence surfaced most often in large urban newspapers, although the ethnic press in some smaller communities also addressed the issue from time to time." Figure 4.8 provides an example of coverage that varies in favorability from one part of a state to another.

TABLE 4.11 Dominant Focus of Network News Coverage of Intervention in Yugoslavia[a]

| | Number of News Segments With This Focus of Coverage | | | |
	CBS	NBC	ABC	Total
Pro-intervention	6	11	8	25
Anti-intervention	5	20	10	35
Wait and see	71	51	60	182

a. This is a fictitious example.

TABLE 4.12 Dominant Stakeholder Perspective on Issue of School Violence[a]

| | Number of News Segments Favoring Stakeholder Perspective | | | |
	CBS	NBC	ABC	Total
Parents	20	22	17	59
Gun lobby	45	48	50	143
Youth	6	3	1	10
Teachers	11	9	10	30

a. This is a fictitious example.

TABLE 4.13 Testing for AIDS in the Workplace[a]

| | Number of Articles | | | | |
Source	Favorable	Unfavorable	Neutral	Balanced	Total
Los Angeles Times		14			14
New York Times		7	7		14
Chicago Tribune	3	20	7		30
New York Post	2	23	3	3	31
Detroit News	7	23	3	7	40
Newsday (Long Island)	1	5			6
Philadelphia Inquirer	2		6	2	10
Cleveland Plain Dealer	4	2			6
Baltimore Sun	1	8		5	14
Houston Chronicle	5	8	2		15
Miami Herald	3	4	4	3	14
Total	28	114	32	20	194
Percentage	14	58	16	10	100

a. The articles are broken down according to tone of comment. This is a fictitious example.

TABLE 4.14   Origin of Argument

New Argument on Topic	City of Origin	Media Source	Journalist
Medical uses	Los Angeles	*Los Angeles Times*	Willett
Benefits to economy	Colorado	*Denver Post*	Kane
Difficulty in enforcing laws	Arizona	*Phoenix Herald*	Jones

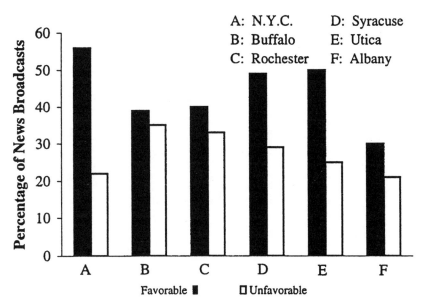

A: N.Y.C.   D: Syracuse
B: Buffalo   E: Utica
C: Rochester F: Albany

Favorable ■   □ Unfavorable

Figure 4.8. Tone of Coverage of Merger (by Six Local Stations)

Measurement of column inches enables the analyst to make statements such as "The percentage of the news hole captured by pro-life groups increased between January 1990 and May 1999" or "The total amount of space devoted to the topic of industry violations of the National Safety Code has increased dramatically since 1995." Measurement of column inches also enables the analyst to make many of the same kinds of statements noted in the previous discussion of frequency of coverage. For example, the analyst can comment on control of the media agenda in terms of time allocation, space devoted to the perspectives of different stakeholder groups, time or space devoted to certain themes, or time allocated to supportive versus critical comment on issues by particular journalists or newspapers (Tables 4.15 and 4.16).

TABLE 4.15 Financial Difficulties of Company X

Newspaper	Column Inches Devoted to Topic
Indianapolis Star	38
Christian Science Monitor	84
New York Times	84
Chicago Sun	50
San Francisco Examiner	20
New Orleans Times-Picayune	28
Washington Post	65
Total	369

TABLE 4.16 Time Devoted to Union Position on Issue X, by Network

| Date | Time (Seconds) | | | |
	ABC	NBC	CBS	Total
March 13, 1999	50.3	46.7	58.6	155.6
March 14, 1999	70.0	68.3	55.3	193.6
March 15, 1999	94.9	89.8	73.4	258.1
March 16, 1999	89.5	88.6	75.4	253.5
March 17, 1999	91.0	67.5	76.7	235.2
March 18, 1999	95.8	35.2	61.4	192.4
March 19, 1999	77.9	84.2	86.6	248.7
Total	569.4	480.3	487.4	1,537.1

See the report on media analysis of GMOs in Appendix B for an example of an analysis that employs standard content analysis techniques. This example also illustrates the way in which the content categories respond to the kinds of questions posed in Chapter 3.

Testing for Reliability and Validity

After completing a content coding exercise, an academic researcher checks for reliability of results. The most common method involves a test for intercoder reliability. That is, after completing a content analysis, the researcher gives written instructions for coding the communication content to at least two additional coders (preferably four or five). In a case involving a large quantity of content, the researcher may select a random sample of the material to give to the coders.

After the coders complete their tasks, the primary researcher analyzes the results for consistency of responses (among all coders, including the primary analyst). The researcher calculates the percentage of agreement for each test item. The resulting statement could read as follows: "Agreement was 100% on 309 of 322 responses." In other words, the coders were unanimous in their assessment of 96% of the content included in the sample. Of the 13 items that generated disagreement, the coder and panel members reached 75% agreement on 7 items, leaving only 6 items with less than 75% agreement. Although the percentages vary from study to study, content analysts tend to use 90% agreement as a common measure of acceptable levels of correspondence. The higher the level of agreement, the higher the level of reliability.

Other scenarios for testing reliability also exist. The researcher can rely totally on others to code the content, checking periodically for intercoder reliability. This circumstance occurs in the case of large-scale projects managed by lead researchers. Alternatively, in an organizational context, tests can be conducted for intracoder reliability. This kind of test is useful when large numbers of coders are not available to the organization or researcher. In this scenario, the same individual codes the same material at different points in time. The results of the coding exercises are compared for consistency of responses. The researcher can generate statements about levels of agreement in the same way as in intercoder tests for reliability.

When levels of intercoder or intracoder agreement are lower than desired, the researcher must revise the subject categories to ensure that the categories are valid (they ask what the researcher wants them to ask). Pretesting sessions enable coders to contribute to the renaming of categories and the revision of category sheets. Such sessions also enable coders to become comfortable with the definitions and the procedures. Furthermore, the training sessions allow analysts the opportunity to discuss problems or to question the organization of the data.

Pretesting a category system is one way to increase the validity and reliability of content analysis results. The term *validity* refers to the extent to which any test or exercise measures what it is supposed to measure. *Reliability* refers to repeatability with consistency of results. In pretesting sessions, analysts discuss the results that they have obtained from working with a test sample. They compare their interpretation of categories with the interpretations of others involved in the study. Where interpretations vary widely, researchers may conclude that they are working with invalid subject categories. That is, not everyone is interpreting the subject categories in the same way. By rewording, combining, or eliminating subject categories, the analysts can reach a common understanding that improves validity and, ultimately, reliability of results. These pretesting sessions allow researchers to discover problems prior to completion of the study; thus, they save time and money.

Interpreting the Data and Writing the Report

Although researchers use the information from the data sheets to generate the basic structure of a public opinion report, they also include other points, quotations, and examples. This additional explication adds value to the results of the quantitative analysis. Sometimes, the analyst notes the context in which the coverage occurred—other events that could have influenced the coverage, catalysts that drove the coverage, and so on. The best reports combine the results of quantitative data with qualitative judgments.

The analyst should note limitations in data presented in the report. For example, people who write to organizations, expressing their points of view on issues, may or may not represent the general public. Most issues have their crusaders. Gary Rosenfeldt of British Columbia, whose son was a victim of mass murderer Clifford Olson, writes on a regular basis to Canadian newspapers arguing for stronger victims' rights and for the death penalty. In general, people who are negatively disposed toward a proposed policy or course of action are more likely to write than those who either agree with or have no strong feelings on the subject. Many of the letters received on any issue are the product of write-in campaigns driven by advocacy groups.

Rightly or wrongly, organizations tend to attach less importance to letters that come from such advocacy efforts (e.g., form letters) than to correspondence that originates with the writer. Some organizations also differentiate correspondence from "experts" on a topic and correspondence from the general public, and they tend to attach more weight to expert opinion. Finally, the analyst should note that a time lag can occur between an event and the arrival of correspondence on the issue. Opinion leaders require time to organize dissent.

Similarly, readers of newspapers comprise a special public with characteristics different from those of the general population. Studies have shown, for example, that regular consumers of newspapers tend to be better educated and more informed on public affairs than less frequent readers. Specialized cable programs, such as the *MacNeil/Lehrer Newshour* and CSPAN, have begun to rival newspapers and news magazines as suppliers of long-term political knowledge, and an increasing number of people rely on television and the Internet for their news. People's usage patterns for different media vary, depending on subject matter and demographic affiliations. Despite the fact that many readers have abandoned newspapers for television and the Internet, some studies show that newspapers remain America's "premier source of public affairs information" (Robinson & Levy, 1996, p. 135).

The analyst should note the audiences whose views are not reflected in the report. For example, mainstream media coverage of the drug problem will not reflect the views of street youth or those most at risk. Nor will the mainstream media reflect the views of many environmental activist groups that rely on specialized publications and interpersonal contact. Media analysis of newspapers, popular magazines, and network newscasts will probably not reveal the opinions of ethnic groups who face linguistic barriers to media access or lobby groups that are in the early stages of organizing.

Sometimes, it can be important to note the omission of items from an analysis. What has been omitted can be as important as what is included (Durham, 1998; Entman & Rojecki, 1993; Ferguson, 1994; Ragin, 1987). Neumann (1997) commented on the importance of noting "negative" evidence: "It may seem strange to look for things that did not happen, but the nonappearance of something can reveal a great deal and provide valuable insights. . . . The historical comparative researcher asks why some things were not in the data (e.g., no reports of child abuse)" (p. 434).

After failing to identify a dominant story frame in the telling of the crash of TWA Flight 800, Durham (1998) commented on the importance of this negative evidence: "As a point of comparative method, studying negative cases can contribute much to our understanding of what is happening in positive cases of reporting" (p. 100). As a doctoral student, I learned this lesson in a very concrete way. Engaged in a study of the rhetoric of the military coup d'etat in Latin America, I discovered a singular absence of any mention of coups in many cases. That is, the newspapers were under such restrictive censorship that they contained absolutely no references to the political changes under way in the country. Instead, journalists reported the social events of the day—weddings and other routine events (Ferguson, 1976).

Lewis and Lewis (1980) noted several different kinds of negative evidence, including events that did not occur (e.g., groups that did not participate in events), lack of awareness of events (e.g., people do not know about some event or issue), or someone wants to hide the event (e.g., people refuse to discuss certain behaviors or events). The study of coup rhetoric in Latin America reflected this last kind of negative evidence.

Training and Using the Analyst

Media analyses carried out within the organization are often the product of one analyst. However, the greater the time to complete an analysis, the higher the likelihood that multiple persons will be involved at some stage in the analysis. For example, analysis of video content will almost never be carried out by one person or be completed in-house. Similarly, correspondence analyses and large-scale print media analyses often involve multiple coders. Outside firms often use multiple analysts to study a single large issue that is being tracked on an ongoing basis. In all instances in which multiple analysts are employed in the study of a single issue, careful training of the analysts is essential. Training will enhance the possibility that different analysts agree on defining subject categories and classifying and interpreting the data.

Because learning the language of any new area takes time, organizations will do best to designate expert analysts for specific content areas. Like chameleons, issues take on new colors over time, and an analyst acquainted with the history and development of an issue can more easily detect variations in form. When training sessions with new analysts are conducted by individuals who have tracked the issues over a long period of time, the organization can short-circuit the inconsistencies that would otherwise surface in a situation involving multiple analysts.

Media analysis is one of the most subjective of processes. Because issues take on new dimensions over time, one training session will not suffice to ensure quality analyses. Ongoing sessions, conducted at regular intervals, will help to guarantee consistency in interpretation of data. The end result of these training sessions will be a set of detailed instructions to all those who participate in the study. These instructions, which typically include examples, serve to shorten the learning time for new analysts who join the team.

For these same reasons, organizations without an in-house capacity to conduct research will do best to establish a long-term contract with one consulting firm rather than asking many different firms to carry out analyses. To ensure quality control, organizations can meet with analysts in the early stages of the research project, review subject categories, determine whether any ongoing steps are being taken to refine concepts, and ask about training sessions for personnel. A representative of the organization can attend occasional training sessions.

Whether organizations obtain the services of someone inside or outside the organization to conduct the analysis, they should consider the following points. The smaller the unit of analysis, the more time needed to complete the research. The more questions to be answered, the greater the time needed to find the answers. Finding the answers to some questions (e.g., determining frequency of arguments and tone of content) requires significantly more time than finding answers to others (e.g., measuring column inches of coverage). The former activities also require a higher level of expertise. Less impressionistic analyses require more time than those based only on "gut feel." If the organization opts for analysis of video transcripts, the time for analysis will be less but the analyst will lose a large part of the content. Anthropological studies indicate that more than 90% of human communication is nonverbal. Faced with a choice between believing the verbal and nonverbal, the large majority of people believe the nonverbal. The most reliable information acquired from video transcripts will be the frequency with which specific questions and arguments appear. Tone of coverage is more difficult to assess.

Unless a transcript is furnished, analysis of audio materials will require more time than analysis of print media materials because few people can skim or speed read an audiotape. Analysis will require stopping and starting the tape, rewinding, and making notes before the researcher can even begin the analysis. The same rationale applies to video material, but the process becomes even more complex and, thus, more time-consuming. Unless the analyst is working with a transcript, he or she must analyze verbal and nonverbal content, which is a highly subjective process.

Whether dealing with print or broadcast media, an analyst who is learning a content area will require more time than one who has carried out work on the same topic over a longer period of time. A large part of analysis is learning to recognize what is new, what is no longer present, and what subtle shifts have taken place in arguments over time. Acquiring this contextual framework is time-consuming, but an analysis carried out without the necessary background risks being superficial. A request for more time for a first analysis is reasonable.

Therefore, an organization should expect to pay more for an analysis that makes increasingly fine levels of discrimination in content, asks more questions, poses questions that are more sophisticated in their nature, requires higher levels of expertise, depends on more than intuitive "feel" (even though intuition is an important asset to an analyst), involves the analysis of audio or video content, or calls for the involvement of an analyst who is new to the subject areas.

Generating a media analysis is a labor-intensive activity. Because the work involves research and constant exercising of judgment, it is also a fatiguing activity. Employees who are expected to do this type of work 5 days a week, 7.5 hours a day will soon experience burnout or will look for another job. Monitoring services experience high turnover for similar reasons. Because it is difficult to achieve the level of concentration necessary to do media analysis for a task that requires "entry time," the time necessary to reconnect with the subject matter, analysts should have access to large time segments in which they can concentrate on their analysis tasks. Analytical work requires immersion in the task for relatively long periods of time. Also, supervisors should attempt to induce some variety into the work of media analysts when circumstances allow (e.g., at the conclusion of an analysis project).

Computers can assist but not replace the analyst. Although programs can help to identify trends, no computer program understands narrative in the same way as a human analyst (Fuld, 1991; Herring, 1991; Weber, 1990). For example, fine distinctions are lost when single words have multiple meanings. Currently, no computer program is capable of drawing inferences from material. Researchers at the Yale Artificial Intelligence Laboratory have attempted to create a computer program that understands narrative and responds to questions about text. In their attempt to program computers with the capacity to make inferences about matters that are only implied, they have experimented with syntax and language, objectives, plans for achieving objectives, affect or emotions, events and scripts concerning events, interpersonal relations, social roles, reasoning and beliefs, settings, and abstract themes (Dyer, 1983). Despite the ambitious efforts of researchers in artificial intelligence, most scientists still regard this field of study as being in its infancy. The Yale system, for example, can understand only a limited number of topics, and experts note that it is dangerous to expect too much too soon, especially considering the cost of developing appropriate techniques and programs. Similarly, many organizational specialists warn against overreliance on computer technologies. Coors and Banc One, which downplay the role of technology in deciding the success of intelligence operations, note that computerized data banks do not substitute for expert analysis (Fuld, 1991). My own experience—more than 12 years of training people to carry out the research and analysis function in the Canadian government—confirms this observation. Nonetheless, computers can be a valuable tool to store data, track the development of trends in content, generate visual displays of quantitative analyses, and preserve the results of research efforts in a way that was not possible even a decade ago. These programs can identify where ideas originate (the source and location), mutations in the message as it moves from one medium to another, and the source of mutations.

Conclusion

When engaging in content analysis of media, researchers consider the purposes of their research. On this basis, they limit the study, deciding what to include and exclude with regard to sources, and their selection of a sample takes different factors (including organizational culture) into account. After deciding on the smallest unit of analysis, they generate categories, or "pigeonholes," for their data. Tabulation of frequencies and space or time follows coding of the data. Finally, the analyst interprets the data and prepares the report. Table 4.17 provides tips on packaging the public opinion report. As noted earlier, the conclusions reached in an analysis may be based on information gleaned from the work of many people over which the organization has little or no control. Unless the research firm conducts adequate training sessions with personnel and refines categories of analysis over time, the organization will probably obtain reports of questionable validity.

Note

1. Peggy Binns, Privy Council Office of Canada, suggested this presentation format.

TABLE 4.17   Tips for Packaging Opinion Environment Reports

Content

• Some organizations offer a choice of different kinds of products to clients, including daily or weekly media summaries, media analyses of specific issues, or monthly trend reports that examine the performance of various issues in relationship to each other. Some analyses are backward-looking; some are forward-looking. Most should project trends at some point in the report.

• The time frame and sources used in the report should be identified and included in an opening paragraph or preliminary statement. The report writer may want to italicize or bold the statement.

• Analyses should indicate convergence or divergence of opinion, as reflected in different sources. For example, do the results of media monitoring confirm the results of public opinion surveys? Does the correspondence from the general public and interest groups support the results of media analysis and public opinion surveys?

• Analytical reports should draw conclusions and suggest implications. That is, the analyst should "add value" to the facts and statistics. Recommendations or highly speculative sections of the report, however, should appear as a separate page that can be distributed to some readers and not to others. For example, policy experts in government may want to receive the recommendations of a consultant; they may not want to circulate those recommendations to all readers, however, if the suggestions are at variance with current policy directions.

Style

• The report should rarely exceed 7 pages in length, plus appendix materials. If a longer document is prepared, a table of contents should be included.

• Writing style should be clear, direct, and unambiguous. The writer should avoid jargon and long, rambling sentences.

• The report writer should avoid using too many quotations within the text.

• The writer should avoid using too many numbers in the discussion. Quantitative data should appear in the appendix to the report.

• The writer should avoid being "clever." Reports remain in files for long periods of time, but witticisms often have a short shelf life.

Presentation

• Every report should include a 1-page executive summary.

• A cover page should include a distribution list, a contact name, telephone number or e-mail address, and logo, cartoon, or other visual to capture interest.

• The organization may want to attach a log of other reports that are available for review.

• Color coding can indicate first or second draft or type of report.

• Some writers include representative quotations as boxed text or as an appendix to the report.

• An evaluation form, also attached as appendix material, can request feedback from the readers regarding what they found useful or not so useful in the report. Alternatively, the report writer can make a one-line request for feedback in the cover material.

• The public opinion analyst may want to provide ring binders to those who receive hard copies of the report.

• Special web sites can be designed for on-line users of public opinion environment reports.

PART
III

Research Methodologies

5

Survey Design and Sampling

In contemporary U.S. politics, the practice of consulting the latest poll has become a ritual like consulting the oracle was to the ancient Greeks. . . . Polling is not just an instrumental means to manipulate or reflect public attitudes, but is also a cultural form that sustains and affirms deeply held founding mythologies about community, democracy, and vox populi.

—Lipari (1999, p. 83)

E very major presidential candidate or president since 1976 has had poll-sters as influential advisers. For example, President Clinton's advisers commissioned weekly national polls between June and Labor Day during the 1992 presidential campaign (Baumann & Herbst, 1994). The Roper Center's POLL database contains nearly a quarter million poll questions that were asked of the American public between 1935 and 1998 (Lipari, 1999). In the Year 2000, governments of all political persuasions appear to have accepted the view most colorfully expressed by consultant Lionel Sosa: "If you fly by your guts, you're nuts" (Witherspoon as quoted in Taras, 1990, p. 180). The popularity that polls enjoy with American politicians and governments has spread to other countries. Government under long-time Canadian leader Pierre Trudeau was dubbed "leadership by Goldfarb" (Taras, 1990, p. 181), and the Conservative government that followed Trudeau contributed to the development of its competitor Decima Research into a "polling powerhouse with an international reputation" (Taras, 1990, p. 182).

RESEARCH METHODOLOGIES

Rationale for Surveying

What the poll is to the politician, the survey is to the bureaucrat and the CEO. Surveys have been dubbed "the most powerful tool in the practitioner's arsenal of scanning and evaluation tools" (Dozier & Repper, 1992, p. 200). In addition to media tracking, focus groups, and consultations, surveys provide a rich source of environmental data. Policy analysts argue that public opinion surveys make a vital contribution to the policy-making process—and ultimately to society. This view is held most strongly by those who consider the policy-making process interactive, with the public influencing the policymaker and the policymaker influencing the public (Yeric & Todd, 1989). Discussing the rationale behind surveys, Canadian broadcast executive Elly Alboim (as quoted in Taras, 1990) said,

> The only way I can evaluate what is really germane . . . is by [surveying]. I have to see what the issue subset is. I have to know what the rank order is. I have to understand the relationship between leadership and issues. (p. 191)

Aware of the significance that governments attach to public opinion surveys, corporate decision makers are avid followers of the latest results of Harris, Gallup, Roper, and other polls. They keep a close check on the pulse of government because government has the power (a) to decide the winners and losers in disputes between firms and their publics, (b) to close down one firm and protect another, (c) to exercise discretion regarding environmental and regulatory policies, and (d) to provide support for favored parties in the form of public goods and services (Arundell, 1988).

They also know that financial traders and members of elite groups read and act on survey results. Although governments do not always volunteer the results of their opinion research (especially if public sympathies, as expressed in surveys, diverge from public policies), businesses, universities, and nonprofit organizations can acquire access to the results of most surveys. Freedom of information legislation requires that citizens be able to access information generated with public funds. Thus, pressure groups often access survey results in the hope of obtaining evidence of public support for their issue stances (Mauser, 1991).

Sometimes, corporations commission their own surveys to understand shifting public priorities and attitudes that could translate into government initiatives (Reid, 1988b). At other times, they follow the latest government-

or media-sponsored surveys. Even when organizations do not conduct their own surveys, the majority appear to recognize the benefits of becoming sophisticated consumers of data from surveys conducted by other groups.

Media also find uses for surveys and polls. News organizations "winnow" the number of candidates to be covered in a political contest by deciding on frontrunners (Meyrowitz, 1994; Nimmo & Combs, 1990). Polls are one of the easiest ways to determine whose campaign merits attention. For this reason, many media organizations commission their own polls. Between 1972 and 1988, the number of media-sponsored polls increased from 2 to 259 (Ladd & Benson, 1992). At least five polling organizations in the United States work for major newspaper chains: "The mating dance between polling firms and news organizations is facilitated by the fact that polling firms often agree to do polls for media outlets at bargain basement prices in the hope of gaining a windfall of publicity" (Taras, 1990, p. 187).

Despite the popularity of polling, some consider the practice to be antidemocratic—a tool for centralizing control and shaping policies (Lipari, 1999; Sears as cited in Taras, 1990). Pollster Angus Reid (1988a) said that "like prostitution, polling has become one of the most controversial professions" (p. A4) and subject to much hypocrisy, with leading citizens and journalists publicly rebuking the practice but privately contracting the services of pollsters. Critics worry about political and commercial motivations for commissioning polls, the consequences to the political system, the inability of journalists to interpret polls, and the failure to cross-check results. Sometimes, media organizations use polls as a "vehicle for self-promotion," celebrating their own polls and downplaying or ignoring polls carried out by other news organizations (Taras, 1990, p. 187). At other times, in the absence of more interesting stories, journalists use tracking polls to create news events (Rhee, 1996, p. 214). "Finger-to-the-wind" politicians, who rely heavily on polls, may focus on the short term (Greenberg as cited in Asher, 1988, p. 15). When used to decide who stays or leaves a political race, polls compromise the political process. Some critics allege that heavy reliance on polls encourages bandwagon responses and creates apathetic publics. Many journalists lack the expertise to interpret either poll or survey results (Frizzell, 1989; Neumann, 1997). One observer noted, "I could count on one hand the number of journalists that are competent to analyze polls" (Sears as quoted in Taras, 1990, p. 187). Few attempts are made to cross-check the results of surveys.

Despite these reservations, polling and surveying practices are not a transient phenomenon, and journalists, the public, and critics are more keenly aware today than in the past of their uses and limitations. Thus, this chapter examines the first two steps in conducting a credible survey. After deciding on research objectives, and before writing the questionnaire, the person charged with conducting the survey needs to select a survey research design and gather a sample.

Selecting the Research Design

After specifying survey objectives and identifying the target population, the researcher selects from several types of survey research designs. The most common forms are the cross-sectional survey, the longitudinal survey, and the multiple-sample survey.

A *cross-sectional survey* collects data from the target population at a single point in time. Examples are surveys to determine employee support for a collective bargaining agreement prior to a union vote or, alternately, exit interviews after the vote. A *longitudinal survey* collects data from target populations at different points in time, sometimes from the same people and sometimes from different people. The longitudinal survey seeks to identify shifts in opinion over time. This survey may take several different forms, including trend studies, cohort studies, and panel studies.

Trend studies consider a general population at different points in time, with different people participating each time the survey is conducted. For example, researchers may want to find out how first-year employees view their jobs over time. Their study design may call for sampling and interviewing employees hired in 2000, 2004, and 2008. The specific employees who are queried may be different each time the survey is conducted. This is the nature of a trend study: the same general population, different points in time, and different individuals in the sample. In this case, the results of the study will tell the company whether first-year employees in 2004 and 2008 have different workplace attitudes and values than employees hired in 2000. Marketing researchers use trend studies (also called "tracking studies") to track customer satisfaction over time.

Cohort studies resemble trend studies, except that cohort studies focus on a specific subgroup of the larger population. That is, cohort studies consider a bounded population at different points in time, with different individuals participating each time the survey is conducted. Assume, for example, that a researcher wants to know how employee attitudes toward a company change as employees acquire seniority. Using the previous example, a cohort design would obtain its sample from all workers first employed by the company in 2000. Then the researcher would sample again from this same population in 2004 and 2008. The use of random sampling techniques permits different employees to participate in each survey (although in some cases they could be the same employees). Some employees may have left the company, moved, died, or otherwise become inaccessible. The researcher, however, must draw the sample from the population of people first employed in 2000 and omit those hired in any other year.

Panel studies are similar to cohort studies, but they require surveying exactly the same individuals at different points in time. Assume that the survey researcher wants to know how employee attitudes toward their work change as they gain seniority with a company. If Joe Smith is in the first survey on employee attitudes, he must also be in the next survey in the case of a panel design. Policymakers use panel studies to learn about people's attitudes toward parties and candidates for office. The pollster meets, at several different times during the course of an election campaign, with the same panel of people. The researcher questions the panel members about their voting intentions and probes to learn if changes have occurred.

A weakness of this approach (compared to the cohort study) is the bias introduced in a winnowing of the group by attrition or the sensitization of respondents who have previous experience with the survey questions. It is difficult to keep track of a group over time and costly to locate and survey panelists who have relocated. Some people refuse to participate in subsequent sessions. Despite their shortcomings, panel studies are useful for answering some kinds of questions. For example, if the researcher wants to know the effects of medications on people over time, he or she might want to survey the same individuals included in his or her first study. Panel studies are most feasible in short time spans.

An alternative to cross-sectional and longitudinal surveys is the *multiple-sample survey,* which involves studying more than one sample at the same time. A multiple-sample study enables the researcher to identify, describe, and explain relationships among two or more populations. For example, the researcher could survey a sample of lower-level employees, middle managers, and senior managers to compare how their views on employment equity differ or converge.

Choosing the Sample

Survey researchers typically select a representative sample from the population that they wish to study. The term *sample* implies a group smaller in number than the total population. *Representative* implies that the smaller group must be sufficiently like the larger group (in terms of the characteristics being studied) to allow the researcher to generalize survey findings to the larger group. Two broad kinds of sampling procedures, probability and nonprobability, can be used to select a sample group.

Probability Sampling

Pollsters and academics commonly use probability-based techniques. Probability theory (also known as random sampling) states that a sample will be representative of the population from which it is selected if every member of the population has an equal chance of inclusion. This can only occur through a process of random selection. Furthermore, probability theory enables the researcher to calculate mathematically the chances that a given member, "unrepresentative" of the "true" population, has been included in a sample by mistake. Described as "sampling error," unrepresentative samples can skew or bias the results of a study. Error can be due to random chance or to systematic sources of bias. For example, if two groups receive different versions of a survey, group differences in variables such as age and social class may be accounting for the different responses rather than survey manipulation. Probability sampling techniques include simple random sampling, systematic sampling, stratified sampling, and multistage cluster sampling.

The most common probability sampling technique is simple random sampling. A random sample is drawn from a sampling frame or "population roster" (Smith, 1988, p. 77). This roster lists all members of the target population (e.g., a telephone directory of all organization employees, a voter registration list, or a list of shareholders for a given corporation). After numbering all members of the population, the researcher draws a random sample from a table of random numbers (Table 5.1) or uses a computerized random selection process or draws names from a hat. If the desired sample size is 150, the researcher draws 150 names. Assuming that the names of all potential members of the population have been included and that no one is missing from the list, this technique should yield a representative sample.

TABLE 5.1 Table of Random Numbers

0.028	0.036	0.080	0.461	0.957	0.341	0.840	0.925	0.044	0.141	0.616	0.029	0.036
0.126	0.938	0.351	0.414	0.646	0.714	0.522	0.246	0.924	0.323	0.868	0.961	0.810
0.488	0.717	0.156	0.943	0.002	0.307	0.026	0.977	0.835	0.886	0.850	0.228	0.794
0.798	0.432	0.932	0.393	0.625	0.165	0.498	0.615	0.809	0.502	0.312	0.460	0.441
0.013	0.778	0.937	0.303	0.900	0.822	0.614	0.073	0.872	0.088	0.031	0.143	0.665
0.152	0.581	0.833	0.566	0.782	0.563	0.579	0.909	0.480	0.154	0.284	0.265	0.385
0.232	0.566	0.347	0.985	0.456	0.448	0.783	0.719	0.495	0.226	0.010	0.848	0.750
0.417	0.782	0.507	0.434	0.138	0.679	0.560	0.304	0.820	0.484	0.611	0.724	0.813
0.655	0.997	0.403	0.422	0.410	0.005	0.713	0.578	0.689	0.994	0.659	0.960	0.437
0.324	0.241	0.534	0.973	0.832	0.708	0.123	0.134	0.647	0.204	0.714	0.316	0.305
0.712	0.054	0.225	0.523	0.224	0.473	0.346	0.182	0.526	0.642	0.725	0.386	0.877
0.809	0.747	0.926	0.914	0.708	0.757	0.282	0.868	0.826	0.049	0.519	0.097	0.297
0.630	0.606	0.805	0.635	0.926	0.851	0.621	0.887	0.329	0.770	0.753	0.332	0.282
0.922	0.956	0.671	0.969	0.294	0.189	0.767	0.009	0.266	0.211	0.542	0.420	0.995
0.521	0.518	0.271	0.711	0.604	0.269	0.859	0.810	0.204	0.457	0.089	0.076	0.598
0.147	0.957	0.697	0.687	0.312	0.450	0.184	0.778	0.914	0.521	0.680	0.946	0.461
0.659	0.035	0.050	0.942	0.874	0.082	0.414	0.234	0.068	0.068	0.110	0.232	0.958
0.148	0.363	0.850	0.885	0.736	0.038	0.024	0.496	0.841	0.689	0.982	0.681	0.997
0.918	0.007	0.632	0.439	0.567	0.121	0.939	0.023	0.829	0.052	0.824	0.039	0.976
0.957	0.971	0.417	0.760	0.685	0.923	0.682	0.336	0.265	0.947	0.010	0.962	0.039
0.428	0.577	0.590	0.794	0.352	0.370	0.062	0.521	0.618	0.930	0.109	0.951	0.263
0.508	0.734	0.416	0.887	0.056	0.886	0.330	0.543	0.197	0.290	0.847	0.851	0.541
0.852	0.104	0.475	0.109	0.388	0.978	0.416	0.153	0.218	0.648	0.820	0.341	0.627
0.598	0.788	0.631	0.977	0.899	0.131	0.213	0.825	0.998	0.725	0.338	0.860	0.792
0.694	0.698	0.834	0.219	0.271	0.227	0.084	0.168	0.760	0.023	0.550	0.337	0.663
0.512	0.094	0.840	0.752	0.970	0.435	0.209	0.641	0.877	0.812	0.150	0.453	0.688
0.960	0.088	0.473	0.096	0.222	0.848	0.637	0.082	0.056	0.219	0.098	0.807	0.441
0.810	0.264	0.785	0.578	0.734	0.344	0.649	0.166	0.705	0.369	0.453	0.632	0.276
0.911	0.093	0.579	0.849	0.669	0.268	0.739	0.018	0.090	0.035	0.903	0.333	0.019
0.093	0.716	0.292	0.917	0.096	0.054	0.489	0.180	0.334	0.815	0.408	0.406	0.075
0.488	0.390	0.365	0.269	0.478	0.693	0.073	0.033	0.403	0.994	0.148	0.279	0.910
0.278	0.392	0.807	0.325	0.001	0.480	0.348	0.054	0.462	0.321	0.568	0.141	0.478
0.167	0.705	0.402	0.517	0.607	0.554	0.734	0.848	0.073	0.025	0.512	0.092	0.975
0.073	0.343	0.530	0.893	0.382	0.123	0.619	0.717	0.757	0.035	0.817	0.059	0.565
0.573	0.789	0.825	0.080	0.196	0.451	0.377	0.844	0.864	0.517	0.877	0.255	0.775
0.346	0.452	0.718	0.758	0.535	0.578	0.262	0.017	0.042	0.198	0.863	0.411	0.195
0.846	0.666	0.858	0.727	0.706	0.510	0.129	0.911	0.627	0.007	0.402	0.277	0.789
0.798	0.847	0.478	0.018	0.472	0.354	0.946	0.595	0.609	0.299	0.670	0.642	0.402
0.794	0.384	0.812	0.515	0.866	0.762	0.592	0.506	0.351	0.297	0.352	0.203	0.427
0.354	0.129	0.005	0.940	0.842	0.030	0.346	0.241	0.817	0.570	0.868	0.974	0.114
0.803	0.073	0.525	0.158	0.593	0.831	0.004	0.167	0.042	0.686	0.745	0.714	0.900
0.792	0.837	0.579	0.290	0.386	0.084	0.562	0.194	0.759	0.450	0.129	0.847	0.232
0.677	0.154	0.319	0.952	0.843	0.677	0.908	0.516	0.110	0.857	0.255	0.597	0.218
0.821	0.470	0.242	0.810	0.141	0.932	0.247	0.781	0.579	0.144	0.152	0.380	0.363
0.611	0.276	0.689	0.136	0.335	0.568	0.166	0.646	0.775	0.009	0.791	0.319	0.280
0.050	0.432	0.808	0.756	0.601	0.275	0.076	0.755	0.801	0.494	0.204	0.037	0.098
0.565	0.646	0.194	0.728	0.294	0.394	0.151	0.340	0.416	0.716	0.731	0.471	0.614
0.491	0.284	0.199	0.986	0.271	0.659	0.003	0.511	0.265	0.944	0.556	0.724	0.983
0.170	0.096	0.221	0.748	0.627	0.293	0.962	0.093	0.416	0.975	0.791	0.978	0.367
0.308	0.191	0.932	0.703	0.410	0.690	0.433	0.541	0.935	0.980	0.553	0.318	0.274

A second probability technique is systematic random sampling. Systematic sampling can also generate a representative sample. First, the researcher randomly picks a starting point for drawing the sample. This process can be as simple as closing one's eyes and placing a finger at some point on a table of random numbers. Then the researcher systematically draws the rest of the sample (e.g., every 10th number of the population represented in the sampling frame until the researcher reaches his or her quota).

A problem can arise from systematic sampling frame periodicity, a situation in which a list has a particular organizational pattern such as an alphabetical arrangement. For example, in a World War II study of soldiers, researchers drew their sample from a list of all men in a military unit. Each roster had 10 names. Using systematic sampling techniques, the researchers selected the first name on each list. Had the names appeared randomly on the list, there would have been no problem; in this case, however, the men were listed by rank, with sergeants' names appearing first on the rosters followed by corporals and privates. Thus, the final sample contained only sergeants, scarcely representative of the military squads they headed (Babbie, 1990). Randomizing the lists prior to sampling can eliminate the problem of periodicity. The ease of using systematic sampling makes it very popular, despite this potential problem.

Rather than being an alternative to simple random sampling or systematic sampling, stratified random sampling is a variation on the two forms. Before drawing the random sample, the researcher divides the population into relatively homogeneous subgroups. The criteria for generating the subsets depends on research purposes. For example, does the study seek to know the differences in attitudes expressed by male and female employees? If so, it is necessary to separate the population into males and females before randomly sampling the population. Does the study have the objective of determining how people in different parts of a business organization view a given issue? If so, it is necessary to break the population into different business divisions (e.g., finance, marketing, manufacturing, and research and development). To consider both sex and division variables, the researcher must organize the population list by males and females and, at the second stage, subdivide the list into different business divisions. In other words, the researcher must classify the population by gender and division membership before drawing the sample. Once stratified, the researcher can use simple random sampling or systematic sampling techniques to choose the sample. Stratified sampling ensures that all relevant subgroups are represented in the final sample. For example, if the population is 55% male and 45% female, the stratified sample should be 55% male and 45% female.

To sample from a very large population (e.g., all members of a multinational corporation), the researcher may need to use multistage cluster sampling. Multistage cluster sampling breaks the process of drawing the random sample into two or more stages. The number of stages varies depending on the size of the population. For example, the researcher who wants to generate a national sample of hospital administrators can do so in three or more stages. In the first stage, the person randomly selects states to be included in the study (from a list of 50 states). In the second stage, the researcher randomly selects towns (from the previously selected sample of states) large enough to have hospitals meeting specific criteria. The third stage involves randomly picking hospitals to be studied (from a list of all hospitals meeting appropriate criteria in the selected towns). The administrators of these randomly chosen hospitals constitute the final population sample.

Even when researchers are diligent about selecting random samples, there can be problems with response rates. Response biases occur when certain portions of the sample complete the survey to the exclusion of others. For example, women and retired individuals are more likely to be home during the day to answer phone calls. Therefore, surveyors who call during the day are likely to find greater portions of females and the elderly in their samples than reflect the actual population. To circumvent such problems, surveyors may make calls in the evening when more people are home and ask to speak to people according to some random criteria (e.g., the person with the most recent birthday). Alternatively, they may oversample certain groups which they know will be less likely to respond (e.g., asking to speak to the youngest person in the house to compensate for any bias in age). There may also be characteristics of people who agree to complete surveys that make them different from those who do not (e.g., those who complete surveys may have more free time or they may feel more strongly about the topics being surveyed). These types of issues mean that samples that are initially random become less random during the process of survey completion. Researchers will try to avoid such problems by offering incentives to respondents, such as money or services, to help increase response rate. If, during statistical analysis, researchers notice that their samples do not match the characteristics of the population (referred to as systematic error), they may compensate through weighting.

No matter how much care the researcher takes in selecting a sample frame, picking a sample, and ensuring that as many people as possible respond to the survey, the results will probably stray (at least slightly) from the characteristics present in the larger population (due to random error). Factors that affect the degree to which the sample represents characteristics of the larger population are the size of the sample and the homogeneity of the population (similarity of its members) from which the sample is drawn. The larger the random sample, the greater the likelihood that the sample contains all important characteristics and, therefore, the smaller the likelihood of error (called "margin of error"). The smaller the margin of error, the greater the likelihood that the researcher will generate unbiased data, or information, on which to base his or her report. The more homogeneous (similar to each other) the population, the smaller the sample can be and the smaller will be the margin of error. This is because it is possible to generalize with greater accuracy from a group with similar characteristics.

Probability theory provides a way to calculate both the odds that the results are in error (different from a "true" score) and the probable degree of divergence. The terms statisticians use to express the odds of error are confidence level and confidence interval.

Confidence level refers to how confident a researcher can be that the statistics represent the population that the person is trying to understand—for example, confidence level may suggest that the researcher's judgment will be correct 95 times out of 100. *Confidence interval* suggests the probable extent of discrepancy (or difference) in estimates if the researcher is wrong. For example, a confidence interval of 3% suggests that, in a survey that reports 48% of the employees favor a corporate takeover, support for the takeover might be as low as 45% (−3) or as high as 51% (+3). The researcher can obtain both an acceptable confidence level and confidence interval by selecting a sufficiently large sample size. Table 5.2 can serve as a guide to appropriate sample size.

First, the researcher decides on a desired confidence level and interval. Perhaps it is sufficient for results of a survey sample to be accurate within ± 5% of the larger population's true score on an issue, and the researcher is willing to accept a 95% probability that the survey will yield results within this confidence interval. Next, the researcher must cross-reference the desired confidence level with the desired confidence interval to arrive at a minimum sample size. For the confidence interval of ± 5% and the confidence level of 95%, the minimum recommended sample size is 384 persons.

TABLE 5.2   Sample Sizes Required for Different Confidence Levels
and Intervals

Confidence Level (%)	Confidence Interval (%)									
	1	*2*	*3*	*4*	*5*	*6*	*7*	*8*	*9*	*10*
99	16,577	4,144	1,842	1,036	663	460	336	259	205	166
98	13,533	3,383	1,504	846	541	376	276	211	167	135
97	11,772	2,943	1,308	736	471	327	240	184	145	118
96	10,547	2,637	1,172	659	422	293	215	165	130	105
95	9,605	2,401	1,067	600	384	267	196	150	119	96
94	8,836	2,209	982	552	353	245	180	138	109	88
93	8,190	2,048	910	512	328	228	167	128	101	82
92	7,656	1,914	851	479	306	213	156	120	95	77
91	7,183	1,796	798	449	287	200	147	112	89	72
90	6,765	1,691	752	423	271	188	138	106	84	68
89	6,400	1,600	711	400	256	178	131	100	79	64
88	6,045	1,511	672	378	242	168	123	94	75	60
87	5,730	1,433	637	358	229	159	117	90	71	57
86	5,439	1,360	604	340	218	151	111	85	67	54
85	5,184	1,296	576	324	207	144	106	81	64	52

Commercial polling firms, such as Gallup and Harris, often aim for a confidence interval of ± 3%, with a confidence level of approximately 95%. To arrive at this confidence interval and level, they must use a sample size of 1,200 to 1,500 people in a national survey. The numbers in Table 5.1, based on the standard normal distribution, apply to relatively heterogeneous populations. With more homogeneous populations (e.g., many stratified samples), a smaller sample size can yield representative results. Generally, a sample size of 30 is considered sufficient when surveyors are confident that their samples are truly representative of the population.

Nonprobability Sampling

Unlike probability sampling techniques, nonprobability sampling techniques do not usually claim to generate a representative sample. Nonprobability sampling relies on nonrandom selection methods, including convenience sampling, quota sampling, and purposive or judgmental sampling.

Convenience sampling involves selecting the sample from readily available people (e.g., on the streets, in supermarket parking lots, or in malls) in public. The benefits of convenience sampling derive from the ease and low cost of using this technique. Because the sampling process is nonrandom, however, the sample will not be representative of the larger population being studied (unless the research question involves these specific groups). For example, morning shoppers in suburban malls will have a certain demographic profile (probably more females than males, usually more old than young shoppers, and probably more unemployed than employed individuals). People intercepted on city streets or in parking lots have other profiles. Shoppers emerging from Neiman Marcus or the Trump Tower will scarcely represent low-income individuals. Convenience samples present threats to external validity—they do not allow one to generalize to greater populations. If one is surveying only shoppers at Neiman Marcus, one should restrict conclusions to individuals who shop at that particular store.

Quota sampling, which aims to generate a nearly representative sample, is not a probability technique. Quota sampling involves the following steps:

1. Construct a matrix based on stratification of the population using all relevant subsets (e.g., age, gender, ethnicity, educational level, income, regional affiliations, political orientation, and other demographic and psychographic variables).

2. Decide what percentage of the population is classified into each cell of the matrix.

3. Collect data from individuals who have the characteristics of a given cell.

4. Use proportionate weighting (in terms of the larger population) to determine the sample size for each cell.

5. Use nonrandom techniques to select the sample.

Essentially, quota sampling provides interviewers with appropriate quotas for their study (e.g., two black male urban professionals and three white female urban professionals). Unfortunately, the procedure is time-consuming, and it offers few guarantees that the researcher will have generated a sample with the characteristics of the larger target population. If researchers learn that the sample does not represent the population, they can weight the data in such a way as to compensate for the shortcoming. That is, they may mathematically put more weight on the responses of the group with too few members.

The most often recounted incident of a poll gone astray (as a consequence of failure to use quota sampling) occurred in 1936 when the *Literary Digest* predicted that republican Alf Landon would defeat incumbent democratic President Franklin Roosevelt by a margin of 57% to 43%. In defiance of the *Digest* predictions, Roosevelt was returned to office by a landslide (the biggest in history), with 61% of the popular vote and 523 electoral votes. Landon, however, received only 8 electoral votes (Squire, 1988). The inaccurate poll results were blamed on an unrepresentative sampling frame. Pollsters had drawn their sample from lists of telephone subscribers and automobile owners—people who were scarcely representative of a Depression-mired population. At that time, fewer than 40% of American households had telephones, and only 55% of the population owned automobiles. Of the 2 million people sampled, the survey drew from a disproportionately large number of people who were wealthy or at least relatively so (Frey, 1989). The disillusioned poor were the ones who turned out in unprecedented numbers to vote in the 1936 elections, however.

George Gallup, using a different sampling procedure, accurately predicted that Roosevelt would win a second term. Through quota sampling, Gallup ensured the inclusion of people at different levels of the social and economic strata (Babbie, 1990).

With purposive or judgmental sampling, the researcher decides who is to be included in the sample. He or she makes a personal judgment about who is representative, or typical. For example, a pollster might decide that, based on historical precedent, certain voting districts will be key to an election victory for the Democrats. He or she samples only from the districts that are perceived to be critical. In other cases, the pollster might sample the potential voters in bellwether precincts to obtain an idea of how other precincts will vote. Sometimes, the researcher is interested in certain subgroups within a population (e.g., employees with a specific profile, travelers who have certain characteristics, or companies with a unique management style). He or she decides which employees, travelers, or companies fit the profile. After making this judgment, the person may use probability sampling techniques to acquire the final sample. The quality of the final sample depends on the quality of judgment in the initial selection phase. The judgments used in these processes do not differ greatly from judgments that are made by customs officials who stop some travelers and let others pass. The randomness of the checks is mediated by the control that is exercised by customs officers.

Conclusion

After discussing the reasons that people survey, this chapter examined the first two stages of conducting a survey research project—selecting a research design and choosing a sample. The researcher can choose to conduct a cross-sectional survey, longitudinal survey, or multiple-sample survey. Cross-sectional surveys collect data from the target population at a single point in time. Longitudinal surveys (trend, cohort, and panel studies) collect data from target populations at different points in time, sometimes from the same people and sometimes from different people. Multiple-sample surveys involve studying more than one sample at the same time. A multiple-sample study enables the researcher to identify, describe, and explain relationships among two or more populations.

When selecting a sample, researchers can use probability or nonprobability sampling techniques. Probability sampling techniques include simple random sampling, systematic sampling, stratified sampling, and multistage cluster sampling. Nonprobability sampling relies on nonrandom selection methods, including convenience sampling, quota sampling, and purposive or judgmental sampling.

Once the researchers have chosen the proper design and selected a sample that is representative of the population in which they are interested, they are ready to design the questionnaire. Chapter 6 discusses survey development, including questionnaire design, and Chapter 7 discusses methods for administering the questionnaire.

6

Survey Development

Sherry Devereaux Ferguson and Alexandra Hendriks

S urvey development is a complex process that requires careful consideration. Researchers must consider a variety of methodological issues. The wording of a question and the information requested will affect the researcher's ability to obtain valid and reliable results that can be generalized to the greater population. This chapter provides information on how to effectively write, construct, and order survey questions and discusses the types of preface materials that should be included with any questionnaire.

Wording Survey Questions

The quality of any survey ultimately derives from the validity of the questions that are asked. Ambiguous, unclear, and loaded questions produce unreliable results. Therefore, it is not surprising that the results obtained by one research firm may bear little resemblance to the results reported by a second firm. Scott (1997) notes,

> Because the questions and methods vary from one polling house to the next, it's not surprising that their polling numbers differ too. If you're like most casual ob-

servers of polls, you probably look at the numbers in the headlines to find the score for the main parties in an election. But the pros and political insiders say you have to understand exactly how the polling house created the final numbers in order to evaluate the results. (p. A1)

Issues commonly associated with questionnaire design relate to language choice, the use of percentages, and the psychology of the respondent (including selective memory).

Problems Associated With Language and Percentages

Common errors in the framing of questions include the use of loaded and leading questions, unclear and ambiguous questions, and questions with a hidden agenda. Other problems include the use of relative language, acronyms, double-barreled questions, double negatives, hypothetical and unqualified questions, and requests for information in the form of percentages.

Loaded and Leading Questions

Although loaded questions are usually easy to spot, many consumers of surveys never see the wording of questions. One study showed that 88% of media reports do not reveal the name of the researcher; 82% do not reveal details on how the study was conducted (Singer as cited in Neumann, 1997). University of Montreal professor Edouard Cloutier states (as quoted in Scott, 1997, p. A1) that he looks first for the wording of the question: "Normally I don't find it, and that can make all the difference."

Consider the following statements, in which the respondent is asked to agree or disagree:

> "I believe that the government should drop all surtaxes that could impair the ability of businesses to attract international investors."
> "I believe that Americans should have the right to defend themselves against intruders."
> "I would like my children to have the opportunity to receive quality day care."
> "I believe that we should help small businesses to stay competitive by allowing them to remain open on Sundays."
> "I am proud that America helps people from other countries to flee despotic regimes."
> "I believe that every American should have the right to three good meals a day."
> "Are you in favor of helping the needy?"

All these examples cue the respondent as to the most acceptable answer. Lengthy preambles can also bias responses.

Although favorable survey results may give some measure of reassurance to senior management, in the long run they will distort their reading of the public mood and invite rather than deter external threats. In the case of one Quebec poll, the survey firm asked the respondents 34 questions before "popping the big one about voting intentions" (Scott, 1997, p. A1). Jean-Mark Leger, head of another polling firm that obtained significantly different polling results, said that "contaminated the answer because people have been prodded to think about leaders, issues, and the fact that the sovereignist Bloc has no intention of forming a government before they're asked which party they support" (as quoted in Scott, 1997, p. A1).

Unclear and Ambiguous Questions

The researchers who carried out a national crime survey in the United States discovered that not all people consider the same acts to be crimes (Converse & Presser, 1986, pp. 17-18). They discovered (as have many groups that work with victims of elder abuse, child abuse, and spouse abuse) that it is necessary to educate people to recognize certain forms of family violence as crimes. Given this ambiguity of interpretation, it is easy to see that if a survey asked respondents to identify past experiences in which they have been victims of crime, some might limit their list to acts of theft or robbery. Similarly, responses may vary greatly to requests for basic demographic information, such as employment or marital status. Someone who is actively searching for work may consider himself or herself unemployed. Someone who gave up searching for work 3 years ago may also consider himself or herself unemployed. The legal system may not accord a gay couple the benefits of marriage, but the individuals may nonetheless define themselves as married. Pretesting a questionnaire can help to anticipate these kinds of discrepancies of interpretation (Fowler, 1992).

Questions With a Hidden Agenda

Questions sometimes contain underlying premises that may be erroneous. Most of us would see the inherent bias in the questions, "Have you stopped beating your wife?" or "Have you given up your life of crime?" Some hidden assumptions, however, are not so obvious. Consider the following question: "Do you support the idea of large multinational corporations controlling our economy?" This question contains loaded language (terms such as "controlling" and "multinational"). The question also contains the underlying assumption that multinational corporations do control the economy.

Terms that suggest restraints on freedom or liberty tend to evoke negative responses (e.g., "constrain," "ban," "restrict," "control," or "forbid") (Converse & Presser, 1986, pp. 13-14). Another example also illustrates the idea of hidden assumptions: "I believe that Americans should have the right to choose their own doctors." By itself, this question is innocuous, and most Americans would agree with it. It is problematic, however, when it appears in association with other questions. For example, if the question appears in a survey that asks about state-subsidized health care, this question (if asked early in the survey) implies that changes from the status quo could result in a loss of the right to choose one's own doctor.

Relative Language

The movie *Annie Hall* illustrates the difficulties of using vague qualifiers in group comparisons. Schaeffer (1991) notes,

> In the movie *Annie Hall,* there is a split screen. On one side, Alvie Singer talks to his psychiatrist; on the other side, Annie Hall talks to hers. Alvie's therapist asks him, "How often do you sleep together?" and Alvie replies, "Hardly ever, maybe three times a week." Annie's therapist asks her, "Do you have sex often?" Annie replies, "Constantly, I'd say three times a week." (p. 395)

The psychiatrist's question has evoked a relative response. The use of semantic differential and other intensity scales can help to alleviate, but not totally resolve, these kinds of problems. The word "often" generates particular difficulties for survey respondents. In the case of an unusual event, such as an earthquake, hurricane, or flood, "often" could be once every 10 years or more. Applied to the frequency of gunfire in action films, "often" could be 50 times in a movie. A person's feelings toward an event can also influence the response. For example, for someone who dislikes taking buses to work, "often" could be once a week. Providing choices such as "more than usual," "less than usual," and "about the same as usual" can elicit more accurate responses than relative terms such as "often" (Schaeffer, 1991).

Ambiguous questions such as the following also lead to inconsistent responses and unreliable results (Fowler & Mangione, 1990):

"Should the United States be making more substantial contributions to Russia?" (How much is substantial? What are we giving now?)

"Do you believe that U.S. policies regulating the flow of immigrants from Mexico to the United States are fair?" (Fair to whom? Mexicans or Americans?)

"Should we be taking stronger measures to protect the environment?" (Is the reference to individuals or government? What is meant by "stronger measures"?)

"Should women under 40 have regular medical checkups?" (What is meant by the term "regular"?)

Some questions do not make much sense, no matter how one interprets them (e.g., asking people in different age groups whether they are satisfied with their level of physical activity). How is an 80-year-old individual to answer? What will a person with a physical limitation say? What does it mean if a 20-year-old indicates that he or she is not satisfied with the level of physical activity? Does the person want more or less activity? The finding that 40-year-old individuals are not satisfied with their level of physical activity and that 70-year-old persons are satisfied is meaningless. The researcher could interpret the data as saying that people in their 70s have accepted their limitations. Alternatively, he or she could interpret the data as saying that most 70-year-old people believe that they lead active lives, on the same terms as a 40-year-old person.

"Acronymonious" Language

Simple, clear language should characterize survey questions. The interviewer should use common terms to reach the lay public and should avoid compound and complex sentence structure. The person should restrict the use of jargon or specialized terms to interviews with professionals who understand the language. Bureaucrats, for example, often speak to each other in a language that means little to the average person. They talk about "target publics," "politically correct decisions," "strategies," "people-at-risk," "demonstration projects," "bilateral programs," "portfolios," and "initiatives." They have specific meanings for these terms, in the same way as the military specialist speaks of "collateral damage," "sweep and escort missions," "delivery of ordinances," "dropping of payloads," "incontinent ordinants," and "targets of opportunity" (which sometimes turn out to be hospitals and the Chinese embassy).

The terms allow these groups and individuals to communicate with each other in a precise way while they restrict communications to the public. Single words can carry a cargo of meanings to the insider, but to the lay public the terms often sound like Lewis Carroll's jabberwocky. Like bureaucratese, acronyms have meaning for those in the organization (e.g., the FDA [Food and Drug Administration], the FCC [Federal Communications Commission], MIA [missing in action], and the GNP [gross national product]). Acronyms allow people in the same culture to communicate in shorthand. Sometimes, the abbreviated version of words becomes so common that people forget the original terms. Nonetheless, as a general rule, surveys should avoid the use of acronyms.

Double Trouble

Including two separate points in the same question forces a choice between the two. In other words, the question is double barreled. The following examples illustrate this idea:

> "Do you support reducing taxes and restructuring the tax system to assist middle-income families?"
>
> It is quite conceivable that a person could support reducing taxes but not believe that restructuring of the tax system is necessary.
>
> "Do you believe that immigration rules should give priority to seniors and children?"
>
> Someone may believe that one group should have priority status but not the other. Because each question in a survey should contain only one idea (Cannell & Kahn, 1953), questions should not employ conjunctions such as "and" or "but." Nor should questions ask for information and attitudes at the same time.
>
> "Do you engage in recycling, and how do you feel about your local community recycling programs?"
>
> "Do you intend to vote in the next election, and would you support our candidate's position on make-work programs?"

Respondents are also confused by questions that use double negatives. Suppose that an interviewer asks the respondent to agree or disagree with the following statements:

> "The United States should not give further aid to Nicaragua." (To disagree is to say that the United States should give additional aid.)
>
> "The company should not reduce salaries to protect jobs." (To disagree is to say that the company should reduce salaries to protect jobs.)

Hypothetical Questions

Interviewers should take care in asking for reactions to hypothetical situations, such as "Would you volunteer for military service if the conflict in Yugoslavia turned into a ground war?" and "Imagine our country faced another world energy crisis. In such a situation, would you be willing to give up the use of your automobile for at least 3 days a week?" It is easy to respond "yes" so long as the situation is hypothetical, but a person might think twice before taking the actual step.

Furthermore, it is rare that a hypothetical situation specifies all the ramifications or options. For example, employees might support a merger if they have guarantees their jobs will not be lost, that they will not be relocated, and that they will not have to take a pay cut. To improve the chances of obtaining valid information from a hypothetical question, one should be as specific as possible: "Would you support a merger if it meant that things basically remained the same for you in terms of job security, place of work, pay, etc.?" The question is still hypothetical, but the specifics make it easier for the person to relate to the question on a realistic level. Similarly, researchers should take care in interpreting the results of questions that elicit intention (Cloutier as cited in Scott, 1997, p. A1). Some researchers suggest adding at least one question based on actual experience to balance any questions of that nature. Researchers also suggest probing at least one of the hypothetical questions (Converse & Presser, 1986).

Problems With Percentages

Surveys often ask people to report the percentage of time or money spent on different activities—work, play, computers, television, or other activities. A survey might ask for the percentage of time spent communicating with clients outside the organization, the percentage of the budget devoted to media-monitoring activities, or the relative emphasis placed on different issues. People usually guess about allocation of time and money, and the guesses may be reasonably accurate or extremely inaccurate. If percentages are important, the interviewer should ask a series of questions that enable the respondent to calculate the percentages (Hogan & Smith, 1991). The interviewer should also frame questions so that they ask for "typical" or "average" amounts of time spent on a task or activity: "How many hours in a typical week do you spend watching television, listening to radio, and reading magazines and newspapers?" "How many hours in a typical week do you spend reading magazines?" and "How many hours in a typical week do you spend reading news magazines?" Alternatively, the researcher can break the questions down into even smaller chunks, such as "How much television do you watch between 8:00 a.m. and 12:00 noon? Between 12:01 p.m. and 4:00 p.m.? Between 4:01 p.m. and 8:00 p.m.? Between 8:01 p.m. and midnight?" The answers to these questions enable the researcher to calculate percentages.

Problems Associated With Psychology of Respondent

Whereas the problems identified previously in this chapter lead to confused responses and inadequate questions, the problems identified in the following sections lead to recalcitrance on the part of respondents. The failure of respondents to answer these kinds of questions does not derive from lack of understanding but from fear of appearing dishonest, foolish, or incompetent.

Tendency to Lie When Questions Ask for Sensitive or Embarrassing Information

"Do you cheat on your income tax?" "What is your age?" "What is your income?" Some questions elicit sensitive, embarrassing, or even high-risk information. Because these questions can result in respondents breaking off an interview or refusing to continue to complete a questionnaire, the designers of questionnaires often place these sensitive questions last or at least in the middle of a questionnaire (Babbie, 1990). An interesting example of people's lack of willingness to respond honestly to certain kinds of survey questions occurred during an anthropological study conducted many years ago. A group of anthropologists studied patterns of food and drink consumption among people living in the southwestern United States. During the day, the researchers went door-to-door, asking people to describe what they had eaten and consumed in drinks in a typical week. To confirm the quality of the data they had obtained, the researchers went through their subjects' garbage cans in the evenings. What they learned is that people are not always honest when they are asked to describe such personal matters as diet. The subjects in the study typically described themselves as following a healthy food regime and consuming few alcoholic beverages. What the anthropologists discovered, however, was that junk food composed a significant part of the diet of the people, and their consumption of alcohol was at a much higher level than reported.

Similarly, approximately 90% of the people who responded to a recent *Dateline* question said that they always answer honestly on income tax forms. If this information is correct, then the government should seriously reduce its expenditures on salaries of Internal Revenue personnel. An alternative explanation is that the sample was contaminated or people gave socially acceptable (and safe) responses.

To alleviate these kinds of response problems, it is necessary to frame sensitive questions in a neutral fashion that encourages honesty. The wording of questions should make it possible for people to give a socially acceptable response (Cannell & Kahn, 1953). For example, the anthropologists could have asked, "Some people include a certain number of foods in their diet that are quick and easy to prepare. Is this the case with your family? What do you eat in a typical week?" With a sensitive topic such as reporting income, the interviewer could probe, "We want to learn more about how Americans view reporting of income. Some people report all of the income they earn in a year. Others report only part of their income. Into which category do you usually fall?"

Sometimes, people are more likely to tell the truth to questions framed in third-party terms. For example, to learn more about how people feel about income tax evasion, the interviewer could say, "Let us assume that Ted and Mary Smith earn $30,000 a year. They report $15,000 of this income. How do you view their income tax reporting practices?" Bracketing age and income can also encourage people to respond to sensitive questions. For example, instead of asking how much someone earns, the interviewer can ask the person to select the appropriate income bracket: "less than $20,000," "$20,000-$29,999," "$30,000-$39,999," and so on. Questionnaires should include at least one bracket lower or higher than required by respondents. Studies have found that people are more likely to be honest if they do not have to place themselves in the lowest income category. Because some people are sensitive about their ages, the best questionnaires offer a choice of different age groupings (e.g., 21-30, 31-40, 41-50, 51-60, and over 60). It is important to ensure that the bracketing of numbers does not include overlapping figures.

Tendency to Want to Please the Interviewer

People who are being surveyed will often look to the interviewer to obtain cues about how they should answer the questions. People do not like to displease the interviewer. Another phenomenon, *acquiescence response set,* refers to a tendency for some people to agree, no matter how a question is phrased. Asking people to agree or disagree with the following kinds of statements encourages an acquiescence response: "Governments should ensure that everyone gets adequate health care" or "Every individual should be responsible for his or her own health care." Asking the question in a different way can help to control for this response tendency: "Should government or the individual be responsible for health care?"

Sometimes, the public will recognize an issue as important on some idealistic scaling, but the issue will rate low on their private agendas. Ranked against domestic issues such as employment, taxes, and health care, most foreign affairs issues assume a low priority. Nonetheless, if queried, people will recognize some of these issues as embodying principles of importance to democratic society. If asked "How important is our country's affiliation with the United Nations?" most Americans would say "very important." Forced to make a choice, they give the rating that they regard to be appropriate to the values embodied in the issue.

To label some issues as unimportant is to violate the American ethic. Issues related to gender equity are linked to human rights and minority rights—concerns that rank high, at least on a rhetorical level, in the American value system. The average American recognizes that he or she is supposed to care about these issues. When asked in a person-on-the-street interview whether the issue of gender equity is "very important," "important," "neither important nor unimportant," "not very important," or "not important at all," many will respond in a predictable fashion. The largest number will probably agree that the issue is "important" or "very important." When the same people evaluate the importance of equity issues against unemployment, escalating health care, and military involvement, however, they may not want politicians to invest a great deal of money in managing the concern. Eliciting views on "motherhood" issues can sometimes lead researchers to the erroneous belief that some issues have a more important weighting to people than is the reality.

Tendency to Hide Ignorance of Issues

No one likes to appear uninformed or unintelligent. Most people assume that if a topic is important enough to appear in a survey they should have a view on the issue or subject. Accordingly, some people will be reluctant to admit lack of familiarity with a topic. Even the uninformed may claim to have an attitude, and the numbers of those individuals may be larger than interviewers like to admit. As early as 1947, Gallup reported that public knowledge in some areas is extremely limited (as cited in Converse & Presser,

1986). Many other studies have reached similar conclusions. An attempt to test people's understanding of economics found that less than one third knew anything about the GNP (Sigelman & Yanarella, 1986). Data derived from the University of Michigan Center for Political Studies confirmed the prevalence of voters who are "lamentably ill informed" about issues and candidates (Yeric & Todd, 1989):

> Between 1956 and 1984 an average of 56% of the people queried were unable to identify the congressional candidates running for election from their district. The surveys were taken at the height of election campaigns, in an environment that has increasingly been saturated by a whole variety of media messages. In studies of more specific issues, citizen knowledge is also low. (p. 105)

A California study that tested public knowledge of the nuclear power issue found that voters were "highly skewed toward the low end of the knowledge scale," with 80% of those surveyed registering below the midpoint on the scale. This finding occurred despite the fact that the researchers gave credit for partial answers (Kuklinski, Metlay, & Kay, 1982). Other studies have found that the American public's factual knowledge of politics is lower than it was in the 1940s and 1950s. Some studies demonstrate that women, younger adults, and the less educated know less about political issues than men, older adults, and the more educated.

At other times, respondents may find the question to be outside their range of interests. Consider the following examples:

"How important is it for the United States to build a dam in Ewaktotok?" (Even if the public recognizes the issue, they may never have had reason to consider it.)
"Do you believe that U.S. corporations should adopt a more global focus?" (The average American may have no idea what this orientation implies, and those who do understand the question may have had no reason or occasion to form an opinion.)
"How important is it for company X to expand its product line into nontraditional areas?" (Only individuals with an intimate knowledge of the functioning of the company will be equipped to answer the question. The average person and sometimes even the average employee may have no basis for forming an opinion.)

The public has relinquished responsibility for many policy issues to their leaders. Unless the issues bear directly on the well-being of the public, they may not follow the issues in the news or discuss them. Despite this fact, few surveys attempt to measure factors such as level of commitment to issues or cognitive involvement (Reid, 1988b). A classic study on the political belief systems of American voters concluded that large portions of an electorate do not have meaningful beliefs, "even on issues that have formed the basis for intense political controversy among elites for substantial periods of time" (Converse, 1964, p. 245). Those who fail to develop "more global points of view" are unable to respond to questions about policies in abstract or ideological terms, and they are unable to relate politics to policy (p. 245). During the 1960s and through the mid-1970s, this situation appeared to be changing as voters showed a higher level of ideological and issue orientation (Nie & Andersen, 1974). Vietnam, civil rights, and law and order were but a few of many issues that claimed the attention of the public. Recent research, however, shows a tendency for today's youth to place considerably less importance on public interest issues that did their peers in earlier years (Easterlin & Crimmins, 1991). Research also suggests that reading of daily newspapers (especially by young people) and viewing of the "flagship" evening news programs on the three major networks are in decline, which are indicators of a less informed populace (Robinson & Levy, 1996).

People will nonetheless often offer an opinion on topics about which they are ill informed or uninformed. Studies demonstrate that between 10% and 15% of respondents "routinely lie to pollsters" (Lewis & Schneider as cited in Taras, 1990, p. 189). One study revealed that almost one third of those queried about an obscure agricultural trade act and a little-known monetary control bill voiced an opinion (Schuman & Presser, 1996). In another instance, one third of those surveyed expressed a point of view on a fictitious public affairs act (Bishop, Oldendick, Tuchfarber, & Bennett, 1980). Some studies have found significant support expressed for nonexistent politicians and bias against some fictitious groups (Lewis & Schneider, 1982). In other cases, deceased individuals garner their fair share of the vote at the polls. University of Toronto political scientist Nelson Wiseman (as quoted in Hoy, 1989) says that many people view surveys as tests they "don't want to flunk" (p. 90).

Researchers suggest that forcing an opinion on a topic about which a person has little knowledge or interest is less than useful. To avoid forcing opinions, some researchers use filter questions (discussed earlier). Filter questions allow a respondent to omit questions on which they have not formed an opinion or that are not relevant to their circumstances. Consider the following filter question: "Have you heard of company X's plan to invest in Russian industry? If *yes,* continue. If *no,* skip to Part II of the questionnaire." In this manner, the survey identifies those who are basically uninformed on the details of the investment scheme. Having a second part to the survey (even if the researcher does not intend to analyze the responses to this section) suggests to the uninformed that they are not alone in their lack of knowledge. The second part of the survey could ask about other issues that respondents consider to be more important or could ask why they have not taken the time to become informed on the issue.

It can also be helpful to establish a frame of reference that will take the level of respondents' knowledge into account. For example, to find out how employees would react to a revised policy that would allow some people to work at home, the researcher could state the following in the preface to a questionnaire or in the introduction to an interview,

> Some people have expressed a preference for working at home. They believe they will be able to accomplish more if they spend fewer hours commuting. However, the present policy requires all permanent employees to be physically present in the office. Do you agree that the company should allow interested employees the opportunity to work at home?

To determine whether the public likes a new company logo better than an old logo, a survey could ask, "You may have noticed that company X recently changed its logo. By logo, I mean the company's trade symbol. If I show you a picture of the old logo and the new logo, could you tell me which one you like better?"

Eliciting the frequency with which respondents discuss the issue with friends and family can alert the researcher to issues of little importance or interest to the individuals (Reid, 1988b). Alternatively, the researcher can ask a series of questions that lead toward the major policy question. Similarly, people may not know why they believe as they do (Converse & Presser, 1986). When researchers ask "why," they may get misleading responses from people who search to find a socially acceptable reason for their beliefs or behavior. As such, some researchers caution against asking "why" questions (Reid, 1988b).

Tendency to Be Impressed by High-Status Sources

Prestige effects can occur when a survey question includes a reference to a prestigious or well-known person (e.g., the president of the United States or the company CEO). The following question could evoke this type of bias: "Do you support the CEO's environmental policies?" This question has two weaknesses. First is its reference to the CEO. The position of this individual is the highest in the company, a position to which the average employee assigns credibility and prestige. Studies indicate that a certain number of people will agree with prestige figures, no matter the question or issue. Second, this question includes an ambiguous term, "environmental policies." Today, most companies' environmental policies have more than one component. Many companies have an entire unit devoted to dealing with environmental concerns.

Framing such a broad question further encourages the person to rely on the prestige source. It is possible that a source could also bias a question in the opposite direction, for example, including a reference to a union leader in a survey directed at corporate executives: "Do you support union leader Robert White's position on the U.S.-Mexico-Canada free trade pact?" If the executive has any doubts about the potential impact of the agreement on the industry, he or she might hesitate to agree with a union leader because the two have traditionally represented different interest groups.

Tendency to Weigh Cost-Benefit Factors

Sometimes, questions do not state the cost of a desired result. For example, most people would respond "yes" to the following question: "Do you think it is important to give increased job opportunities to disadvantaged minorities?" They might not answer in the same way to the following question: "Would you support increased job opportunities for disadvantaged minorities if it meant fewer job opportunities for you?" Similarly, most people would respond positively to the question, "Do you support subsidized food banks for the poor?" Fewer would respond as positively to the question, "Would you favor subsidized food banks for the poor if it meant significantly higher taxes?" Almost everything has its price, but questions often fail to mention that price. At other times, questions do not allow people to state their reservations or to qualify their support.

Polls during the first term of the Reagan administration showed support for a nuclear freeze but only for a "verifiable and balanced freeze agreement." Others might have favored an agreement, but they doubted the sincerity and commitment of the Soviet Union. Still fewer individuals felt positive toward the political activists who were behind the debate (Hogan & Smith, 1991). Support for many issues is conditional, and the most useful surveys try to capture this kind of information.

Problems Associated With Memory, Orientation, and Perspective

Selective Memory

Survey respondents often have problems remembering fine details from the past. Most of us remember the most important life events (births, deaths, anniversaries, and marriages). We also recall major historical events (elections, wars, and crises). Canadians will not soon forget, for example, the massacre of young female engineering students gunned down in the corridors of a Montreal polytechnic institute, and Americans will not soon forget the slaughter at Columbine High School, the carnage at Oklahoma City, or the deaths of such icons as John Kennedy and Marilyn Monroe. The British remember the Falklands, the Americans D-Day, and the Canadians Dieppe. In general, it can be said that people remember the best and the worst. They are selective in what they recall, and they tend to allow lesser events to slip from their memories.

In designing surveys, it is sometimes useful to place questions against some landmark event that people are likely to remember to set the question in time. References to major holidays can also assist people in remembering. For example, "Since the time of the Montreal Massacre, would you say that the women's movement in Canada has (a) grown stronger, (b) remained about the same, or (c) grown weaker?" and "Since last Christmas, would you say that the company has made (a) steady progress toward its goal of achieving quality in customer service, (b) some progress toward its goal of achieving quality in customer service, or (c) no progress toward its goal of achieving quality in customer service?" (Converse & Presser, 1986).

Specificity, the use of graphic, concrete terminology in a survey question, can also trigger recall. For example, to elicit people's views on whether they connect celebrities' on-screen behaviors with their off-screen behaviors, the interviewer could prompt recall in the following way:

Try to remember any scenes of celebrity figures smoking on television. Perhaps in a bar? A restaurant? Relaxing at home or with friends? Would you say that media coverage is probably (a) completely representative of their actual behaviors, (b) somewhat representative of their actual behaviors, or (c) not representative at all of their actual behaviors?

Reducing the reference frame to 6 months or less can encourage recall: "Has your company established any new equity policies during the past 6 months?" and "Has correspondence from shareholders increased notably during the past 4 weeks?" Even with a short reference frame, people will typically go beyond the period for which the interview requests information. Therefore, if the interviewer asks what happened to someone in the past year, the respondent might go back 18 months. If the interviewer asked what occurred in the past 6 months, the respondent might go back 9 or 10 months. Alternatively, they might *telescope,* or underreport, stating that an event occurred more recently than was actually the case. Respondents telescope when they say that they attended a meeting last week but the meeting actually occurred 3 weeks previously (Converse & Presser, 1986).

To cope with problems of overreporting and underreporting time periods, researchers have developed techniques such as *bounded recall,* which requires more than one interview with the same subject. The first interview asks the subject to recall events of the preceding 6 months. A subsequent interview requires the person to remember what has happened in the 6 months since the first interview. By examining both sets of data, the interviewer can identify the events that occurred in the second time period. A variation on the bounded recall technique asks the respondent about what happened in the time period previous to the one in which he or she has an interest; then the interviewer asks about the current time period (Converse & Presser, 1986). Other techniques for dealing with overreporting and underreporting of time periods include using cues to stimulate recall (e.g., asking about participation in a list of events or behaviors), asking respondents to recall landmark events in their lives and to recount events that followed, and verifying responses against more objective records (e.g., attendance records, calendars of events, ledgers, other official records, or accounts of other people) (Frey, 1989).

Political Orientation and Perspective

Public opinion research during the past decade suggests a tendency for "the population to adopt right-wing attitudes on general issues but left-wing perspectives on specifics" (Reid, 1988b, p. 140). For example, public opinion research shows high levels of support for "cutbacks in government expenditures" but strong opposition to "cuts in major expenditure areas such as education and health" (p. 140). Similarly, the public opposes the general concept of increasing immigration but supports allowing larger numbers of specific groups into the country (p. 140). Personalizing more general concepts appears to make a difference to responses to a survey question. The variation in some political polls derives from the fact that some surveys elicit support for parties and others for leaders. People react in different ways to both of these (Scott, 1997).

The responses of respondents also vary when they are asked to view an issue from different perspectives, according to the perspective they take (Reid, 1988b). For example, if asked to respond as consumers, they will answer one way. If asked to respond as citizens, they will respond differently. As consumers, they may like the idea of legalized gambling. As citizens, they may oppose legalized gambling, believing that it will bring crime into the community. The framing of the survey question will influence the response.

Constructing and Ordering the Questions

Questions usually elicit some of the following categories of information from respondents: knowledge or awareness (how much they know about the topic), degree of concern (level of interest in the topic), attitudes (predisposition to act), motivations (why respondents act as they do), the intensity with which they hold their beliefs and attitudes, salience (the perceived importance of the topic), readiness to act, perceptions (how respondents view the issue or topic), background characteristics (demographic variables such as age, sex, and place of residence), behavioral patterns (in terms of participation, voting, and consumer habits as well as other categories of information), and preferences (in terms of products, services, companies, or policy alternatives) (Frey, 1989).

Designing a survey involves determining the appropriate level of measurement for all questions, deciding on scaling techniques, deciding whether to ask open-ended or closed-ended questions, assessing reliability and validity, organizing the questions in such a way as to encourage a high response rate and to avoid question order effects, and developing appropriate instructions.

Levels of Measurement

When constructing questions, researchers need to consider the desired level of measurement. The way that a question is worded and the information that it requests will affect the surveyor's ability to run statistical tests on the data and to draw various conclusions during the analysis phase of the study.

Nominal-Level Measurement

Nominal measurement is the most basic level of measurement. At this level, researchers classify responses into categories; they verify whether the construct is present or absent. Variables such as gender, race, employment status, and marital status are nominal because responses can only fit into one category (e.g., they are either male or female). Questions that ask for "yes" or "no" responses or for people to check categories that apply to them are also nominal (e.g., "Which of the following television shows have you watched in the past week?" and "Which of the following household products do you use?"). Nominal variables allow researchers only to count the frequencies with which categories occur; they do not allow them to determine magnitude. For example, a nominal question does not allow one to determine how masculine or how feminine a person is or how often someone watches a particular television program—only whether the person watches it or not.

Statistical analyses using nominal variables are restricted to those that employ the mode and frequencies (e.g., chi-square and binomial test). Qualitative researchers using techniques such as content analysis operate at the level of nominal measurement; they count how often variables appear (e.g., the number of aggressive acts that appear in a film segment or the number of references to an organization). Sometimes, researchers do not want more sophisticated levels of analysis; they are satisfied with simply comparing categories. If researchers want to conduct powerful statistical analyses on their data, however, they should consider substituting higher levels of measurement for nominal variables.

Ordinal-Level Measurement

The second level at which questions operate is the *ordinal* level of measurement. Ordinal measures increase statistical power because, in addition to providing frequencies, they allow researchers to gain a basic understanding of the relationship among variables. Ordinal scales typically ask the respondent to rank order a series of items, from most preferred to least preferred. For example, subjects can rank order the five issues that are most important to them, with "1" indicating the most important and "5" indicating the least important. Sometimes, a person is asked to select the top three or four choices from a longer list. Some ranking scales involve paired comparisons (Zikmund, 1988), which ask respondents to indicate whether "A is better," "B is better," or "they are the same." Figure 6.1 provides an example of a paired comparison.

We would like to know your opinion of the following two approaches to foreign aid. "Approach A" says that we should emphasize technical assistance (expertise, tractors, equipment). "Approach B" says that we should emphasize monetary assistance (dollars).

_____ A is better   _____ B is better   _____ They are the same

---

Figure 6.1. Example of a Paired Comparison

Q sorting techniques ask respondents to indicate their attitudes by arranging cards or other items. Each card represents some concept, policy, or other item. A respondent, for example, could be asked to Q sort issues into groups on the basis of their perceived importance, visibility, or impact on the organization or the individual. The *cafeteria reward system* asks respondents to assign priorities to ideas or issues (Zikmund, 1988). The person is asked to divide a set sum of money or points among different categories, as shown in Figure 6.2.

Suppose that you have $100, and you can give varying amounts to the following categories of services for seniors. How would you divide the $100?

_____ Housing subsidies
_____ Transportation subsidies
_____ Recreational programs
_____ Pension income
_____ Health care

Figure 6.2. Example of a Cafeteria Reward System

Questions with unequal category levels are also classified as ordinal. Consider, for example, a question that asks how long people have lived at their residences. A question with the response options "(a) less than 1 year, (b) 1 year to less than 3 years, (c) 3 years to less than 5 years, and (d) 5 years or more" is ordinal because the quantities in each category are not equal. That is, "a" covers less than 1 year, whereas "d" covers any period of time more than 5 years.

Ranked responses are limited in terms of the information they provide. Researchers learn preferences but not how much respondents like or dislike the items in question. Similarly, they do not know the relative differences between items that are ranked first, second, third, and so on. It is possible, for example, that individuals really like their first-ranked item but hold more neutral attitudes toward the remaining options. Value surveys typically ask people to rank order values rather than to rate them on scales. The difficulty with forcing choices, however, is that sometimes two or more values will be equally important to an individual (e.g., loyalty and morality may have equal weighting). Forced to choose, the person makes arbitrary selections. Ordinal-level measures should be restricted to use with nonparametric statistics that employ the median (e.g., Mann-Whitney U test, Wilcoxian signed-ranked test, and Spearman correlation).

Interval- and Ratio-Level Measurement

Interval and ratio scales go a step further than ordinal scales: They allow individuals to understand not only the type of difference but also the magnitude of the difference. With interval-level data, equal intervals exist between the numbers, but no absolute zero point exists (i.e., the absence of the variable is not an option). Regarding the example of the television show ratings, researchers might ask respondents the degree to which they agreed with the statement "*The Practice* is a television show of high quality." They repeat this question for each of the programs of interest. In this case, the scale could include 5-point anchors ranging from "completely agree" to "completely disagree." With interval scales, researchers understand how much respondents like or dislike the particular shows. Likert scales use interval-level measurement because they assume equal distances between responses, but they do not include an absolute zero (a neutral response is the nearest to zero that can be obtained).

Ratio-level measurement includes an absolute zero in its scale. Open-ended questions that ask for raw numbers and percentages (e.g., "How often do you go to the gym in a typical week?" and "How much money do you spend on long-distance telephone calls in an average month?") are usually considered ratio-level data because they allow for zero responses (e.g., I never go the gym; therefore, I respond with a "0"). To transform the ordinal-level question about housing into a ratio scale, the question must be open-ended and allow respondents to enter the amount of time they have lived in their current residences. Interval- and ratio-level data provide substantially more information than nominal and ordinal data because researchers can run parametric statistical tests (e.g., t test and analysis of variance).

Researchers need to be aware of the level of measurement they are using to understand the types of interpretations they can make (e.g., researchers cannot reach conclusions regarding magnitude of response when they use ordinal data) and the types of statistics to use for analysis. Although some questions cannot be converted from formats that require nominal responses, often researchers can transform questions into higher levels of measurement with relative ease.

Types of Scales

The Guttman scale is a popular survey tool used to evaluate a body of existing data. Using this scaling device, researchers can identify hierarchical relationships in the data. For example, if an individual agrees that cocaine should be legalized, he or she will probably also agree that marijuana should be legalized. Many more people will probably agree with the legalization of marijuana than with the legalization of cocaine. In other words, the hierarchical relationship presumes that if respondents agree with a higher scale item, they will also agree with the lower scale item. Thus, Guttman scaling enables the researcher to predict one response on the basis of another response. When the researcher selects the items to be included on a list of indicators, the person assumes a logical relationship among some factors.

Clogg and Sawyer (1981) used Guttman scaling to study American attitudes toward abortion. They examined different conditions under which people thought abortion was acceptable (e.g., the mother's health was in danger or pregnancy resulted from rape). They discovered that 84.2% of responses fit into a scaled response pattern (Neuman, 1997). In another case, McIver and Carmines (1981) analyzed the roll call votes of U.S. senators on 12 proposed amendments to consumer protection legislation. They concluded that the voting pattern of the senators conformed to a "Guttman scalable pattern 92% of the time" (as quoted in Neuman, 1997, p. 168). The hierarchical nature of the Guttman scale means that it fits into the ordinal level of measurement; responses provide the researchers with a ranking of items but not any indication of how much more strongly one attitude is held compared to the others.

The Likert scale asks respondents to indicate how strongly they agree or disagree with statements designed to elicit attitudes toward some object, concept, or person (Likert, 1932). These carefully constructed opinion statements are followed by three or more options. The most common options are "strongly disagree" (1), "disagree" (2), "uncertain" (3), "agree" (4), and "strongly agree" (5) (Figure 6.3). The most favorable attitudes carry the greatest weight. The analyst determines a total summated score based on the weight attached to each response. For example, if the questionnaire contains 10 statements to which the respondent reacts, the responses could carry the following hypothetical weights: 5, 5, 3, 1, 5, 4, 4, 4, 4, and 1. The sum of the responses in this example is 36. Some criticize the method because they believe that dramatically different attitudinal patterns can generate identical or similar totals.

The new legislation that restricts pornographic content on the Internet is badly needed.

Strongly disagree	Disagree	Uncertain	Agree	Strongly agree
(1)	(2)	(3)	(4)	(5)

Figure 6.3. Example of a Likert Scale

Another popular rating scale is the semantic differential (Osgood, Suci, & Tannenbaum, 1957). Semantic differential scales use bipolar adjectives placed at opposite sides of a 7-point continuum. Respondents place a check mark along the continuum corresponding to how they rate the organization, its products, or its handling of an issue. Three dimensions are represented in semantic differential scales. The first is the evaluative dimension, indicating the degree of favorableness that someone feels toward a word, personality, or concept. Examples are "good-bad," "cold-warm," "efficient- inefficient," and "fair-unfair." The second dimension is the potency dimension, exemplified by adjectives such as "strong-weak," "heavy-light," and "hard-soft." The third dimension is the activity dimension, represented by bipolar adjectives such as "fast-slow," "dynamic-static," and "active-passive." Issues, personalities, companies, governments, and policies can be rated on a semantic differential scale such as that shown in Figure 6.4. In interpreting the results, the analyst attaches a weight to each position on the rating scale.

Starr's Handling of the Lewinsky Affair

Efficient _____	Inefficient
Fast _____	Slow
Static _____	Dynamic
Active _____	Passive
Progressive _____	Regressive
Dull _____	Sharp
Cold _____	Warm
Soft _____	Hard
Dirty _____	Clean
Expensive _____	Inexpensive
Moral _____	Immoral
Unfair _____	Fair
Strong _____	Weak
Light _____	Heavy
Old-fashioned _____	Modern
Good _____	Bad

Figure 6.4. Example of Semantic Differential

Typically, choices are 7, 6, 5, 4, 3, 2, 1 (ranging from the most positive to the least positive), scored as 3, 2, 1, 0, -1, -2, and -3. The researcher varies the placement of the adjectives from left to right. That is, sometimes the more positive adjective appears on the left side of the rating scale, whereas at other times it appears on the right side of the continuum. Similar to the semantic differential, numerical scales rely on bipolar adjectives (Figure 6.5). Some studies suggest that numerical rating systems work as well for educated populations as the more descriptive semantic differential scales.

The government has been debating the question of revising our health care system. Please indicate how important it is to you to have access to a health care system that does not charge user fees.

Extremely important   7   6   5   4   3   2   1   Extremely unimportant

---

Figure 6.5. Example of a Numerical Scale

A Stapel scale measures the intensity and direction of a person's attitude (Zikmund, 1988). The Stapel scale substitutes a single adjective or a phrase for the bipolar adjectives used in a semantic differential scale. This word (or words) will appear in the center of a 7-point scale that ranges from 3 to –3. With this scaling device, the researcher attempts to measure the proximity of a concept to the descriptive term. Stapel scales such as the one depicted in Figure 6.6 are easy to construct and use.

Company X
3
2
1
Environmental policies
–1
–2
–3

Figure 6.6. Example of a Stapel Scale

A special type of rating scale is a magnitude estimation scale (Converse & Presser, 1986), which is used to measure various aspects of public opinion (e.g., the perceived usefulness of a piece of legislation, the perceived effectiveness of a policy, or the seriousness of a crime). The researcher might ask, "If robbery is given a rating of 6, what would sexual assault be?" Alternatively, a survey could ask, "If the earlier policy had an effectiveness rating of 4, how would you rate the current policy?" It is interesting to note that this technique is employed with patients who believe that they may be experiencing a heart attack. The doctor in attendance will typically ask, "How would you rate this pain on a scale of 1 to 10? Compared to earlier experiences, how would you rate your present level of discomfort?"

Some rating scales employ graphic techniques (Fink & Kosecoff, 1998). With the line-production method, a person is asked to draw a line to represent the perceived importance of an issue (e.g., the ozone problem) to the government in power. The individual may then be asked to draw a second line to indicate how important the issue should be to the government. In another instance, a graphic scale might request that the respondent place an "X" at the place along the continuum that best represents the person's attitude (Figure

6.7). To interpret the results, the analyst will need to divide the line into equal intervals and assign a quantitative value to each response. Not all graphic scales involve straight lines. Research studies that involve children may use a technique called the self-assessment mannequin. This technique asks the children to identify how they feel based on reference to happy and sad faces. To assess the public's level of confidence in the Clinton administration, the research designer could use ladder scales (Zikmund, 1988). The ladder, which is graphically depicted for respondents, has 10 rungs. Respondents are asked to select a place on the ladder that best represents their level of confidence in Clinton. The top rung represents the highest level of confidence in Clinton, and the bottom rung of the ladder represents the lowest level of confidence.

Please rate each of the following issues in terms of their importance to you. Place an "X" on the line at the place that best indicates your rating of the issue.

Lowering taxes	Not important _____ Important
Increasing welfare benefits	Not important _____ Important
Reducing the deficit	Not important _____ Important

Figure 6.7. Example of the Graphic Technique

A similar rating instrument is the feeling thermometer, developed by the National Election Study (Wimmer & Dominick, 1997; Yeric & Todd, 1989). Originally designed to measure a person's feelings toward political candidates, the feeling thermometer has been adapted to measure attitudes toward issues, policies, organizations, and their leaders. If someone feels warmly toward a policy, for example, the person places the policy close to the 100-degree mark on the thermometer. If he or she feels neutral toward the policy, he or she places it close to the 50-degree mark. If the person has cold feelings toward the policy, he or she locates it at (or near) the zero point. The person does the same in representing feelings and attitudes toward personalities and organizations (Figure 6.8).

Whereas the previously discussed rating scales measure attitudes and perceptions, other scales measure behavioral intentions and expectations. For example, a survey can ask respondents about the likelihood that they will vote for a certain political party in the next election (Figure 6.9).

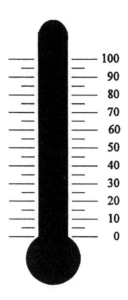

Figure 6.8. The National Elections Study at the University of Michigan Developed the Concept of the "Feeling" Thermometer

---

How likely is it that you will vote for the Republican party in the next election?

_____ I definitely will vote for the Republican party in the next election.
_____ I probably will vote for the Republican party in the next election.
_____ I might vote for the Republican party in the next election.
_____ I probably will not vote for the Republican party in the next election.
_____ I definitely will not vote for the Republican party in the next election.

Figure 6.9. Example of a Scale That Measures Behavioral Intentions

The U.S. Bureau of the Census uses a probability scale that ranges from 100% for "absolutely certain" to 0% for "absolutely no chance" (Zikmund, 1988). Respondents indicate their expectations in terms of performance and policy outcomes.

Open-Ended Versus Closed-Ended Questions

Questions can be open-ended or closed-ended. Open-ended questions call for unstructured oral or written responses such as the following: "What are the most important issues on the public agenda?" "How do you feel about the new abortion legislation?" and "If a Democrat came into the room, what would the person look like?" Researchers can learn much from open-ended questionnaires, especially in the exploratory stages of research. Open-ended questions do not anticipate a response; rather, they give people the freedom to generate their own answers, they encourage in-depth responses, and they can probe why a person answered in a certain way. This technique is time-consuming, however, and quantifying open-ended responses is more difficult and subjective than quantifying closed-ended responses. Responses to open-ended questions are sometimes ambiguous. Asked what is most important in a job, employees may say "pay." Does the respondent, however, mean "good" pay or "steady" pay (Converse & Presser, 1986)? Open-ended questions sometimes tap only the superficial concerns of people and fail to reveal their fundamental attitudes. Finally, the person conducting the survey has less control. To anticipate these kinds of problems, researchers may ask open-ended questions in pretests and closed-ended questions in the larger confirmational phase of research.

Alternatively, they may ask open-ended questions in the early part of the interview, followed by closed-ended or fixed-response questions that probe underlying attitudes and beliefs. Open-ended questionnaires often employ vignettes, or stories, to encourage the expression of opinions and attitudes. For example, a state government, considering legislation to release large numbers of mentally disturbed people from hospitals, could write a vignette that gives several alternatives to the status quo, including legislation to tighten the criteria for admitting and keeping mentally disordered individuals in hospitals. Respondents would be asked their views on the topics. In another situation, a committee formed to deal with the problem of prostitution in the city's market area could write a vignette that describes the situation. The public would be asked to suggest solutions to the problem. The attractiveness of vignettes, or scenarios, is their concreteness. To avoid respondent fatigue and boredom, the survey should limit the number of vignettes to 15 or fewer cases (Converse & Presser, 1986). Some suggest that open-ended questions should precede closed-ended questions to avoid response bias caused by leading questions (questions that suggest a desired response).

Unlike open-ended questions, responses to closed-ended questions force respondents to choose from the alternatives provided. Examples of closed-ended questions are multiple-choice questions and those that ask for "yes-no" or "agree-disagree" answers. Others ask respondents to check all applicable items on a list or inventory. A survey that employs closed questions forces respondents to make choices. Compared to open-ended questions, closed-ended questions require little time or effort to answer. The results are easy to analyze and quantify. The choices, however, may not reflect the true range of possibilities. Situations may change between the time a questionnaire is written and the time it is administered. If the survey asks people to select the most important issue facing the country but omits a critical or emerging issue from the list, the consequence can be invalid data. The addition of categories such as "other," "not applicable," and "no opinion" to forced-choice answers enables researchers to obtain an estimate of the usefulness of the categories. Some researchers, however, do not like to include a "no opinion" or "don't know" category because one eighth to one third of people surveyed will choose these responses if given the opportunity (Converse & Presser, 1986). Telephone reviewers solve the dilemma by recording "no opinion" and "don't know" when respondents seem unsure or reluctant to choose an answer, but they do offer this category as an option to respondents. Forcing an opinion choice (when the respondent has no opinion on the issue) creates misleading readings.

Correctly written closed-ended questions should not include overlapping or vague categories from which people must choose. That is, response categories should be mutually exclusive. Notice the following common mistakes:

> *Example 1.*   People are asked to indicate an age category. The choices are "less than 20," "20-30," "30-40," "40-50," and "50 and over." People who are 30, 40, or 50 will not know which category to mark.
>
> *Example 2.*   People are asked to indicate a period of time. The choices are "less than 6 months," "6 months to 1 year," "1 to 2 years," and "2 to 5 years." People who would choose 6 months, 1 year, or 2 years would not know which category to mark.

A special type of closed-ended question is the filter question, which directs some subgroups of respondents to additional questions. The following are examples:

> *Example 1.*   Do you subscribe to any monthly news magazines? If yes, please continue. If no, skip to Part II of the questionnaire.
>
> *Example 2.*   Do you agree or disagree with the statement, "Implementation of career planning is key to the future development of the company?" If you agree, answer the next question. If you disagree, skip to question number 5.

Reliability and Validity

Once survey developers have constructed their questions, they need to ensure that the surveys are reliable and valid. Reliable and valid scales will minimize error and lead to greater confidence in one's results.

A scale is considered reliable if it is stable and produces consistent results over time. *Test-retest reliability* refers to the requirement that the instrument produce the same results when administered to the same subjects on different occasions (given similar circumstance). For example, researchers asking for adult height should not obtain different results from one week to the next. If results differ, they need to examine the design conditions to determine the cause of the differences. A correlation coefficient allows researchers to determine the extent to which their scales are stable. *Interrater reliability* is obtained when different raters obtain similar results when using the same measurement tool on similar subjects.

Researchers also need to ensure that scales composed of multiple items are internally consistent (i.e., all measure the same construct). For example, indicators designed to measure depression (loss of appetite, lethargy, etc.) need to measure depression and not another construct, such as frustration or poor health. Statistical techniques such as Cronbach's alpha and factorial analysis provide ways to measure the reliability of scales. An alpha level of .7 or higher is generally considered an acceptable measure of reliability.

In addition to being stable and consistent, a measure also needs to be valid; it should measure the construct under study and nothing else. A survey developed to measure fright reactions in children, for example, should measure fear rather than excitement or anxiety. *Face validity* is determined by examining the items to verify that they appear to measure what they are supposed to measure. Sometimes, individuals not involved with the study can provide guesses as to what the scales measure. *Convergent validity* uses statistical analysis to determine the degree to which the measure correlates with other acceptable measures of the same (or similar) constructs. For example, a questionnaire that measures attitudes toward politicians can be compared with election results. *Discriminant validity* ensures that the instrument is measuring the construct under study and not additional constructs (e.g., attitudes toward politicians and not political party affiliation). Finally, *construct validity* refers to the need to measure the construct in an adequate and comprehensive way. This end is usually achieved by including multiple questions that measure the same construct.

Ordering the Questions

Few rules are available to guide the researcher in deciding question order. Survey administrators, however, believe that a well-ordered survey encourages the maximum number of responses. The most common view is that general questions should precede specific ones, and related topics should appear together. Others argue that the "inverted funnel" order (specific to general) is best (Smith, 1988). They believe that the ease in answering more specific questions motivates people to continue the survey or interview. As noted earlier, some believe that open-ended questions should precede closed-ended ones so as not to lead respondents in a predetermined direction.

Several different kinds of order effects can occur. First, people are more likely to agree to opinion items that appear early in a survey than to those that appear later in the same survey (Smith, 1988). Second, people learn as they participate in a survey. They use cues from some questions to answer other questions. A question that appears early in a survey may ask an employee to rate the quality of some employment equity practices that have been undertaken by an organization (e.g., "fast-tracking" women and visible minorities, affirmative action hiring policies, access to career counseling for employees who are members of minorities, increased access to training programs for these same individuals, and cross-cultural training for managers to sensitize them to minority group needs and cultures). If a later question asks the respondent to evaluate the company's commitment to employment equity, the earlier question will have influenced the response. Similarly, the answer to the question "Do you believe in opening up more markets in which U.S. industry can sell its goods?" will be quite different if the interviewer precedes the question with the query, "Do you believe in allowing other countries freer entry to the U.S. market?" If a question about job losses precedes a more general question about corporate performance, the earlier question will influence the response to the latter question.

Question-order effects occur most frequently with less-educated respondents (Benton, 1991). Some researchers recommend randomizing the order of questions to overcome these kinds of problems, but others believe that randomizing question order can result in a disordered and confusing questionnaire. Respondents may react negatively to the seeming lack of coherency to the questionnaire, and researchers may find it more difficult to identify contextual biases. The best approach may be to become sensitive to the potential for order effects. Alternatively, the researcher can give different versions of the questionnaire to different respondents. Some researchers recommend pretesting questionnaires, using different formats, to determine order effects. This latter approach would facilitate identification of problem areas.

Preparing Introductory Material

The following kinds of preface materials should introduce all questionnaires:

- A short informal cover letter that includes a general explanatory statement
- The name of the organization or individual conducting the survey
- A contact name and number in the event that people have questions
- The nature and purposes of the survey
- Assurances that confidentiality will be maintained
- A promise to send results of the survey to participants (if it is feasible to do so)
- References to incentives (if incentives are offered)
- Assurances that answering the questionnaire will not consume too much of the person's time (if the questionnaire is relatively brief)
- An explanation of why the questions are necessary (if the survey includes personal questions)
- Estimate of time required to answer the questionnaire
- A self-addressed stamped envelope in the case of a mail survey

General directions for responding to the survey appear on a cover page or in a paragraph that precedes the first question. More specific directions accompany individual sections of the survey. These preliminary materials also explain key terms (Fowler & Mangione, 1990). The appearance of questionnaires is important in generating responses. The questionnaires should be free of spelling or grammatical errors, attractively formatted in sufficiently large typeface so as to be readable, uncluttered in appearance, and characterized by sufficient white space. (What is deemed "sufficient" varies from situation to situation, depending on the audience [e.g., the publications of seniors require more white space than those of middle-aged adults].)

Conclusion

To successfully measure and analyze concepts of interest, survey researchers must consider a variety of factors when developing their questionnaires.

First, they need to write questions that employ unbiased, clear, and concrete language that does not lead respondents to desired answers or force them to respond to statements about which they have no opinion. Survey developers must also consider how psychological factors and problems with memory affect the responses they obtain. Questions should use reliable and valid scales (e.g., Likert or Guttman) that test at the level of measurement appropriate to research purposes, and researchers should order questions in such a way so as to avoid eliciting biased responses. Finally, surveyors should prepare preface materials that provide subjects with a general overview of the procedural requirements of the study. If all these steps are successfully completed, survey developers can feel confident that their results are sound and not corrupted by errors in the measuring instrument.

7

Survey Administration

Afterresearchers have developed a questionnaire, they must follow proper procedures in administering the questionnaire. Before actually distributing the survey, many individuals run pretests to identify potential problems. (See Chapter 6 for examples of possible problems.) This chapter also examines problems associated with interpreting and reporting results.

Pretesting the Survey

Pretests usually consist of one-on-one interviews in which researchers review questions with respondents after they have completed the questionnaires. This in-depth interview process allows researchers to learn how subjects interpreted the questions, whether the instructions were clear, and whether the response options were adequate. Sometimes, researchers realize that respondents have skipped questions or responded in erroneous ways (e.g., giving percentages rather than raw numbers). Pretests also allow researchers to time respondents to get a sense for how long it takes to complete the survey. Once researchers have run enough pretests to feel confident that the survey questions are clear, they can begin to administer the survey to their sample of subjects.

Administering the Survey

Oral administration of surveys involves setting an appropriate pace and allowing sufficient time for considered responses. In administering a survey, an interviewer should not ask, for example, "Would you strongly agree, moderately agree, neither agree nor disagree, moderately disagree, or strongly disagree that the government should reinstate capital punishment?" Instead, the person should say, "Some people say that the government should reinstate capital punishment. Would you strongly agree, moderately agree, neither agree nor disagree, moderately disagree, or strongly disagree with that point of view?" The interviewer may need to explain why the organization is conducting the survey. With a written questionnaire, these instructions will appear in preface materials, as discussed previously. Additional rules apply to the administration of different types of surveys.

In some cases, researchers administer surveys to groups rather than individuals. The interviewer may read the questions aloud to low-literacy groups. Response rates in group interviews are generally high. Also, the availability of the interviewer to answer questions and address problems means that respondents leave few blanks or unanswered questions. Group interviews cost less than face-to-face or telephone interviews. Respondents may assume, however, that upper management has sanctioned the group-administered survey, and this conclusion can influence responses to individual questions. Respondents may also fear that their responses will become known to management. Mixing different classes of respondents (e.g., respondents from different levels of the organization) is not recommended.

Researchers should judge whether they have asked an appropriate number of questions. No survey (mail, group, or one-on-one survey) should exceed 1 hour in length. Telephone surveys should not exceed 20 minutes, and mall intercept surveys should not require more than 10 minutes of the respondent's time (Wimmer & Dominick, 1997).

Personal Interviews

Generally conducted in the workplace or at the respondent's home, personal interviews can be structured or unstructured. A structured interview allows little room (with regard to the content or format of the interview) for improvisation on the part of the interviewer. In contrast, an unstructured interview allows the interviewer to generate new questions, probe freely, and shift the order of questions. The interviewer can acquire more in-depth information in the latter survey situation. Dubbed "a conversation with a purpose" (Kahn & Cannell, 1957, p. 149), the unstructured interview contains open-ended questions, and the respondent plays an important role, sometimes guiding a discussion in directions not foreseen by the interviewer. Although unstructured interviews are more costly (in time) and require a higher level of interviewing expertise, they can yield unexpected insights. The establishment of good rapport with interview subjects can increase the chances of obtaining responses to sensitive questions. Unstructured interviews are particularly appropriate in pilot studies or in the exploratory stages of a study. The results enable organizational researchers to frame closed questions, which can be administered to larger numbers of people at a second stage of the research.

Personal interviews enable the researcher to acquire large amounts of information in a relatively short time. Typically, they take 45 minutes to 1 hour. The interviewer can, and often does, use "show cards," photographs, and other visual materials. Observation can supplement other kinds of data obtained from the interview. The organization of the questions is often topical, and the interviewer obtains demographic data at the beginning or end of the interview (Babbie, 1990). Critical to the success of the interview, training and instruction manuals tell whom to interview, when to interview, how to dress, and how to behave during the interview. They also tell the interviewer how to record information and what to do when people are not available. They outline procedures for callbacks, which are necessary when people are busy or unavailable. They also outline procedures for verification of results.

The following are disadvantages of the personal interview:

- Relatively high cost
- Possibility for interviewer bias (with the age, sex, race, dress, and verbal or nonverbal behavior of the interviewer influencing the results)
- Data overload with an unstructured interview
- The possibility that the interviewer will not be competent or honest
- Tendency to suspect people who come to the door requesting an interview
- Possibility that the respondent may try to please the interviewer

Respondents often look to the interviewer to obtain cues about how to answer. The nonverbal behavior of the interviewer (e.g., a smile, a nod, a grimace, a frown, or a look of boredom) can influence the response to a question because respondents do not like to displease interviewers.

The elite interview involves an audience with "the influential, the prominent, and the well-informed people in an organization or a community"

(Marshall & Rossman, 1989, p. 94). Information acquired from these individuals can be of more than ordinary value to the organization. Selected for interviews on the basis of their expertise in the social, political, financial, or administrative spheres, elites often have a sophisticated understanding of the legal and financial structures of their organizations. They occupy positions with the power to influence policies, plan future courses of action, and place past events in context.

It is necessary, however, to realize that some interview techniques work better than others with elites. Elites tend to enjoy an active exchange with the interviewer: "Elites respond well to inquiries related to broad areas of content and to a high proportion of intelligent, provocative, open-ended questions that allow them the freedom to use their knowledge and imagination" (Marshall & Rossman, 1989, p. 94). Because elites often attempt to assume the questioner's role in an interview session, the interviewer must be poised to recover control by displaying a thorough knowledge and understanding of the topic areas discussed. Obtaining appointments with elites, however, may not be easy. To gain an audience with these influential individuals, the interviewer may need to rely on referrals, recommendations, and introductions. Although it is possible to gain many valuable insights from elites, the interviewer must recognize that these views may not be generalizable to the larger population.

Telephone Surveys

Telephone surveys also require the use of special materials, such as an instruction manual and training materials. The instruction manual will include information such as whom to call, when to call, and how to record information. Simulations of the survey situation at training sessions give interviewers the opportunity to discuss problems. The organization designates a central location for receipt of survey information and for monitoring (Presser & Zhao, 1992). Although it is necessary to make callbacks when respondents are not available the first time they are called, interviewers usually make no more than two callbacks to busy lines or no answers. Some studies have found that as many as six callbacks can be required to reach 95% of all targeted individuals. Three callbacks produce a response rate of approximately 75% (Wimmer & Dominick, 1997). Interviewers often try to reach respondents in the evening who were not available during the day. Answering machines do not appear to be generating serious problems for telephone interviews because most answering machine owners are "reachable and willing to communicate" (Tuckel & Feinberg, 1991, p. 217). The answering machine is more of a problem on weekends than on weekday evenings.

Care should be taken so that the contamination of samples does not occur at the time of survey administration. For example, in the United States, many polling firms refrain from polling on Friday evenings because studies show that the more affluent are less likely to be home at this time. Polls conducted on a Saturday evening, however, can lead to underestimating the level of support for liberal government policies. Younger voters are less likely to be at home on a Saturday night than are their older counterparts (Reid, 1988b). Conducting all interviews during the day, when seniors and women with young children are most likely to answer the telephone, can contaminate a sample. Some polling firms have other rules that they observe, routinely asking for the adult with the next birthday, the youngest man, or the oldest woman. At other times, they question whoever answers the phone or rely on choices generated by a computer, which are programmed to use different methods (Scott, 1997). All these methods, however, can alter the final result.

Verifying the results of telephone interviews involves selecting a small subsample of respondents for callbacks. These individuals respond to two or three of the original questions. When omissions are found to have occurred, the most likely pertain to sensitive areas that interviewers do not like to question. Therefore, verification teams often include these questions in callbacks. Tabulation of the final data involves a computation of the response rate, including the number of disconnects, no answers, and refusals.

In administering telephone surveys, interviewers observe the following rules:

- Speak clearly and slowly.
- Read the questions as written and in the order in which they appear in the questionnaire.
- Repeat questions that are not understood.
- Probe unclear responses with neutral questions.
- Appear interested and appreciative.
- Record responses verbatim for open-ended questions.
- Thank the respondents for their participation.

Behaviors to avoid include prompting answers, showing approval or disapproval for responses, and asking for explanations that are not part of the planned interview.

The advantages of telephone interviews include the following: higher level of control over the interview, higher response rates than with mail surveys, lack of transportation expenses, access to WATS lines that facilitate the collection of national survey data, reasonable costs, fast responses, ability to reach almost everyone, less likelihood of interviewer bias, and the possibility for the client or contracting firm to "listen in" on the telephone interviews (especially in the early stages of interviewing). In this way, the firm can identify problems, get a sense for how the interviews are proceeding, and learn whether respondents understand the questions.

Disadvantages of this interviewing medium include the limited kinds of questions that can be asked, the cost (telephone interviews are more expensive than mail surveys), the possibility for the interviewer to influence the results, the inability of the interviewer to use visual aids, the tendency for some respondents to view the telephone interview with suspicion, lack of commitment that comes with anonymity, lack of nonverbal feedback, incompleteness of some telephone listings, and inaccuracy of other listings. Failure to call back individuals can result in a contamination of the original sample.

Some telephone surveys are computer-assisted. These surveys are more error-free because the interviewer does not make unprogrammed "skips" of questions or ask the wrong questions (Frey, 1989). Although this type of survey takes more time to administer, the research firm saves considerable time at the data processing stage because the data are already in the computer. Also, there is no possibility for errors in data transfer. With computer-assisted interviews, the computer screen prompts interviewers at each step of the interview, telling them what to say. Skips prevent respondents from answering the wrong questions. Ensuring that the computer program is "bug-free" is time-consuming.

Computer-Administered or Internet Surveys

Computer-administered surveys are becoming increasingly popular. These surveys can take several different forms. Sometimes, firms send diskettes with questionnaires to respondents. The limitation of this technique derives from the fact that people have to have access to computers. Therefore, the population may not be representative of all groups in the population. To alleviate this problem, research firms can bring subjects into computer labs to have them fill out surveys on-line because it saves data entry time and eliminates data entry errors. This technique is advantageous because the research firm acquires cleaner data. As for computer-assisted telephone surveys, researchers construct programs to do skips to ensure that respondents answer the correct questions.

Many businesses, government agencies, and nonprofit organizations are building web sites that ask visitors to fill out questionnaires. These questionnaires elicit demographic data, motivation for visiting web site, hobbies and interests, and other information. The disadvantage of Internet surveys is their inability to test the validity of the information recorded. Internet users are mostly anonymous. Also, Internet users share characteristics that cannot be generalized to the mass public. They are probably better educated and more technologically sophisticated than the average nonuser. Nonetheless, the current impetus toward a computer-mediated society means that these kinds of questionnaires will become more popular in future years.

Mail Surveys

The mail survey can generate large quantities of information drawn from many different constituencies. Requiring a minimum expenditure of time and money, they are the least expensive of the survey techniques. Nor do they require a large survey team. Specialized mailing lists and selective sampling make it easy for the organizational researcher to reach target audiences. Respondent anonymity is possible with mail surveys. People can complete the questionnaires anywhere—in the privacy of their own homes, and at their own pace. This mode of surveying eliminates interviewer bias.

An analysis of 115 studies that appeared in more than 25 business, education, marketing, political science, psychology, sociology, statistics, and other journals indicated the following ways to increase the response rate from mail surveys (Yammarino, Skinner, & Childers, 1991):

- Use a cover letter that includes appeals.
- Limit the survey to less than 4 pages.
- Include a stamped or metered return envelope.
- Include a small incentive.
- Give preliminary notification that the survey will arrive at a later date.

Self-administered questionnaires should begin with the most interesting questions, grouped by topic, with the demographic questions at the end. Questions that elicit sensitive information should appear after the middle or near the end of the questionnaire (Babbie, 1990).

With business reply envelopes, the researcher pays postage charges only for returned questionnaires. For best results, the first follow-up mailing takes place after 4 weeks. Some studies indicate that telephone calls may be as effective as letters in "prodding nonrespondents to return mail questionnaires" (Frey, 1989, p. 24). Studies also confirm the advantages of sponsorship, personalization, anonymity, prior commitment, and attractive presentation of questionnaires (including format and layout) in prompting high return rates (Sanchez, 1992). The Eagle Group (cited in Wimmer & Dominick, 1997) found that response rates increased with the inclusion of telephone cards activated only when the questionnaire is returned, a $10 bill, or reference to a drawing for a prize (CD player or TV).

Other suggestions relate to the content of the mail survey questionnaire. Studies indicate that closed-ended questions are preferable to open-ended questions, and response rates increase with a survey shorter than 4 pages. Explanations should be clear and concise. Many professional associations and marketing research organizations sell mailing lists to researchers and advertisers, but obtaining the results of mail surveys is often a slow process. Moreover, researchers never know for certain who answered the survey. The major disadvantage of the mail survey, however, is its low return rate. A typical survey achieves a return rate of 10% to 40%, even with follow-ups (Wimmer & Dominick, 1997). Studies confirm significant decreases in response rates during the past four decades. When the author requested that one *Fortune* 500 company respond to a survey, a representative wrote back saying that the number of requests had become so overwhelming that the company could employ a person to do nothing but fill out surveys. Many other companies returned a form letter response that indicated lack of time to participate in the survey.

Only the most interested people participate in surveys, and high-status groups are more likely than low-status groups to return mail surveys. Many marketing companies use the "phone-mail-phone" survey. An initial phone call enables the marketing group to learn (a) whether the respondent meets the sampling criteria (e.g., conforms to the desired quota group) and (b) if the person would be willing to complete a mail survey (for an incentive) that will be mailed later the same week. Surveys are mailed to those qualified individuals who agree to participate. The firm obtains the responses, by phone, a week after the mailing. Although the process is lengthy, the marketing firm obtains significantly higher response rates and maintains greater control (Ferguson, 1999).

TABLE 7.1   Survey on Environmental Policy

Survey on Environmental Policy	Number of Employees	Percentage of Employees
In favor of	46	48
Opposed to	35	37
No opinion	14	15
Total	95	100

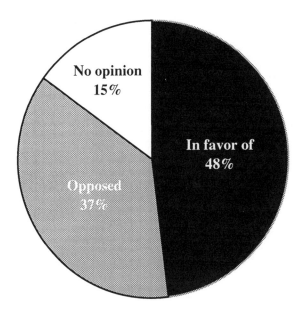

Figure 7.1.   Survey on Environmental Policy

Interpreting and Reporting the Results

In the most basic terms, the first task in analyzing survey results is to count the number of participants who fall into each question category. Perhaps the researcher wants to know, for example, how many employees support or oppose a company policy. Next, he or she translates the numbers into percentages. These numbers and percentages can appear in the form of simple frequency distribution tables (Table 7.1) or pie charts (Figure 7.1). Sometimes, the researcher will choose to compare percentages (e.g., between the responses of different groups of respondents or different regions). Contingency

TABLE 7.2 Survey on Corporate Merger

Survey on Corporate Merger	Number Surveyed	Percentage for Merger
Employees with shares	65	60
Employees without shares	90	30

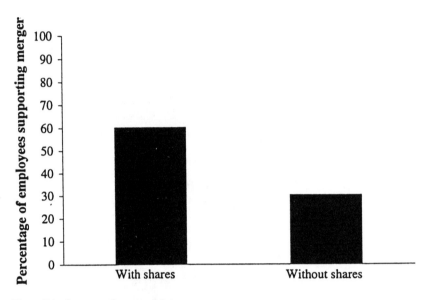

Figure 7.2. Survey on Corporate Merger

tables depict the relationship between a respondent characteristic and answers given to survey questions. The contingency table in Table 7.2 compares the responses of employees who hold shares in a company and those who do not. Although pie charts show simple frequency distributions, bar graphs are more useful in presenting the kind of information found in contingency tables (Figure 7.2).

Complex breakdown tables show the relationship between respondent answers and more than one variable. A complex breakdown table, for example, breaks respondent data down by variables such as gender, age, region, and income bracket. A contingency table, however, includes only one of these variables. Complex breakdown tables also include total numbers of respondents in each subgrouping (Table 7.3). To identify the relationships depicted in these tables, the survey must have collected the necessary kinds of data from

TABLE 7.3   Views on Abortion[a]

Views on Abortion	Number Surveyed	Percentage Pro-Life	Percentage Pro-Choice	Percentage No Opinion
Gender				
Male	285	26	55	19
Female	333	35	59	6
Age				
16-18 years	115	37	42	22
19-25 years	237	21	64	16
26-39 years	164	35	61	4
40 and older	102	41	53	6
Income				
Under $20,000	257	37	60	3
$20,000-$39,999	175	20	56	24
$40,000-$64,999	141	30	53	16
$65,000 and over	45	40	56	4
	618	31	57	12

a. This is a fictitious example.

participants (e.g., age, gender, ethnicity, residence, and memberships). The nature of the survey dictates the specific questions. As discussed earlier, inadequate numbers of respondents in a given category may mean that the researcher cannot break down the percentages by subgroups. Unless oversampling compensates for the limited numbers of respondents, the researcher may have to forego examining certain relationships.

Researchers can use statistical techniques such as *t* tests to determine whether statistically significant differences exist between two groups. (These tests compare the means of the two groups.) Analysis of variance allows for comparisons among more than two groups. For example, these tests can allow researchers to determine whether males differ from females in terms of purchasing behavior or whether individuals from different ethnic groups have different criteria for selecting products. Correlations allow researchers to detect whether relationships exist between variables. For example, a correlation can indicate whether a relationship exists between the number of negative political advertisements and candidate success at the polls. A correlation of 0 indicates that no relationship exists, a correlation of 1 indicates a perfect positive relationship (when the number of negative advertisements increases, the popularity of the sponsoring candidate increases), and a correlation of −1 indicates a perfect negative relationship (when the number

TABLE 7.4   Employee Confidence

Month	Number Surveyed	Percentage Confident
March 1999	203	77
April 1999	187	72
May 1999	190	68
June 1999	215	58
July 1999	167	52
August 1999	185	45

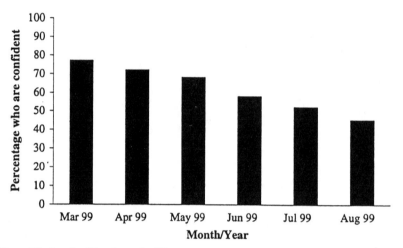

Figure 7.3. Levels of Employee Confidence

of negative advertisements increases, the popularity of the sponsoring candidate decreases). The closer the correlation is to 0, the weaker the relationship. Although these are some of the most popular statistical methods used for data analysis, many different techniques exist that cater to specific data analysis needs. Several of the methodology books referenced in this chapter offer a good source of information on additional options.

Sometimes, the researcher searches for changes over time or the emergence of trends. Both bar and line graphs can be useful formats for presenting these changes. Bar graphs tend to be more appropriate when the number of time periods is relatively few or the researcher wants to view the data as being given at discrete points in time or both. The information in Table 7.4 (employee confidence) translates well into bar graph format (Figure 7.3). Line graphs, however, are useful when there are a fair number of time intervals or the data can be viewed as continuous over a period of time or both. Table 7.5

TABLE 7.5   Opinions Related to Cloning of Body Parts: Example of Data That
Would Translate Into a Line Graph

Year	Number of People Surveyed	Percentage Who Accept Cloning of Body Parts
1990	15,083	10
1991	15,678	14
1992	15,238	18
1993	15,403	22
1994	15,233	23
1995	15,809	26
1996	15,456	30
1997	15,908	30
1998	15,345	32
1999	15,290	33
2000	15,870	36

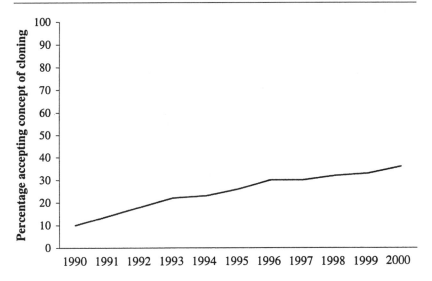

Figure 7.4. Acceptance of Cloning of Body Parts

(opinions on cloning) provides an example of tabular data that translate into
line graph format (Figure 7.4). Researchers use multiple bar and line graphs
to compare trends between or among two or more sets of data. Table 7.6 compares the percentage of companies with 500 or more employees that have initiated sexual harassment policies with the percentage of companies with
fewer than 500 employees that have initiated sexual harassment policies.
(Figure 7.5 translates this information into line graph format.)

TABLE 7.6   Companies Initiating Sexual Harassment Policies

Year	Companies With 500 or More Employees	Companies With Less Than 500 Employees
1	20	4
2	25	7
3	32	3
4	37	5
5	45	8

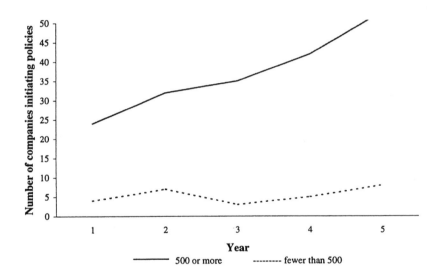

Figure 7.5. Companies Initiating Sexual Harassment Policies

Problems associated with the interpretation and reporting of survey results include the tendency to extend the results of a survey beyond the date of surveying, to misread results, and to inject bias into the reporting of survey results.

Tendency to Extend Results Beyond the Date of Surveying

Despite their 1936 experience, the pollsters (including Gallup) proved their fallibility again in 1948 when they predicted that Thomas Dewey would win over Harry Truman. It is now believed that the polling exercise finished too soon to predict the steady trend toward Truman. The largest number of those who were undecided apparently voted for Truman. Experts believe that shortcomings in quota sampling techniques contributed to this inaccurate prediction (Babbie, 1990).

A recent example of the same phenomenon occurred in 1980 when pollsters predicted that Ronald Reagan would win over Jimmy Carter by only the narrowest of margins. They reported the race as being too close to call (Yeric & Todd, 1989, p. 231). Like Truman's win, the extensiveness of Reagan's victory was explained by the failure of the pollsters to pick up last-minute voting trends. Those who continued to survey until election day were more successful in gauging the margin between victor and vanquished. Whereas Gallup and the *New York Times*/CBS polls ceased their operations 4 days prior to election day, the ABC News/Harris organizations polled up to election day. Whereas the earlier polls showed a 1% margin in favor of Reagan, the latter polls showed a 5% margin. More aware of what was happening, Patrick Caddell, Jimmy Carter's pollster, is said to have warned Carter of a severe hemorrhage of support in the final days before the election (Yeric & Todd, p. 232).

Journalist Neil Reynolds cites instances in which the results of polls conducted during the 1988 U.S. presidential campaign varied by dramatic degrees, even within the same time frames. The *Los Angeles Times* published one poll, for example, that gave George Bush a 9-point lead over Michael Dukakis. On the same day, it published a second poll that showed that the two contenders were tied. In September 1988, the results of seven survey organizations varied from an 8-point lead for Bush to a 6-point lead for Dukakis. The same day that the *Washington Post* gave Bush his breakthrough lead, the *New York Times* published a poll that showed the two men were neck-in-neck.

Survey results taken a month before a major Canadian referendum revealed that the "yes" camp for a new constitutional accord had 42% support, the "no" camp had 41% support, and the undecided vote was at 17%. These data fluctuated from day to day by a significant number of points, showing that public opinion was capable of being moved in either direction, depending on who was interviewed by media representatives on a particular day. It was not unusual for politicians to boast that they had "dramatically increased the odds for their points of view since yesterday." On another occasion, three polls conducted within 1 week of each other varied by dramatic percentages (Scott, 1997, p. A1). Some analysts say that these kinds of results prove the fluidity of public opinion, which is attributable not to public apathy or igno-

rance of political process but to an increasing cynicism and a general erosion
of confidence in traditional institutions and authorities (Ladd & Ferree,
1981). Others claim that flawed methodologies explain the variations.

Tendency to Misread Results

Canadian pollster Angus Reid (1988a) said that polls are often misunderstood and sometimes misinterpreted by the media (p. A4). The inexperienced
may read increases in support for one candidate as losses for the other candidate. In fact, the increases may come from a hardening of the undecided vote
rather than a loss of confidence on the part of supporters. Reid describes an
example of poll results being misinterpreted because people failed to keep
track of the undecided vote:

> Soon after the first televised leaders debates in the 1984 election, a stunning ver-
> dict was delivered by the polls. Liberal support among decided voters had
> dropped a full seven points. For Canadians, this news implied that many thou-
> sands of Liberal supporters had switched their allegiance to the Conservatives.
> What actually happened was the number of undecided voters had dropped from
> 30% to 20%, and most of these went to the Conservatives. (p. A4)

A certain percentage of any campaign vote is soft (i.e., voters have only
weak party allegiances). Leaners can and often do switch direction. Therefore, it is important for surveys to take commitment into account: Measures
of commitment are harbingers of what lies in store for the public opinion formation process. Used to detect areas of strength and vulnerability, they
should be included as a central element in any public affairs undertaking
(Reid, 1988a, p. A4). It is also important to remember that public opinion
polls are only snapshots in time (Yeric & Todd, 1989, p. 233), with limited applications: Today's poll is tomorrow's history. The results of a good poll reflect the opinion of the target population when the questions were asked. People can and will change their minds for all sorts of reasons in an instant or over
time (Mangiacasale, 1992, p. B3). Another problem arises from the fact that
different pollsters deal with the undecided vote in different ways. Some firms
divide the undecided vote along the same lines as the decided vote. Others
weight the vote on the theory that "people who can't decide or won't say are
more likely to favor the status quo" (Scott, 1997, p. A1). Another technique
divides the undecided vote along demographic lines (based on statistics gen-

erated by the decided members of those demographic groups). Obviously, the
results will vary according to the methodology.

Tendency to Inject Bias or to Be
Indiscriminate in Reporting Survey Results

In translating survey statistics into language that is more palatable to the
public, journalists may inject unintentional bias into their reporting. Because
of the problems associated with reporting of poll results, the U.S. National
Council on Public Polls has published a guide to interpreting poll results titled *Twenty Questions a Journalist Should Ask About Poll Results* (as cited in
Mangiacasale, 1992). Many journalists do not distinguish between the results obtained in biased and misleading surveys and those of more professional, rigorous studies (Neuman, 1997). More than 88% of media stories
omit the name of the researcher; 82% do not describe how the survey was conducted (Singer, 1988). As a result, British Columbia now requires that media
publish the question, the date, and the sponsor of a poll (Scott, 1997, p. A1).

At other times, bias in reporting surveys may be more intentional. Assume
that a public opinion survey finds that 49% of Americans favor ground military action against the Serbians and 51% oppose such action. A newspaper
can publish several different headlines, including "Near Majority of Americans Favor Ground Action Against Serbs," "Americans Oppose Ground Action in Yugoslavia," or "Americans Ambivalent About Deployment of
Ground Forces Against Serbs." In essence, the headline writer can report the
glass as "half empty" or "half full." Bias within the community or media hierarchy for one point of view over another often influences the choice. It can be
speculated that the higher the profile of the issue, the more likely that the majority opinion of the community or news organization or both will be represented in the headline.

Sometimes, organizations encourage erroneous reporting of survey results. Just as surveys can function as *input* (an instrument for learning), they
can also serve as the basis for *output* (a means of legitimizing what the organization has already decided to do). In the second case, organizations conduct
surveys to obtain confirmatory data, which they then use to sell proposed policies, acquisitions, research and development activities, products, services,
and programs. Individuals in the Marketing Science Institute's group of companies note that more than 60% of the studies they undertake are confirmatory—that is, "designed to reinforce or sell a decision that has already been

made" (Day, 1992, p. 48). In such a case, the research may lack rigor or produce deceptive results (Neuman, 1997). The proliferation of surveys in all areas of our lives and the often conflicting results leave many people, including the general public, confused. The individuals who design confirmatory surveys may be more interested in obtaining useful information than valid or reliable information. This supposition can explain the sometimes wild variations among survey results and legitimize the claims of those who believe that public opinion surveys manufacture public opinion (Yeric & Todd, 1989, p. 241). At other times, researchers use "pseudosurveys" to persuade someone to adopt a point of view or take action (Neuman, 1997).

Interacting With Survey Research Firms

Few corporations, governments, or voluntary associations have the necessary expertise and resources to carry out all their own research projects. Often, the company or government unit contract out an entire research project or components of the project. The following should be kept in mind when purchasing research services from outside suppliers (Reid, 1988b):

- Request the services of a senior researcher for projects requiring high levels of senior management input. The use of junior researchers for more field-intensive projects can lower the overall cost of the project.
- Expect the research firm to introduce your organization to a range of alternatives and to explain the strengths and weaknesses of each alternative.
- Request detailed information on how the firm will select the sample. Consider not only sample size but also other factors such as the potential quality of the sample.
- Ask how much of the work will be carried out by the firm from whom you are buying services and how much will be subcontracted.
- Evaluate the expertise of those who will conduct the survey interviews.
- Visit the interviewing centers periodically during the project to conduct quality checks.
- Attend briefing sessions or ask for audio recordings of pretest interviews. This information can help in assessing the validity of the survey instrument.

Because the cost of surveying is generally greater than that of other means of tracking public opinion (media analysis, focus groups, and some forms of consultation), the survey option is not available to all organizations. A remedy has recently emerged, however. The omnibus survey permits clients to add a designated number of questions to a multipurpose survey at a prorated cost. The omnibus survey may contain a mix of questions pertaining to products, issues, policies, or personalities.

Conclusion

The past several chapters demonstrate the rigorous process required for survey research. The steps in conducting a legitimate survey include the following: using standard techniques to select a research design and choose a sample, constructing and ordering the questionnaire, preparing introductory materials, pretesting and administering the questionnaire, analyzing the results, and interpreting and reporting on the results. The more complex the issues addressed by the survey, the more important it is to assess the research capabilities of the consultant firm.

Many specialized textbooks contain an in-depth consideration of how to statistically analyze survey results. They explain how to calculate average and median responses to questions, how to assess the reliability of instruments and procedures, and how to apply advanced multivariate techniques to the analysis of survey data. Many computer packages also allow researchers to input data for statistical analysis, perform reliability checks, and conduct other calculations. This book does not aim to accomplish these purposes. Its purpose is to help the organizational communication researcher to gain heuristic insights into how surveys work, to learn how to design questionnaires, to pinpoint problem areas, and to interpret the results of survey research. If a research project is properly designed, the questionnaire is well-constructed, and accepted procedures are followed, any competent statistician can generate a useful analysis of the data.

8

Focus Groups, Delphi Technique, Stakeholder Assemblies, and Q Methodology

M any different methodologies can be applied to the study of public opinion. These methodologies include focus groups, stakeholder assemblies, Delphi techniques, and Q methodology.

This chapter places a greater emphasis on focus groups because opinion researchers rely most heavily on this methodology. Focus groups have become an increasingly popular tool for tracking opinion on key organizational issues. Whereas the corporate world once used focus groups almost exclusively for market research purposes, they now apply these techniques to study corporate reputation, to test creative communication concepts, to learn more about public awareness and knowledge of organizational issues, and to evaluate the extent to which key publics have accepted company policies. Bureaucrats find focus groups to be a relatively inexpensive way to learn more about the opinions of various demographic populations and key publics, differentiated on the basis of age, sex, region, language, ethnicity, and other variables. Politicians use focus groups to track shifts in public opinion on salient issues, to make choices on issue stances, and to discover weaknesses in the opposition's stance on issues.

Most large organizations (business, government, and nonprofit) also employ focus groups to learn more about the views of internal clients and employees. In other words, focus groups have become the methodology of choice for many organizations whose leaders are concerned about the opinions of key stakeholders, inside and outside the walls of the organization.

Focus Groups

Despite the fact that the corporate and political communities have co-opted the focus group, its origins are academic. Emory Bogardus (1926) originated the concept of the group interview, considered by Kitzinger (1994) to be the earliest precursor to focus group research. By the 1940s, researchers were using the "focused interview" to assess the reactions of listeners to radio programs (Lazarsfeld & Stanton, 1941, 1944). Following World War II, Robert Merton developed a manual on focus group research (Merton & Kendall, 1946), and Paul Lazarsfeld suggested the application of this research strategy to commercial purposes (Lunt & Livingstone, 1996). Despite its academic origins, universities mostly abandoned focus group research between the 1940s and the 1980s, at which time academics joined market researchers, politicians, and corporations in making frequent use of the methodology (Morrison, 1998).

What Is a Focus Group?

Focus groups are a "discussion group with a purpose" (BT Organisational Development, 1997, p. 23)—a special kind of group interview or variant of quota sampling techniques (Babbie, 1990). Although some focus groups are "self-moderated," most involve a moderator and 4 to 12 participants, typically unacquainted with each other. Researchers tend to disagree on the optimum number of participants. Restricting the number of participants to 4 or 5 (as researchers such as Watt and Van Den Berg [1995] advocate) makes it easier for the organization to fill the focus group and to establish a close friendly atmosphere, but some researchers worry that the small number of participants can translate into less participation, fewer insights, and less learning for those conducting the session. Nonetheless, Fern (1982) found that increases in group size from 4 to 8 did not result in a doubling of the quantity of ideas or a significant increase in the quality of ideas.

Focus group participants meet at a predetermined location at a given time to discuss a single topic, although the topic may have many facets. The discussions may center on a candidate, corporate image, a product, a concept, or issue. Syracuse University used focus groups to help plan a major fund-raising drive, and a county mental health department set up focus groups to plan a program (Baskin & Aronoff, 1992). In the context of this discussion, I am interested in examining how focus groups can elicit information on issues, corporate reputation, leadership, or assessment of communication strategies.

Relatively unstructured, the focus group has a flexible format that can be adjusted by the moderator. The moderator introduces the subject and encourages the group members to discuss their perceptions, feelings, and opinions on the topic. Occasionally, the moderator asks additional questions to stimulate interaction or to focus the discussion on areas of interest to the organization sponsoring the focus group.

As previously noted, organizational researchers use focus groups to investigate new areas of interest, to search for unexpected insights, or to refine existing insights. They also use focus groups to gain a better understanding of why people hold certain attitudes and beliefs or behave as they do. Senior managers like the fact that this methodology gives them an opportunity to acquire a more sophisticated understanding of people's reasoning processes. Some researchers argue that the focus group is the only research method that can be used successfully in discussing highly sensitive issues (e.g., insurance fraud, tax evasion, or human rights violations) (Reid, 1988b).

Whereas surveys identify the positions of Americans on the most salient issues, focus groups often identify emerging or less prominent issues that may not appear in surveys. For example, Republicans conducted focus groups during the 1988 presidential campaign to identify the weaknesses of the opposition candidate Michael Dukakis. The results suggested that Americans strongly disagreed with Dukakis on two issues. They did not approve of Dukakis's support for weekend furloughs for criminal offenders, and they believed that Dukakis should support legislation that would force teachers to lead students in the pledge of allegiance. In the aftermath of these focus groups, George Bush placed his campaign hopes on these two issues rather than on the critical pressing issues of the day, such as the economy and unemployment—a decision that helped to secure the presidency for Bush (Cohen & Moyers, 1989; Kern & Just, 1995). The 1992 Clinton campaign conducted focus groups every 2 weeks until October. After October, they conducted two focus groups on four nights each week (Baumann & Herbst, 1994).

Criteria for Participation in Focus Groups

Research has shown that relatively homogeneous groupings of people (with similar characteristics in terms of education, expertise, income level, age, social class, or interests) work best (Morrison, 1998). Sometimes, the perception of a common interest or cause can override the other variables; for example, social class was an unimportant variable in focus group research into the bereavement process in widowed women (Morgan, 1988). In general, however, people who perceive themselves to be inferior to other group members in educational accomplishments, socioeconomic status, or expertise tend to be poor participants. Uncomfortable voicing their views, they often defer to the opinions of higher-status members. Similarly, bringing together individuals of widely varying ages can generate adult-child interactions, whereby some members behave paternalistically and others rebel against authority figures. Although experts may populate some focus groups, it is not wise to place one or two experts in a larger group of relatively uninformed individuals. The presence of the expert can deter full-group participation, and the expert may dominate the discussion (BT Organisational Development, 1997).

Focus group designers must also take the interaction patterns of men and women into account. Studies show that men tend to dominate discussions in which women are present. The domination manifests itself when men interrupt women or answer questions not addressed to them. Also, men often initiate new topics of conversation rather than acknowledging or responding to comments by women. Delayed listening responses, overlapping comments, and interruptions serve to have a subduing impact on women. Men also tend to "perform" for women (Krueger, 1994), and they are more apt than women to discuss controversial subjects in a public forum (Noelle-Neumann, 1993).

Women complain that they have a difficult time getting and holding attention in group situations that involve men. Some women tend to take on "stroking" behaviors such as nodding and confirming the contributions of men with "yes," "mmh," and so on (Wood, 1996). At other times, women use tag questions, which involve asking for follow-up confirmation after an assertion (Bate, 1988; Borisoff & Merrill, 1992). The following is an example of a tag question: "We really should push for some legislation to stem the violence in schools, don't you think?" Some studies suggest that women tend to "realign" their conversations to be supportive and inclusive, whereas men react in more judgmental and divisive ways in verbal encounters (Tannen, 1993; Wood, 1996). Others have found that men accept less influence than women in task groups populated by both genders (Witte & Davis, 1996).

Such differences in patterns of communication imply the need for separation of the sexes in focus group situations. In instances in which focus groups are composed of husbands and wives, it has been observed that wives tend to defer to the views of their husbands. Even when a wife disagrees with her husband, she may remain silent. Therefore, focus groups composed of four married couples yield the results that a focus group of four individuals might generate (Krueger, 1994). Other studies have found that younger participants are more likely than their older counterparts to discuss controversial subjects (Noelle-Neumann, 1993). Ethnicity can also influence patterns of participation (Witte & Davis, 1996).

The introduction of too many different arguments and viewpoints into one focus group can also confuse the results. For example, when members of different business units interact in one focus group, they tend to engage in territorial behaviors, defending their special organizational interests. To learn the perceptions of several different categories of people, the researcher should conduct a series of focus groups, with different kinds of people in each group (Zikmund, 1988). In such a case, a maximum of four focus groups, composed of individuals with similar characteristics, is generally required (Fowler & Mangione, 1990). Some believe that it is wise to evaluate the findings after the third focus group. If the third group fails to generate any new information, the researchers may not need a fourth focus group. If additional insights emerge from the third group, plans for an additional group may be warranted. More sessions may be required when the groups are highly heterogeneous (Krueger, 1994). Statewide or nationwide studies can necessitate as many as a dozen focus groups (Taras, 1990).

Selection Procedures

Groups can be selected randomly or nonrandomly (see the discussion on sampling techniques in Chapters 4 and 5). Names can be pulled from existing membership lists, directories, or organizational files or solicited from relevant organizations, perhaps with a promise of a donation to the group. Intercept techniques can also be used, whereby individuals are recruited "on location." For example, participants may be recruited at an exhibit or other activity likely to be visited by individuals with the desired characteristics. In this latter instance, the researcher is relying on "convenience sampling," a common technique in putting together a focus group (Watt & Van Den Berg, 1995). Telephone screening involves randomly selecting names from a telephone directory and then calling to find out if the individuals possess the required characteristics to become focus group participants. Success with this technique depends greatly on the interpersonal skills of the person conducting the screening. With snowball sampling techniques, the researcher asks participants to bring a friend to the focus group.

Alternatively, at the end of sessions, participants can be asked to suggest the name of a friend or family member to participate in some future group. Some researchers warn against having friends in the same group (Neuman, 1997). Friends mean loss of anonymity. Often, they endorse the other's view even if they hold a conflicting point of view (Stewart & Shamdasani, 1990). When they "pair off," they cause a breakdown in group process because private conversations disrupt and inhibit the expression of views by others (BT Organisational Development, 1997).

Public institutions and nonprofit organizations use a variety of techniques to solicit participation in focus groups. Some of these techniques, such as newsletter announcements, form-letter invitations, and announcements at meetings, have been found to yield poor results. Major flaws include a failure to personalize invitations, to follow up the original invitation, to build on existing social and organizational relationships, to take seasonal demands into account, and to offer incentives (Krueger, 1994). People resent being asked to attend a discussion on a seemingly insignificant topic. They need to understand why they have been selected to participate in the focus group. Follow-up correspondence to the original invitation should include meeting times that do not conflict with work schedules, sporting events, or the beginning of fall network TV shows. Follow-up letters should arrive approximately 1 week before the meeting time. Last-minute reminders, either via phone or mail on the day before the meeting, help to ensure high participation rates. Experts suggest the need to overrecruit by 20% to ensure sufficient group numbers (Morgan, 1988; Morrison, 1998).

Focus group participants may receive the offer of a small incentive in the form of money, a gift, or a meal. Typical cash incentives range from $20 to $50 in the United States (Krueger, 1994) and between £12 and £15 in Great Britain (Morrison, 1998). Gifts (e.g., alarm clocks, calculators, and telephones) range in value from $5 to $20. The size of the incentive is tied to the level of difficulty in securing the cooperation of people in that group of society (Krueger, 1988). For example, an incentive of $25 may secure the participation of members of the general public, such as male or female heads of households, an incentive of $50 may be necessary to fill a focus group with middle managers or engineers, and incentives in excess of $100 may be required to secure the participation of physicians and lawyers. Holding a session at a prestigious location, serving refreshments, conducting sessions at the location of participants, and explaining the value of the study further enhance the chance that people will agree to participate and will arrive at the designated place on time.

To prevent the likelihood that some individuals will plan their responses in advance (e.g., discuss the situation with friends and family), advance publicity will offer limited information on the purpose of the focus group. Specific information on the sponsorship and purpose of a study, however, will be given at the end of the focus group session.

Criteria for Physical Setting

Focus groups are conducted in many different kinds of settings. Organizations that conduct much marketing research may have meeting rooms equipped with two-way mirrors. Others will rent hotel or motel rooms for the sessions. When available, conference rooms are used. Participants should feel at ease in the focus group situation, and one way to establish this sense of well-being is to choose a pleasant physical environment for the central meeting location—easily accessible and nonthreatening. Some believe that the use of mirrors or holding sessions on site at the workplace can create a threatening environment in which participants do not feel free to express their feelings (Krueger, 1993). Buildings and their layouts influence the interactions of the group, and the nature and size of a room are important. More positive exchanges tend to occur in "beautiful" rooms (Maslow & Mintz, 1956; Mintz, 1956). Levels of noise and lighting, degree of privacy and noise, color, and location also influence interpersonal interactions (BT Organisational Development, 1997; Ferguson & Ferguson, 1988). Moderators should prepare the room and adjust the temperature before the participants arrive.

Whereas some settings encourage interaction (e.g., chairs placed in circles bring people together), other settings discourage interaction (e.g., bolted down chairs in airports hold people apart). The placement of chairs, desks, and sofas in a room influences both the quality and the quantity of communication. Individuals seated at the end of long rectangular tables have an advantage over others in terms of perceived dominance, whereas persons occupying the corners of such tables contribute least to discussions (Strodtbeck & Hook, 1961). A squared-off or circular table, however, maximizes eye contact, minimizes distance between group participants, and encourages more participation and sharing of power (Hanna & Wilson, 1991). Others recommend a horseshoe arrangement or broken circle around a low coffee table (BT Organisational Development, 1997). They believe that a "coffee klatch" or "bull session" atmosphere works best for focus groups (Axelrod, 1975).

Where larger numbers participate in a focus group session (6-12), the moderator can place the table in a central location, sufficiently large to accommodate all participants. Some researchers recommend placing experts and loud participants next to the moderator and more reticent participants directly across from the moderator. Studies show that eye contact encourages responses, whereas lack of eye contact discourages interactions (Hare & Davies, 1994).

Focus groups conducted at work locations can be problematic because superior-subordinate interactions can impede the process. Employees may be reluctant to speak openly and honestly in front of their superiors, and superiors may feel the need to mask their true feelings and motivations in front of subordinates. Status factors can be powerful inhibitors to group discussion. High-status individuals are not only more willing to express their point of view but also more likely to enter into discussions on controversial topics (Noelle-Neumann, 1993). High-status individuals accept less influence than low-status individuals; they exert more influence over others, however (Witte & Davis, 1996). The moderator, however, must establish an atmosphere that is conducive to openness and sharing. People must be made to feel that their ideas and contributions are important to the success of the meeting. A facilitator who relates well to people will have the best chance of establishing this kind of tone. Name tags help participants to become acquainted and make it easier for facilitators to call on people by name. In some situations, however, especially if sensitive topics (e.g., sexual harassment, family violence, or supervisor-subordinate relationships) are the subjects of discussion, participants may not want to be recognized by their last names. In this kind of situation, the moderator may opt to invite individuals to share private thoughts or experiences on paper, which they pass to the moderator. The moderator maintains the anonymity of the contributor but shares the idea or experience with the group.

Appointing an assistant, who attends to details such as videotaping or sound recording sessions, can free a moderator to concentrate on the group discussion. The assistant ensures that the physical needs of participants are met and welcomes late arrivals.

Steps in Conducting the Focus Group

Focus group discussions typically involve the following stages (Mariampolski, 1984): (a) a rapport-building stage that establishes relations and clarifies the task; (b) an exploratory stage that allows participants to answer broad questions; (c) a probing stage that narrows the topic areas of special interest to the researcher; (d) a task stage that could entail, for example, writing a slogan or using projective techniques; (e) an evaluation stage that may include some stimulus to create interaction; and (f) a closing stage that elicits any final input from the participants and allows the moderator to ask unanswered questions. Not all stages will occur in every focus group. Some researchers use supplementary questionnaires to solicit additional information from the focus group. Other researchers believe that responding to a questionnaire can bias later responses in the focus group or, conversely, the focus group interaction can bias how the participants respond to the questionnaire (Morgan, 1988). They believe that questionnaires should be used to elicit only demographic information.

Introducing the Session

In opening the session, the moderator welcomes group members, gives a brief and general overview of the topic, and previews the agenda for the focus group session. The moderator discusses the basis on which the participants were selected and stresses the importance of hearing from all group members. The moderator also emphasizes that there are no right or wrong answers but only different points of view. He or she solicits negative and positive observations. The moderator should indicate if confidentiality is to be protected. Alleviation of anxiety and stress is critical to achieving effective results with focus groups (Hare & Davies, 1994).

If sessions are to be recorded, the moderator should explain the purpose for these recordings. In the introduction to the session, the facilitator should refer to the length of the discussions, break times (if any), availability of refreshments, and policies on smoking. The moderator should also establish ground rules (e.g., expectations regarding turn-taking). The group facilitator then asks members to introduce themselves. The moderator will ask group participants to withhold specific information in making their introductions if the information could bias later interactions (e.g., occupational status or position in the community).

Once introductions have been concluded, the first question should be an "ice breaker." Focus group members can be asked to share stories or anecdotes on the topic being discussed. Alternatively, a stimulus can be used to initiate discussion, such as "an object, a drawing, a slide or transparency, a story board, or a complete communication product such as a public service announcement" (Dozier & Repper, 1992, pp. 191-192). Sometimes, a group will be asked to react to a videotape or an audio recording (Wimmer & Dominick, 1997).

Ordering the Discussion Agenda

Most focus group discussions move from the general to the specific. Moderators open a discussion with open-ended questions and follow with more closed ones. They avoid becoming too specific too soon in a focus group. Given the proper context, participants will move in a natural way toward the topic of interest. Nonetheless, although the discussion format remains flexible, the moderator should keep on hand prepared questions in case the group fails to raise critical issues or the discussion dies prematurely. The moderator memorizes key questions (usually no more than 10) in advance of the focus group session. To stimulate creativity, moderators may divide an issue so that the group considers each part of the larger question separately (Wilson & Hanna, 1993). Rules governing the development of questions for focus groups will be similar to those discussed in Chapter 7 on survey questions.

Focus groups have purposes, and throughout the discussion the moderator gauges the extent to which those purposes have been met. The experienced moderator never loses sight of where the group should be at the end of the discussion. At some point, the moderator may encourage a narrowing of focus to address main areas of interest. Occasional summaries and gentle prompting can help to refocus a group that has strayed from the topic. The moderator monitors the mood of the group and, when interest flags, he or she must be ready to move the group toward the next issue.

Recording and Observing the Session

An assistant researcher often observes the focus group from behind a two-way mirror, taking notes on verbal and nonverbal behaviors of participants. Representatives of the group that commissioned the study may also be present (e.g., company executives or senior managers). Sometimes, researchers videotape or audiotape sessions for later study. In such a situation, it is best to use an omnidirectional microphone, which is compatible with the tape recorder. The microphone should be centrally located on the table in clear view of the participants. As the discussion proceeds, participants (sometimes even the moderator and his or her assistant) will tend to forget the equipment is present. Even if the session is being taped, the moderator and assistant moderator should take notes. The assistant moderator takes more detailed notes than the moderator and should be careful to record quotable statements and names of speakers (Jackson, 1999). These observations and notes can be useful in postsession analyses. This extra measure is important because tape recorders do not always function, comments can be lost when tapes are switched, and background noise can interfere with the quality of the recording. The moderator's note-taking, however, should not impede the flow or spontaneity of the discussion.

Part of maintaining a friendly interpersonal environment is beginning and ending a focus group session on time. Group members can become openly hostile if held beyond the time for which they have been asked to meet. Therefore, the moderator must manage time well (i.e., keep the group sufficiently on track to cover all points that are raised while not stifling or shutting off discussion too soon in important areas). The average focus group session lasts 1 or 2 hours.

Analyzing the Results

At the conclusion of the exercise, one or more judges can analyze the results, either in a formal (content analysis and other statistical techniques) or informal way (impressionistic analysis or simple descriptive summaries). Exploratory studies often employ more impressionistic techniques, whereas full-scale studies rely on content analysis (Watt & Van Den Berg, 1995). Content analysis involves creating categories, classifying the information according to these categories, and tabulating the frequencies with which different categories appear. Computer programs can subject the data to more sophisticated quantitative analysis. Transcripts of the focus group sessions are required for content analysis. For a detailed description of how to conduct content analysis, see Chapter 4. The quantity of data, both verbal and nonverbal, that can be generated in a focus group poses the most serious challenge to the analyst.

Tables 8.1 and 8.2 illustrate how focus group comments can be presented in a shorthand form for easy consumption. Recently, companies have begun to pay for video recording of focus group sessions, and production firms edit the videotapes to show representative comments by members. (The written permission of participants is required for inclusion in a videotaped presentation; otherwise, confidentiality has been violated.) In either case (written or videotaped), the comments should be "typical" of the general tone of the discussions. These comments give a "flavor" of the interactions that have taken place. Descriptive summaries and analyses of the data should complement any charts or videotaped presentations.

Interviewer Styles and Moderator Characteristics

Facilitators for such groups can use directive or nondirective interviewing techniques. Nondirective techniques derive from the Hawthorne studies of the late 1930s and early 1940s when researchers discovered that they could gain more insight into employee motivations when they asked open-ended rather than closed questions. Nondirective interviewing allows control to shift occasionally during the interview (i.e., from the interviewer to the interviewee and back again). Although the interviewer supplies the topics for discussion, the focus group process remains highly interactive.

Although a more directive interviewing style can result in many topics being covered in a relatively short span of time, this approach can result in the facilitator shutting off some avenues of discussion before they yield interesting results. In such a case, learning will be single loop (i.e., the moderator elicits only information within the confines of existing knowledge). Some of the most productive focus groups open new avenues to moderators—areas of interest that the moderator may not have anticipated. For example, a discussion that begins with commentary on a company's social events may end with a critique of its position on the environment. A directive style of interviewing shuts off this option.

It has been said that the best approach to moderating focus groups may be some combination of the two extremes of directive and nondirective. For a 2-hour focus group, the moderator will generally ask 10 to 12 questions (Krueger, 1993). The facilitator maintains sufficient control to keep discussions on track and focused but allows temporary excursions into unforeseen territory. Moreover, before arriving at the discussion, the facilitator reviews the purposes of the session and chooses a style that is most appropriate to achieve these purposes. For example, if the intent of the focus group is to generate new and creative insights, a free-wheeling approach may be best. If the purpose of the gathering is to isolate problem areas, a more directive ap-

TABLE 8.1 Representative Comments From a Focus Group[a]

Question	Responses by Region				
	Southeast	Northeast	Midwest	West	
You're probably aware that pharmaceutical companies sometimes receive unexpected publicity on their products. Can you think of any examples in recent years to illustrate this point?	Viagra Aspirin	Hismanol Some diet pill	Breast implants A new diet pill	Seldane Viagra	
One of you mentioned product X. What have you heard about this product lately?	Side effects Heart attacks	Don't remember hearing anything Heart problems	Heard something on TV Can't recall details	Can induce heart conditions	
Where did you receive this information?	Television	Newspaper Radio Television	Television	Television Newspaper	
Has this information influenced your purchasing habits? If so, in what way?	Yes: No longer buy product	No: Don't use product	Yes: Follow maker's instructions	No: Don't use product	
What do you think that the company could do to restore public confidence to former levels?	Do more testing Correct problem	Depends on whether reports are correct	Nothing unless reports can be proved to be false	Run public announcement campaign on TV explaining how to use product safely	

a. Assume that Company X has recently received national publicity on one of its products. Although the company does not believe the claims are valid, it has decided to conduct a series of focus groups to determine the short-term impact of the negative publicity. The company is hoping to acquire insights from the focus groups that would enable it to address the concern of consumers. This is a fictitious example that does not reflect on the companies mentioned.

TABLE 8.2 Representative Comments From a Focus Group

	Responses by Region			
Question	Southeast	Northeast	Midwest	West
How do you feel about Florida as a possible place to relocate?	No real interest in Florida Florida's OK I like the sun	Would be a nice change Wouldn't be a bad place to live	Sounds like a nice place Wouldn't want to live there	Never really thought much about Florida, sounds OK though
What do you find attractive about the state?	Have family there I like the ocean	No snow! Florida has great beaches I like warm places	Disneyland is there Warm weather	You can play a lot of golf A lot of tourist attractions
What do you find unattractive about the state?	Too hot The threat of hurricanes Too many drug problems	Too much drug trafficking Dangerous because of hurricanes and tropical storms	Would miss the change of seasons Hurricanes are scary Might be too hot	Too far away from friends and family Wouldn't want to have to worry about hurricanes
If you relocated in Florida, would you choose to rent or buy?	Would probably buy Definitely rent	Buy Might rent for a while	Would depend on what was available Would like to buy	Would rent first to see how I like Florida, then buy if I decided to stay for a prolonged period

What kinds of factors would influence your decision?	Finances Market situation How likely the place could be lost to a hurricane	How long I planned to stay If I bought a condo, could keep it even if I moved again	If I was going to be there for a long time, I would buy I don't think I'd have the money to buy	I know I wouldn't want to stay there permanently, so I would just rent How much it cost
Some states, such as California and southern Atlantic coastal states, are prone to damage from natural disasters. Do you believe people pay much attention to the possibility of earthquakes, hurricanes, etc., when they buy property?	People probably don't think about it too much Think people are more afraid of earthquakes than hurricanes Crime is more of a problem	I definitely would not buy in an area where everything could be lost in an earthquake or hurricane, and insurance wouldn't cover it People forget People go where jobs are	I think that hurricanes and earthquakes might influence my decision on whether to move there but would not really affect my decision on whether to buy or rent	People are concerned about these things, but financial and other aspects seem to be greater influences

a. Assume that a recent hurricane has brought a fair amount of unfavorable publicity to Florida. The real estate industry has become concerned. This concern has led a real estate association to hold a series of focus groups in different regions to determine how much impact the hurricane is likely to have on people's decisions to relocate to Florida. This is a fictitious example generated to illustrate focus group comments.

213

proach may be better. In a focus group, the moderator should limit the use of "why" questions (Krueger, 1994; Reid, 1988b). Although some people recommend calling directly on individuals to respond to questions or going around the table and asking for positions on an issue, such techniques can be counterproductive. Some researchers claim that a weakness of focus groups is a tendency for the moderator to "overdirect." The moderator may embarrass a person by asking for an opinion on certain topics. An individual who does not have an opinion on a particular topic may feel pressured to take a stance. Uninformed individuals may be similarly forced into a position. Having stated a position on an issue, a person may feel obliged to defend that position. Progressing systematically around a group can be boring for participants. The lack of spontaneity in the situation can generate disinterest in completing the session. In such a forced situation, some group members will answer at length, whereas others will give short peremptory responses.

The best moderators take care not to signal acceptance or nonacceptance of an idea through verbal or nonverbal behaviors (e.g., nodding the head or saying "that's an excellent point"). Successful moderators treat participants as equals, being careful not to give responses that could be construed as championing some points of view and negating others. A focus group moderator should avoid expressing or revealing personal opinions or biases. Moderators should be good listeners. Friendly, consistent behaviors exhibited throughout the session can make participants feel that their views are valuable. A moderator who wants to encourage balanced group participation can catch and hold the eye of nonparticipants when asking a question. If the person closes the communication channel by averting his or her gaze, the moderator does not push the point. Avoiding the gaze of an individual who tends to dominate the discussion can prove to be an equally useful technique (Wilson & Hanna, 1993). If one panelist has a much higher level of expertise than the rest of the group, the moderator may want to appoint this individual as a resource person to elaborate on designated points or to provide detailed factual information. The individual can be asked to refrain from expressing an opinion or point of view that could unduly influence the course of the discussion.

Some researchers claim that moderators should appear like the participants in manner and dress. Some caution against having female moderators with all-male focus groups or male moderators with all-female groups (Axelrod, 1975). Others believe that females can moderate all-male groups, but males should not moderate all-female groups. Whatever their position on the issue of gender, most agree that facilitators should share some characteristics in common with participants. As much as possible, the moderator's background should match the background and lifestyles of the participants (Watt & Van Den Berg, 1995). Some focus group firms specialize by working exclusively with certain age or demographic groups (e.g., teenagers or ethnic groups) or in certain areas, such consumer research, marketing research, or political communication. A good background knowledge of the topic being discussed, an ability to recognize the critical dimensions of issues, and good group facilitation skills are just a few of the characteristics that the successful focus group moderator should possess. Also helpful are a sense of humor, a basic respect for people, and an enjoyment of interacting with others. The ability to synthesize and see the relationship between ideas is essential. Training in areas such as communication (advertising, public relations, interpersonal, small group, negotiation and mediation, and business), marketing, psychology, and psychotherapy can be useful preparation for a facilitator (Stewart & Shamdasani, 1990).

Common Participant Behaviors

A classical study in group dynamics classified participant behaviors in the categories of group task roles, group building and maintenance roles, and self-centered and dysfunctional roles (Benne & Sheats, 1948). According to this study, group members act out various roles during the course of a group discussion.

Under group task roles, some group members act as *initiators,* proposing new ideas, goals, and solutions. Those classified as *information givers* contribute evidence and opinions to group discussion. *Information seekers* ask for information and seek clarification. *Opinion givers* state their own beliefs, opinions, and attitudes on a topic. *Opinion seekers* solicit the views of others and ask others to clarify their ideas. *Elaborators* clarify and build on ideas presented by other group members; they offer examples, illustrations, and explanations. *Integrators* try to synthesize and make sense of the concepts and ideas contributed by the group. *Orienters* keep a group focused on its goal, offering periodic summaries and clarifying positions of group members. Finally, *energizers* call for higher levels of involvement from group members.

Those in group maintenance roles work to increase group cohesiveness by building and maintaining the interpersonal relationships in a group. The *encourager* praises and compliments others for their contributions. The *harmonizer* works to mediate differences and conflicts, proposing compromise positions for the group. The *tension reliever* uses informality and humor to establish a relaxed interpersonal climate. Through body orientation and eye contact, the *gatekeeper* encourages balanced participation on the part of group members. The *follower* defers to the opinions of others.

Some dysfunctional roles do not contribute to the progression of a discussion or to the maintenance of interpersonal relationships. Rather, members who assume these roles can take a discussion off track or can cause friction and disruption. The *blocker,* who complains and offers only negative comments, objects to more constructive suggestions by others. The *aggressor* insults and criticizes other group members, laughing at perceived faults or mistakes. The *anecdoter* takes the group off course with irrelevant stories and personal experiences. *Recognition seekers* call attention to their own achievements and successes. *Dominators* monopolize group interaction either by flattering or interrupting others. The *confessor* uses the group as an audience for his or her personal problems, revealing inadequacies and fears. The *special-interest pleader* seeks favors or attention for an outside group. The *distractor* (originally labeled as *playboy/playgirl*) relies on antics, jokes, and irrelevant comments to distract a group from more task-oriented goals to more entertainment-oriented goals.

Strengths and Weaknesses of Focus Groups

Focus groups are relatively easy to organize and execute. Compared to the cost of conducting large-scale survey research, the focus group is an inexpensive tool for learning about the opinion of key publics. It is easier for the organization to afford the services of one trained focus group moderator than the services of many skilled interviewers. Data collection in a focus group is fast, and data analysis is relatively easy. Its flexible format allows the researcher to conduct discussion on many topics. The interviewer is able to probe and explore ill-defined areas of thought. Also, the focus group is useful for gaining insights in new areas, for testing concepts, and for learning what motivates people to believe and behave as they do. Unexpected insights often emerge from the creativity of focus groups, and people can build on the ideas of others. The "synergistic output" of focus groups offers the possibility for more natural and spontaneous interactions than in other types of survey situations (Herndon, 1993, p. 41). People speak when they want to speak, not on demand as in the individual interview situation.

There are many problems with focus groups. Seldom are focus group results capable of being generalized to the mass public because few focus groups are representative samples, no matter how carefully the organization proceeds in recruiting participants. Without a competent facilitator, focus groups can be ineffectual. Focus groups tend to vary in characteristics and quality of contributions. In some cases, one or two individuals dominate a focus group, sabotaging the group process. Tendencies of focus groups to move toward conformity can sometimes undermine the process. Studies by Fern (1982) demonstrate that focus groups produce no more or better ideas than the same number of individual interviews. It can be difficult to coordinate the schedules of focus group participants. Participants sometimes follow the lead of those in the group who are experts or who proclaim themselves to be the experts. The views of the verbally aggressive receive more than their fair share of weight in the final results (Berg, 1995). Some moderators "overdirect," reducing the number of opportunities for group members to interact spontaneously. To address these problem, some researchers suggest that companies should conduct "unfocus" groups with less rigid formats and freer flow of communication (Dozier & Repper, 1992).

Although less expensive than the survey, the focus group also entails costs. Major cost factors in setting up and conducting focus groups include the expense of hiring or training a moderator, the investment in incentives for participants, rental fees for the research site, and the cost of making and transcribing tapes of the sessions. The cost of focus groups can more than double with a requirement to obtain the involvement of individuals with specialized expertise or the involvement of more difficult to reach segments of the population (Morgan, 1988).

Many researchers claim that focus group results are most valuable when combined with results from other quantitative and qualitative techniques, such as surveying or interviews with elite opinion leaders or both. For example, a company interested in learning more about public perceptions of its image might commission a focus group before investing in a larger study. The focus group can yield insights into what should be included in the survey questions (Reid, 1988b). In some cases, the sole purpose of the focus group is to test a questionnaire that will be used in a larger study. Some researchers argue, however, that it is not always necessary to follow focus groups with quantitative studies. They claim that some research firms use focus groups as a "stalking horse to lead clients into more expensive surveys" when focus groups can stand on their own (Morgan, 1988, p. 13; see also Calder, 1977).

Other Methodologies

Delphi Technique

A well-known technique for gathering information (often applied within the organization) is the Delphi method developed by the RAND Corporation. The Delphi method involves soliciting the involvement of a group of experts, often from diverse backgrounds. The composition of the group depends on the nature of the problem. For example, interdisciplinary perspectives are more important when the problem is general and abstract. Technical expertise has a higher priority when the problem is specific and technical. In some situations, a balance of specialists and generalists is preferred. The teams often seek input from both theoreticians and pragmatists (Tersine & Riggs, 1988). Unlike focus groups, Delphic methods and nominal groups seek consensus and an agreement on solutions (Krueger, 1994).

Basic steps involved in the Delphi method include defining the problem, determining the type of expertise that is required, selecting a sample of experts, preparing and distributing a questionnaire to these individuals, and analyzing their responses to determine whether consensus has been reached. The consultant then provides any follow-up information and tabulates the responses. The degree of homogeneity in the participants governs the size of the sample. Ten to 15 respondents can be sufficient when the group is homogeneous. With more heterogeneous respondents, a larger number is required. Several hundred persons participate in some Delphi studies. Respondents should have knowledge in the subject area, a good performance record, time to participate, and a rational approach to problem solving.

After deciding on an adequate sample size, the researchers inform participants of the purpose of the study, questions to be addressed, their roles, and the importance of their participation. They locate replacements for those who decline participation in the study. The questionnaire contains a clear statement of the problem, written in specific or general terms, along with a request for the respondent's opinion and reasoning on the topic, important facts that influenced the subject's thinking on the topic, and additional information that the person may require to reach a decision. After identifying areas of agreement and discord, as well as items requiring clarification or amplification, the researcher prepares and distributes a second questionnaire. This questionnaire includes statistical and qualitative summaries of the group responses to the first questionnaire along with additional information or explanations, as requested by participants. After reviewing the summaries and the new information, respondents have the opportunity to revise their positions. Where responses are categorized into an extreme percentile, relative to the other responses, the researchers ask participants to explain their positions. The second round of responses is then circulated to participants for their consideration and reaction. This procedure continues until consensus is achieved. A minimum of three rounds of questionnaires may be required to reach convergence. The final report offers a summary of the goals, process, and results of the Delphi exercise. The company or government division uses this input in various ways, including long-range strategic planning and forecasting (Tersine & Riggs, 1988).

Weaknesses in the technique include the possibility for selection of panelists with inadequate knowledge or motivation, the number of calendar days required to conduct the study, and the possibility that some recommendations will not be implemented in the immediate future, if at all. Nonetheless, Delphi compares favorably to other techniques on factors such as cost and the number of working hours required for participation and processing of results (Tersine & Riggs, 1988).

Stakeholder Assemblies

The Dunvegan Group of Canada markets a concept called "stakeholder assemblies" to interested corporate clients. According to Executive Director Olev Wain (personal communication, December 21, 1992), "a stakeholder assembly is a panel (typically 500 to 1,500 people or organizations) consisting of a representative cross section of stakeholders who have agreed to receive and complete questionnaires sent to them by the Dunvegan Group." Stakeholder assemblies can be used for environmental monitoring (including reactions to proposed changes to policies or regulations), public consultation, or program evaluation. From the point of view of participants, however, stakeholder assemblies offer a forum for communicating with the organization about issues of import or interest. Although stakeholder assemblies employ Delphi-style techniques, they do not restrict membership. Anyone (individual or group) who wishes to become involved has the opportunity.

Typically, 8 to 12 weeks are required to establish an assembly from the list of stakeholders presented by the client organization. The Dunvegan Group argues that both experience and survey research data suggest that stakeholder assembly members do not vary attitudinally, demographically, or behaviorally from nonassembly members.

Advantages of stakeholder assemblies include the following: (a) Geographical, time, and economic restraints do not significantly influence patterns of participation because the medium for communication is the mail; (b) assembly members can complete the questionnaire in their own time, at a comfortable pace; (c) they can also think about the questions and consult with others before replying; (d) responses are more reflective than opinions obtained through other means, such as personal interviews and telephone surveys; and (e) the data are also more comprehensive. For these reasons, stakeholder assemblies are better than public meetings for strategic decision making. They provide extended time for processing complex issues.

The process is highly participatory. Clients, industry groups, and associations can become involved in framing the questions that are asked. Assemblies, however, do not allow "shrill" but unrepresentative voices or high-status voices to dominate the process. People with a fear of public speaking can voice their views in a nonpublic way. Assembly procedures ensure anonymity and confidentiality. The fact that no interviewer is present and that all participants receive the same questionnaire eliminates other sources of bias. Response rates are high (between 60% and 70%).

These assemblies provide an opportunity to develop and maintain contact with participants over an extended period, thus offering the opportunity to study shifts in opinion over time. The research organization can determine how thinking on issues changes, can identify population sectors in which the changes are occurring, and can probe the reason for the shifts. The written nature of the data allows the opportunity to quantify opinions and points of view.

Disadvantages of stakeholder assemblies are the following: (a) Defining stakeholders can be a complicated and contentious process, (b) the client typically provides the list of names from which stakeholders are selected, and (c) the preparatory work can be time-consuming as researcher and client identify issues and develop meaningful questionnaires. Most important to the success of stakeholder assemblies is the requirement for feedback. Assembly members must regularly receive feedback regarding findings. Without this feedback, they lose interest and drop out of the assembly. Businesses tend to agree more readily than governments to this exigency.

The Cape Breton Corporation of Canada holds a public meeting of all interested stakeholders each year, at which time they write their strategic plan for the year. This corporation would seem to be a prime candidate for this type of exercise.

Q Methodology

Like surveys and focus groups, Q methodology seeks to identify the major themes in stakeholder opinions on issues. To accomplish this task, Q methodology asks subjects to sort a series of statements into categories that respond to some criterion (e.g., perceived importance of the issue or level of agreement with the issue). Subsequently, the researchers identify clusters of opinion by statistically analyzing and interpreting the results of the "Q sort" exercise.

Q methodology, unlike public opinion surveys, does not require large population samples to generate meaningful results. According to proponents of this methodology, a Q sort that involves 40 to 50 people can produce the same insights into trends as an opinion poll with 1,000 respondents. The following discussion identifies the major steps in carrying out Q methodology.

The term *concourse* refers to the sum of discourse on a research topic. To gather this concourse, the researcher uses a variety of sources, including newspapers, magazines, correspondence, academic journals, convention proceedings, transcripts of broadcasts, policy documents, and bulletin boards on the Internet. Where the volume of items in a concourse is too great for individuals to sort, the researcher draws a sample of statements. Prior to sampling, the researcher classifies the statements into compartments of a matrix. Then the researcher randomly selects an equal number of statements from each compartment.

Next, the researcher places the statements on cards and asks participants to sort the cards according to some organizational principle or "condition of instruction." For example, they may sort the cards in order from "most agree" to "most disagree" or "most important" to "least important." The researcher specifies the number of piles into which the participants must place the cards. If the researcher uses a Likert-type scale for the exercise (5 to –5), he or she will ask the respondent to sort the cards into 11 piles. Alternatively, the researcher may specify that the piles should be lower on both sides and higher in the middle, in the shape of a bell curve.

Researchers subject the completed Q sorts to factor analysis, which enables them to identify factors common to the Q sorts of several participants. Factor analysis also identifies the statements that most characterize each factor. The final step in Q methodology involves interpreting the findings, determining how the statements fit together. Review of the original concourse and sample statements used in the Q sort can help the researcher to construct a more complete picture. In addition to revealing individual differences in opinion, Q methodology can yield unexpected insights into patterns of opinion.

The previous discussion is based on the work of Steven Brown of Kent University as interpreted by TimeWork Web (*http://www.vcn.bc.ca/timework/q.htm*). Brown (1980, 1999) is one of the leading authorities in Q methodology research, an area of study developed by Stephenson (1953). Brown believes that interest in Q methodology increased, with the initiation of an electronic mail discussion list in 1991, the development of a QMethod freeware package for mainframe computers in 1992, the establishment of a journal/newsletter devoted to Q methodology, and the founding of an international society and William Stephenson Communication Research Center at the University of Missouri. This methodology is being applied in marketing, discourse analysis, and many other areas (Brown, 1999).

Conclusion

This chapter examined several popular methods for soliciting stakeholder input, including focus group testing, Delphi techniques, stakeholder assemblies, and Q methodology. Although researchers can use other techniques, such as field methods and nominal group techniques, they do not tend to apply these methodologies to opinion research. Instead, nominal group techniques are used most often with employees to encourage creative problem solving. Field methods do not enable the researcher to ask direct questions of respondents. These techniques involve drawing inferences based on behavior, which is not always a valid guide to opinion.

PART
IV

Theories on the Impact of the Media

9

Academic Debate
Over Media Effects

The Effects Continuum

As the preceding chapters suggest, organizational leaders, who are shepherding their organizations into a new millennium, hold a firm conviction that media have effects—powerful and rarely without consequence. Adhering to this belief, they spend millions of dollars each year on survey research, focus groups, Delphi techniques, Q methodologies, stakeholder assemblies, and media analysis. They establish intelligence systems to track opinion on key issues, and they feed the opinion data into strategic planning systems used in formulating responses to key publics.

Their homespun conviction that the media act as powerful forces on passive audiences is not shared by all members of the academic community, however, who are positioned along a "media effects continuum." Although some believe that media have powerful and direct effects (evidenced by events such as the 1999 shooting at Columbine High School), others believe that media's more potent influence is long term and cumulative, fashioning a society that sanctions violent and often antisocial behaviors. Other academics, who believe in the idea of "selective reinforcement," agree that causal relationships are complex. The long-term, ongoing debate reveals little movement toward consensus, even after many years of research and argument.

This chapter concludes with a brief review of this debate and comment on what the public believes to be the relationship between media effects and public opinion. By examining the "third-person effects" hypothesis, the chapter seeks to explain the concerns of leaders.

Powerful, Direct Effects Model

In the early years of radio and television, communication researchers viewed media as having powerful, direct effects on audiences. This interpretation of media's effects grew out of several events. First, the Payne Fund studies (1933) demonstrated that participants in an academic survey believed the movies had a direct influence on their play, dress and hair, and emotions as children. Respondents cited numerous examples to illustrate the way in which they had emulated movie stars and film events (DeFleur & Dennis, 1981). Peterson and Thurstone (1933) concluded that films could change children's attitudes toward social issues, sometimes dramatically. For example, they found that prosocial films evoked positive attitudes, and antisocial films evoked negative attitudes toward specific groups targeted in the films. These perceptions sometimes persisted for long periods of time after the viewing of the films. Peterson and Thurstone also concluded that the effects were cumulative—that is, repeated exposure to the same concepts could increase the degree of attitude change. Third, the hysteria provoked by Orson Welles's *War of the Worlds* radio broadcast confirmed the fears of many people that mass media have a dramatic and serious impact on peoples' lives. Studies of media advertising also demonstrate obvious direct effects on consumer behaviors. Finally, the success of Hitler in swaying the emotions of millions of Germans convinced many people that media have a powerful "magic bullet" effect. Just as people once believed that a hypnotist could exercise great powers over a subject— even to the point of convincing the person to commit murder—they also accepted the general wisdom that media could inject people, in the fashion of a "hypodermic" needle, with information that would change their attitudes and behaviors in predictable ways. All these terms came to signify the nature of the powerful, direct effects model applied to mass media.

Limited Effects Model

Academics such as Cantril (1940) were beginning to suspect, however, that other variables influence the strength and nature of popular reactions to mass media. When Cantril studied the response of Americans to the *War of the Worlds* broadcast, he found that people who scored low in critical ability had "tended to accept the invasion as real and failed to make reliable checks on the broadcast; for example, they did not call authorities or listen to other stations" (De Fleur & Dennis, 1981, p. 305). Those with strong religious convictions were especially prone to accept the invasion as the will of God and the end of the world. Education was another deciding variable in whether the listener had accepted the invasion as authentic. In fact, data from CBS revealed that the level of education was the "single best factor in predicting whether people would check the broadcast against other sources of information" (p. 305).

In the 1940s, other psychologists and sociologists also began to focus on individual responses of people (needs, attitudes, values, intelligence, and other factors) within the same environment. Gender, racial, ethnic, age, status, and other variables became the subject of many of these studies. The U.S. Army studied the effectiveness of films designed to instruct recruits and to shape their opinions. In the end, it was concluded that the films had had minimal influence in producing attitude change (Hovland, Lumsdaine, & Sheffield, 1965). Although the films had succeeded in increasing the knowledge of viewers and modifying certain specific beliefs, they had not effected changes in the general belief orientations of viewers. For example, the films had not convinced the recruits that they should pursue the war with great enthusiasm, harbor a strong hatred of the enemy, or have great confidence in U.S. allies. Moreover, the education level of the recruits had mediated the effects—that is, soldiers with more education had learned more from the films. The researchers concluded that the effects of the films were clearly limited. Early studies on the effects of television on children supported the same conclusions (Schramm, Lyle, & Parker, 1961). As in the Payne Fund studies, researchers found that television offered diversion for children and allowed them to escape into fantasy worlds. They also found, however, that factors such as family, intelligence, age, and gender mediated how children used television, and effects varied from child to child and among categories of children.

Limited and Indirect Effects Model

In the mid-1940s, Lazarsfeld, Berelson, and Gaudet (1948) carried out landmark research that provided additional support for the limited effects model, in which demographic characteristics of voters played a key role. This study also added a new twist to the academic debate over media effects when the researchers discovered strong evidence of personal influence. When asked to report on their exposure to political information, they mentioned friends, family, and acquaintances more often than they cited print or radio media. On the basis of these findings, the researchers formulated a hypothesis that they called "the two-step flow of communication." This hypothesis proposes that some individuals, heavily involved in following the political campaign, act as "opinion leaders": "Ideas often flow from radio and print to the opinion leaders and from them to the less active sections of the population" (p. 151). In addition, Lazarsfeld and colleagues found that only 8% of the population had changed their support from one party to another as a consequence of mass media exposure. This benchmark study, reported in *The People's Choice,* moved mass communication theory solidly into an era characterized by a belief in minimal or limited and mediated effects. The study concluded that the media were only one among many influences that helped people to make their political decisions. In documenting the influence of third parties, the study called into question the powerful and direct effects model of the media, often characterized as the "hypodermic" or magic bullet model. Thus, the study also moved theorizing from a model of direct influence to that of indirect influence.

The findings of a follow-up study by Katz and Lazarsfeld, planned in 1944, finally appeared in 1955. *Personal Influence: The Part Played by People in the Flow of Mass Communication* joined its predecessor (*The People's Choice*) as a landmark work in the debate over media effects (Lowery & De Fleur, 1983). Later researchers argued that it is more appropriate to speak of a multistep (as opposed to two-step) flow of communication that "trickles down" through multiple layers of opinion leaders (Rogers & Shoemaker, 1971). It can also be argued that messages have undergone considerable processing before opinion leaders ever become active. For example, the president makes a public statement on television. A "spin doctor" or expert in the subject matter comments on the message. A television personality then comments on "the comment," after which an audience member with opinion leader status offers an interpretation of the expert commentary to a second level of opinion leaders, who pass their interpretations of these highly processed messages to friends and followers (Ferguson, 1994, 1999). Political and social commentators often lament the many layers separating them from target audiences, evidenced in this opinion leader/commentator model.

Limited and "Direct-ed" Effects Model

What could be called the limited and "direct-ed" effects model views audiences as active and involved, seeking information and controlling the uses to which that information is applied. This school embodies the concept of uses and gratifications. Those who adhere to this paradigm believe that the influence of the media is limited because people are active consumers of media. They make choices, they meet needs, and they seek gratification (rewards or satisfaction) through the media. Early researchers, such as Herzog (1940) and Berelson (1949), examined why people use media. Lasswell (1948) identified usage categories such as surveillance, correlation, entertainment, and cultural transmission or socialization. Later researchers, such as Katz, Gurevitch, and Haas (1973), talked about how people use media to enhance their status, strengthen relationships, and meet other social or psychological needs. McQuail, Blumler, and Brown (1972) presented a typology that includes diversion and escapism, personal relationships, personal identity (e.g., value reinforcement), and surveillance of the environment.

Political communication researchers examine how audiences use the media for purposes such as to acquire knowledge about candidates and current issues. Other researchers compare audience preferences for different media (e.g., television vs. newspapers) (Robinson & Levy, 1996). Health communication researchers study patterns of media usage among high-risk groups, such as smokers, people with AIDS, or women at risk of breast cancer (Johnson & Meishoke, 1992). The key idea in this limited effects paradigm relates to the fact that audiences vary in their characteristics, motivations, and habits, and the list of needs and motivations for using media varies from audience to audience (Rubin, 1994). The differences influence how and why people use media.

The work of another group of theorists, European in their traditions, can also be classified under the limited and direct-ed effects model. "Revisionists" (sometimes converts from the critical or radical functionalist traditions) view audiences as highly active and engaged in choosing media content. In this sense, the effects are extremely controlled and limited. Revisionist perspectives emerged in the 1980s from the ashes of the radical functionalist approach. Curran (1996b) noted,

> The most important and significant overall shift has been the steady advance of pluralist themes within the radical tradition: in particular, the repudiation of the totalizing, explanatory frameworks of Marxism, the reconceptualization of the

audience as creative and active. . . . A sea change has occurred in the field, and this will reshape—for better or worse—the development of media and cultural studies in Europe. (p. 272)

Powerful and Cumulative Effects Model

During the 1960s, questions related to the long-term and cumulative effects of television and other media were raised. Concern regarding the increasing amount of televised violence gave rise to research into social learning and modeling behavior (Baker & Ball, 1969). Social learning and modeling theories suggest that individuals adopt behaviors that they observe on television and in the movies. They identify with and seek to emulate the actions of their television or film role models. This research led theorists to believe that the effects of television, even if indirect, are powerful. In other words, few contemporary scholars accept that a single exposure to some act on television motivates an individual to duplicate the act, but many believe that the cumulative effects of many similar exposures can significantly increase the probability that an individual will think or behave in a specific way. Many speculate that pornography and other undesirable materials on the Internet have the same undesirable consequences.

Several conceptual constructs fit within the powerful and cumulative effects model of media influence, including cultivation research, framing, agenda setting, and priming (Lowery & De Fleur, 1983). These theories fall under the broader label of *social constructionism,* the idea that media construct realities for people through symbolic content. Reflecting Lippmann's (1922) belief in mediated realities, social constructionists adhere to the idea that the influence of media is incipient, long term, and powerful, with the potential for cumulative effects. Griffin (2000) claims that social constructionists such as W. Barnett Pearce and Vernon Cronen are social ecologists who, like environmentalists, believe that the effects of communication have a long-term impact on people and societies. The coordinated management of meaning model of Pearce and Cronen (1980) proposes that people construct their own social realities in the process of interacting with each other. The universe created by people of great diversity is, by definition, a pluralistic one. No single truth exists. A multiplicity of interpretations are possible with every event. Drawn to "ambiguity, paradox, and irony" (Griffin, 2000), social constructionists do not hold everyone accountable to the same standards. Curious, they view life as a complex ribbon, ever changing, without end or resolution. Social constructionists become actively involved in what they study rather than seeking positions on the sidelines as observers.

Cultivation Research

In 1967 and 1968, the National Commission on the Causes and Prevention of Violence funded research by Gerbner and colleagues, later sponsored by the U.S. Surgeon General's Scientific Advisory Committee on Television and Social Behavior, the National Institute of Mental Health, the White House Office of Telecommunications Policy, the American Medical Association, the U.S. Administration on Aging, and the National Science Foundation. Cultivation theory emerged from this large-scale, ongoing study of violence in the media (Gerbner & Gross, 1976).

In the early stages of the study, Gerbner's team developed "cultivation indicators" for the study of perceived levels of crime in society. They attempted to document a correlation between perceived levels of crime in society and people's television viewing habits. Current cultivation research examines a variety of areas, as noted by Gerbner, Gross, Morgan, and Signorielli (1994), including the

> extent to which television viewing contributes to audience conceptions and actions in areas such as gender, minority and age-role stereotypes, health, science, the family, educational achievement and aspirations, politics, religion, and other topics, all of which are increasingly also being examined in cross-cultural comparative contexts. (pp. 21-22)

Cultivation theorists question the debate over media effects because they believe that most of those engaged in the debate presume that media produce short-term effects at an individual level. Instead, cultivation researchers argue that media effects are massive, long term, and cumulative, influencing large and heterogeneous publics. *Mainstreaming* refers to the idea that heavy viewing can "absorb or override differences in perspectives and behavior that ordinarily stem from other factors and influences" (Gerbner et al., 1994, p. 28).

Advocates of cultivation theory do not like to use the term "media effects" because they view the shift away from measuring short-term attitudinal changes to long-term cumulative factors as a paradigm shift. In line with this perspective, cultivation theorists talk about "growing up" and "living with" television (Gerbner et al., 1994, p. 37). Critics of this technique believe that

long-term studies tend to be contaminated by other environmental influences, making it difficult to draw cause-effect relationships or to reach valid
conclusions. Other theorists with compatible views argue that media transform societies by changing conceptions of time and space (Innis, 1950;
McLuhan, 1964) or the political process (McQuail, 1994).

Framing

Another current research area, relevant to social constructionist thought,
asks how the media frame stories. The term *framing* refers to a "central organizing idea or story line that provides meaning" (Gamson & Modigliani,
1987, p. 143). The concept of framing links to the work of Berger and
Luckmann (1967) and Tuchman (1978), who talk about the way in which media construct reality. As Tuchman observed,

> News is a window on the world. Through its frame, Americans learn of them-
> selves and others, of their own institutions and those of other societies. But, like
> any frame, news conceals as well as it reveals, giving some occurrences a public
> character while preventing others from becoming public information. What
> events are chosen to be treated as news? How does news get made? What, ex-
> actly, is "news"?

Like later writers, Tuchman talks about how media tell stories. The assumption in framing analysis is that media influence public attitudes on issues by
giving a particular "spin" to their stories (Wimmer & Dominick, 1997). Current researchers in the field include Durham (1998), Jasperson, Shah, Watts,
Faber, and Fan (1998), Pan and Kosicki (1997), Rhee (1997), and Scheufele
(1999).

Agenda Setting

The term *agenda setting* refers to the ability of the mass media to direct attention to specific issues. As Cohen (1963) noted, "The press may not be successful much of the time in telling people what to think, but it is stunningly
successful in telling its readers what to think about" (p. 4). McCombs and
Shaw (1972) carried out the first study designed to test the agenda-setting hypothesis. Confirming the previous speculations, the researchers found a close
relationship between the political issues to which the news media gave their
attention and those that voters viewed as key issues in the campaign.

Agenda-setting effects also emerged in later studies (Eaton, 1989; Iyengar & Kinder, 1987). Some authors prefer to use the term agenda building (Curtin, 1999).

Rogers and Dearing (1988) proposed that three kinds of agenda setting occur: public agenda setting, media agenda setting, and policy agenda setting. A relationship exists between the three types, with media influencing both the public and the policy agendas. Other interactions also occur, with the public agenda exercising an influence on the policy agenda. McCombs, Einsiedel, and Weaver (1991) explain that one cannot examine one kind of agenda setting in isolation from the others because many institutions and groups have an impact on media agendas. Many discussions and applications of these ideas have appeared in the public relations literature (Dyer, 1996; Theus, 1993).

Researchers ask the following kinds of questions about agenda setting: Who sets the media's agenda? How does the media prime audiences through agenda setting? and What variables mediate the agenda-setting process? The answers to these questions define the limits of the organization's ability to get its issues on the public and media agendas. Other studies demonstrate the limits of the public's willingness to accept media agendas. These limits derive from characteristics of the issues, audiences, media, and journalistic practices.

People pay more attention to some issues than others (Weaver, 1994), and they do not view all issues as being equally important (McCombs, 1978). The issues that someone recognizes as most important to the community or nation (issues on the public agenda) may differ from the issues that are most significant on a personal level (issues on one's private agenda). Responses vary according to level of interest in issues, need for orientation, levels of exposure, prior knowledge of issues, education level, and history of political involvement (McCombs, 1994; Wanta & Hu, 1994; Weaver, 1994; Williams & Semlak, 1978). Weaver observed that the impact of agenda setting varies according to "the campaign context, the length of time being considered, and the kind of effects being studied" (p. 348). McCombs and Shaw (1972) and Niemi and Weisberg (1976) concluded that agenda setting influences become more pronounced and consistent in election periods, when voters pay more attention to political news.

Cultural, institutional, and organizational factors also influence the media agenda (Curran, 1996a; Reese, 1991; Tuchman, 1978). McCombs (1994) said that "traditions, practices, and values of journalism as a profession" have a strong impact on the media agenda (p. 9). Every media establishment faces deadlines; every reporter, editor, and producer adheres to these deadlines. Providing prepackaged materials to the media increases the chance that the media will air the organization's viewpoint, particularly when the organizations face short deadlines. To meet deadlines, layout editors often fill last-minute news holes with materials prepared by public relations personnel (Saxer, 1993). McCombs (1994) explains,

> Even the largest and best national newspapers with their huge staffs of reporters and editors, newspapers such as the *New York Times* and *Washington Post,* obtain over half of their daily material from press releases, press conferences, and other routine channels created by governmental agencies, corporations, and interest groups. Only a small proportion of the news results from the initiative and innovation of the news organizations. (p. 11)

Curtin (1999) cites additional studies (Sachsman, 1976; Wilcox, Ault, & Agee, 1995) that confirm that between 40% and 50% of news content in daily newspapers comes directly from press releases. Other authors (Crouse, 1972; Nimmo & Combs, 1990; Taras, 1990) have addressed the phenomenon of pack journalism—the tendency for reporters to borrow from each other and to check with pack leaders to determine what should be the lead story or issue for the day.

Journalists also respond to commercial imperatives (Curran, 1996a). Survival requires that media consider what "sells." Therefore, the stories that ultimately are placed on the agenda are predictable in their characteristics—highly visual, sensational, dramatic, controversial, and supported by celebrity figures. There is a tendency to avoid issues that require interpretation and analysis, which are more time-consuming exercises. Incumbents in office have an advantage over those who only aspire to office because exclusive interviews with influential figures guarantee media coverage. Technical requirements also influence news coverage. Photographers and television camera crews require adequate light, proper facilities to accommodate sound and video equipment, and a good vantage point for filming or witnessing events.

In recent years, critical theorists have argued that the economically powerful in society control and set the media agenda. They believe that media institutions are part of the establishment, owned by a handful of corporations that represent the most conservative forces in society. According to this view, commercial motives drive the media, determining their content and political bent. Critical theorists believe that the effects of media are powerful, with po-

tentially long-term impact. They do not believe that the media are autonomous. Rather, they argue that the concentration of media in the hands of a few
powerful individuals undermines democracy and contributes to the molding
of societies with little commitment to social justice.

Unlike the other schools of thought on media effects that rely on experimental and survey research, these theorists develop their arguments on economic and philosophical foundations. Like the corporate and government
leaders they seek to discredit, they presume that media have effects that are
predictable and destructive; they believe, however, that the negativity occurs
because media represent economic rather than social interests.

Priming

The term *priming* refers to the way in which media set the standards by
which we judge our leaders. Iyengar and Kinder (1987) note that the media
"prime" the public to evaluate the performance of politicians and others on
the issues to which it accords importance. If employment issues are
front-page news, we judge our leaders by how well they manage these concerns. If, however, health care issues capture headlines, these issues become
the standard by which the public judges the performance of politicians and
bureaucrats. Thus, the media "prime" audiences to alter the centrality of issues to which they accord importance. If issues appear for a sufficiently long
period of time on the media agenda, the public begins to judge its leaders on
how they perform on these issues. Other researchers (Jo & Berkowitz, 1994)
apply the concept of priming to other contexts. They talk about how media
(television, radio, and comic strips) prime audiences to act in aggressive or
antisocial ways.

Some researchers caution that we should take care in drawing too heavy a
line between the media's potential to tell us "what to think about" and "what
to think." They believe that increasing the salience of issues can influence
both the direction and the strength of public opinion (Iyengar & Kinder,
1987; Weaver, 1991). They believe that agenda setting can also lead to action
—that people do more than think about issues on the media agenda. Sometimes, they "participate more in elections, attend more meetings, write more
letters, and sign more petitions" (Roberts & McCombs, 1994, p. 354). Voters
must feel a sense of efficacy, however: "Agenda setting can lead to either political involvement or alienation of citizens, depending on whether it is
mainly top-down or bottom-up and whether real issues or pseudo issues are
emphasized" (Roberts & McCombs, 1994, p. 354).

Selective Reinforcement

Like the advocates of cumulative effects, theorists such as Curran (1996a, 1996b) search for a more sophisticated model of media effects. They believe that media systems are "neither fully independent of, nor fully subordinated to, the structure of power in society. . . . They are neither the 'voice of the people' nor agencies of domination" (Curran, 1996a, p. 148). Although they have close links to power structures, they are also subject to countervailing pressures.

Although active, audiences are not always in control. Societal and cultural influences can determine the extent to which audiences accept or reject media content (Morley, 1996). Sometimes, audiences demonstrate high levels of selectivity in choosing media content; at other times, they show little resistance to media influence (Curran, 1996a, 1996b). Jeffres (1997), who examined the social context for processing messages and the dependent variables of audience behavior, notes that media influence audiences to the extent that they allow media to have an influence. People learn about issues in many different kinds of ways, and the relationship between media effects, personal knowledge, and peer influence is complex (Kitzinger & Williams, 1997).

The "Third-Person Effect"

In concluding the chapter (and book), it is interesting to note what the public thinks about the relationship between public opinion and media effects. Whereas 75% of respondents in one survey believe that a body of "public opinion" exists (Glynn & Ostman, 1988), people also believe that media have a greater effect on others than on themselves. Davison (1983) explained that people tend to overestimate the impact of media on the attitudes and behavior of other people. He attached the label of the third-person effect to this happening. Numerous studies have provided evidence to support the existence of this phenomenon (Perloff, 1993). Jeffres (1997) summarized some of the research, citing studies by Cohen, Mutz, Price, and Gunther (1988), Perloff (1989), Larosa (1989), Rucinski and Salmon (1989), Cohen and Davis (1991), Kim, Ahn, and Song (1991), Gunther and Mundy (1993), and Willnat (1994). All these studies demonstrate that people assume that messages have a greater effect on others than on themselves.

Some variables affecting the third-person effect are education (people with higher levels of education are more likely to overestimate media effects on others), knowledge (people with greater knowledge of a topic are likely to overestimate media effects on others), the level of engagement with the topic (more involved people tend to overestimate the effects of media on others), the nature of the communication (people are especially likely to think that negative political advertisements or defamatory messages will affect others more than themselves), association with other audience members (people are more likely to overestimate the influence of a message on the "public at large" or on more remote audiences than on individuals in close physical proximity), and perception of source bias (people tend to overestimate the influence of biased sources on audiences) (Jeffres, 1997).

This third-person effect could explain the tendency of politicians, bureaucrats, and chief executives to overestimate the impact of media on audiences. These individuals fit many of the characteristics described previously. They are well educated, knowledgeable on the issues, highly involved, and often separated in physical distance from their constituencies (the higher the person is placed in the organizational hierarchy, the less likely the possibility that he or she will be associating with members of the public at large). The messages to which they react are often critical in nature, and they perceive the sources to be highly biased. Given the operation of these factors, the perception of media effects may be more exaggerated in this public than in any other public.

Conclusion

This chapter considered the academic debate regarding media effects. The following kinds of questions have been considered: To what extent do studies support the fears of government and industry leaders? and Are media as powerful as they presume? If not, then what are some of the mediating factors that tilt the balance away from a powerful effects model of media influence?

This book began and ends with a discussion of academic discourse in the areas of public opinion and media effects. While recognizing that the debate exists, this book has taken a more pragmatic stance. The fact is that the overwhelming majority of CEOs have ignored or dismissed the academic discourse as irrelevant to their day-to-day survival in a media-saturated world. Similarly, politicians and bureaucrats do not contribute to the political philosophical debate over whether governments should listen to public opinion. Like Machiavelli, they do not believe that they have a choice. Taking this perspective as a given, this book addressed some of the ways in which political and corporate leaders cope with their fears of media influence. The question that they seek to answer is not "if" but "how." How can they best monitor and analyze the views of key publics? From what sources should they collect information? Which methodologies offer the best opportunities to answer different kinds of questions? This book has offered tools for undertaking this task. The audience for this book will be those who believe that the citizens have a role to play in government, that media have a potentially powerful impact on their opinions, and that new-age organizations will be best equipped to function in a new millennium if they seek to understand these opinion environments. As discussed previously, however, this audience will probably perceive itself to be more vulnerable to the effects of media influence than is actually the case.

Appendix A

Communications Environment Analysis Report (October 1992)

An Analysis of Issues and Trends in Alcohol and Substance Abuse

Distributed by: Canada's Drug Strategy Secretariat

Prepared by: Mary Metcalfe, Envirocomm Communications Consulting

Environment

"We'll just have to build bigger band-aids if we don't change the way we do things."

> Danni Boyd
> Saskatchewan Alcohol and Drug Abuse Commission

"We are paying for addiction in the most expensive ways possible—through our health budget, through corrections, through difficulties in our schools."

> Paul Welsh, Executive Director
> Rideauwood Institute, Ottawa

"Une loi qui autoriserait la vente d'alcool la nuit dans les dépanneurs contredirait la volonté gouvernementale de favoriser la santé et le bien-être de la population."

> M. Réal Morin, Spokesperson
> DSC, Québec

Facts and Figures

- Some 15% of all work accidents are linked to alcohol or drugs. (Source: *Montreal Gazette*)
- The annual dollar cost to Canada of substance abuse is in the order of $25 billion. (Source: Conference Board of Canada)
- Alcohol or drug abuse is a factor in about 18% of industrial accidents causing permanent disability. (Source: MacMillan Bloedal, Ltd.)

Environment

The constitutional discussions and resulting referendum overtook much of the media agenda in all regions over the summer months and into the fall. As a result, economic and social issues in many regions were either pushed into the background or became entangled in the public and media debates over constitutional matters.

The economic crunch facing the health care system throughout Canada is, in the view of many field specialists, bringing about a vigorous look at ideas and approaches first broached during the 1970s. Cross-treatment concepts, for example, are being revived as regions and communities come face-to-face with limited human and financial resources and an increased ability to identify at-risk and high-risk individuals and groups.

Chronic Unemployment, Limited Economic
Prospects, and Consumption Patterns . . .

Continuing economic hardship and chronic unemployment in many areas of the country, for example, is raising concern among a number of addictions specialists that there will be noticeably increased demands on drug dependency services in the near future, at a time when funding and resources are already straining to meet demand. Pointing to historical trends, some specialists are concerned that prolonged unemployment and limited alternatives will lead to increased consumption and abuse, along with increased family dysfunction and violence, particularly in smaller rural and isolated communities.

Specific problems, such as the provincewide fishery crisis in Newfoundland and major crop losses in the prairie provinces, may further aggravate an already fragile situation in the many smaller communities in those provinces. In Newfoundland, for example, where the fisheries have been cut dramatically, there is concern that the province may see overall unemployment rates rise to levels not seen since the Depression. In Saskatchewan, where the bulk of the grain crops were damaged by storms and early snow, many communities are seen to be at greater risk than in the past.

At the same time, there is concern that while a major shift to community-based ownership and action on drug and alcohol abuse issues has occurred, community organizations and volunteers need stronger support than is yet available. While there is strong agreement that community-based approaches offer very strong returns, the base of trained and experienced resources which are needed are not yet available and won't be for some time in the view of many specialists across the country. Training and the need to develop information resources for secondary prevention remain priorities in the area of community development.

Public Health Versus Public Revenues

Differences between public health policies, government revenue considerations, and even potential requirements under international trade agreements have been raised by some specialists and have been present for many months in media coverage of federal and provincial budgets which raise "sin taxes." With all governments giving high priority to reducing long-term health care costs through health promotion policies, other areas within those governments continue to rely heavily on the revenues generated by the sale of alcohol and tobacco and on potential increases in revenues through extended access. At a time when health promotion efforts and high prices are being credited with reducing public demand and consumption, moves to lower prices or expand access are viewed as counterproductive and contradictory.

For example, after months of near silence across the province of Québec on nonenforcement-related alcohol and substance abuse issues, a plan by the province to allow 7-day a week, 24-hour sales of beer and wine is meeting strong opposition from the network of hospital community health departments in the province. The province's 34 *Départements de santé communautaire du Québec (DSC)*, with support from a wide range of organizations including the Québec nursing association, the Montréal police, the municipalities of Hull, Gatineau, and Thurso, and the Women's Centres of Québec, have roundly condemned the proposal. According to the DSC, the plan directly contradicts a provincial policy announced in June to reduce alcohol consumption in the province by 15% over the next 10 years. There are also major concerns that expanding availability will increase violence, drinking while driving, drinking by young people, and will aggravate addictions. In Hull, for example, a major effort is under way to have bars closed earlier than the current 3 a.m. closing policy as one way to reduce the significant incidences of rowdyism, violence, and injuries along that city's downtown bar strip. The municipal police force estimates that almost half of their enforcement activities are linked to alcohol.

At the national level, there is also concern that current negotiations on interprovincial barriers to trade and trade with the United States may ultimately affect consumption and, in turn, demand for treatment and rehabilitation services. If prices of beverage alcohol products, particularly beer, are driven down as a result of reduced trade barriers, for example, there is concern that consumption may increase. The potential for lower prices, combined with chronic unemployment and limited prospects in many communities across the country are considered significant factors in increased consumption.

At the root of these concerns is a belief that more discussion and coordination is required in the development of agreements which may require arms-length compliance. Federal and international agreements could, it is believed, ultimately commit the provinces to respond in ways that may run counter to their health objectives. Within provinces, it is believed that increasing accessibility is undermining health policies.

Environment—Cont'd

"We believe in a maximum deterrent. We are more concerned at being tough on the first-time user than we are geared to rehabilitation."
Gil Stein, President, NHL

"It would be more positive for the (NHL) league to consider rehabilitation first, rather than focussing entirely on punishing offending players."
Editorial, *Hamilton Spectator*

"Faut comprendre que les règlements rétrogrades de la Ligue nationale ne favorisent pas le dialogue."
Jean Perron, Former Coach, Montreal Canadiens

Drugs in Sport

The death of NHL hockey player John Kordic from a combination of alcohol, cocaine, and steroid abuse touched off an unprecedented spectrum of media coverage and commentary. Amateur and professional teams throughout the country responded to media and public questions about player use of steroids, alcohol, and drugs and team policies to deal with abuse. The player's death touched off a national controversy in the media over the extent of drug use, with some favouring strong deterrents for the many sports and players who are considered role models for young people. Others favor a combination of deterrents, education, and access to treatment and rehabilitation, citing the enormous pressures and financial enticements given to relatively immature young people. For the most part, however, the issue of alcohol use or abuse by athletes has not been raised. The substance abuse issue in sports accounted for a significant portion of overall media coverage of substance abuse issues in the 3 months under review.

Education and Prevention

"We avoid negative messages or approaches like the plague. Negative messages simply titillate and make for good media coverage but they do not affect people. Positive messaging is a slow process but a very hopeful one."

> Kevin McPherson
> N.S. Drug Dependency Commission

"Scare tactics have gone out the window. The focus is on providing good drug information and decision-making information from a very early age and putting the issues forward in a way that is appropriate to the age."

> Beverley Clark
> Drug Dependency Service
> Newfoundland and Labrador

Education and Prevention

There has long been consensus among those in education and prevention that positive messages and even humor are effective in educating people about various substance abuse issues. There is also consensus that scare tactics and negative admonitions will not work in primary prevention programs, particularly with young people. Despite this, however, well-meaning organizations, with the support of some boards of education, continue to develop primary prevention approaches which include the display of coffins and body bags to grade school children. As well, some television public service announcements continue to promote fear messages to young people.

Defining Risk

While the risk factor approach to identifying at-risk populations continues to predominate, some specialists are beginning to consider "resiliency factors" as influences on people who would generally be considered at-risk and yet maintain a healthy lifestyle free of dependency. The relative importance of factors such as community support networks, strong cultural values, positive role models, and family cohesiveness is, some research is suggesting, an area for future consideration.

Cultural Diversity Is Creating a Need for
Adaptive Approaches and Information . . .

The increasing presence of a wide variety of ethnic groups in many Canadian communities is creating new demands for information, approaches, and resources. With thousands of children entering the Canadian school system, with neither English nor French as their first or second language, mainstream school alcohol and drug awareness programs are not necessarily adequate, according to many in the field. Added to this is the inability of many immigrant parents to even begin to relate to some of the issues being raised with their children in school, particularly where their culture traditionally forbids or sanctions use of, for example, alcohol. With the combined pressures to meet parental expectations, fit into a Canadian youth culture, and the added pressures of adapting to a new country, there is growing concern that a generation of ethnic youth and their parents will require specialized approaches and information.

Fetal Alcohol Syndrome

"Many (people) do not yet link alcohol consumption during pregnancy with possible life-long damage to their children."
> Hon. Benoit Bouchard
> Minister, Health and Welfare Canada

"There's eventually going to need to be a case here. Someone like that (pregnant and abusing alcohol) has to have her rights infringed upon."
> Dr. C. Ferguson, Director
> Winnipeg Child Protection Centre

Fetal Alcohol Syndrome/Fetal Alcohol Effect: An Expanding Issue

While still not an issue in the vast majority of media, the incidence and impacts of fetal alcohol syndrome (FAS) and fetal alcohol effect (FAE) are gaining stronger recognition among addictions specialists, family physicians, community health workers, and others working with or treating at-risk and addicted women. The initial groundwork for bringing the issue to the public policy level is being credited to grassroots efforts. However, there is growing recognition among specialists that federal action, particularly through a House of Commons committee report and a recent symposium in B.C., is rapidly expanding awareness of the issue among professionals.

The emergence of FAS/FAE as a public health policy issue is expected to lead to an initial concentration on training for workers throughout the health care spectrum on identification of high-risk and at-risk individuals; development of effective approaches for secondary and tertiary prevention; and development of materials for education, prevention, and intervention. At present, it is believed that most professionals and community support groups do not have some of the basic information which will be required to address these issues effectively. This health issue is also generating some debate among child care workers and health care professionals over the legal rights and responsibilities of at-risk pregnant women and the future role the courts may play in ordering treatment.

Treatment and Rehabilitation

Even as community-based approaches are becoming the preferred method, there is concern amongst treatment specialists that developing skills in program management, administration, and policy development will need strong support and nurturing from provincial and federal levels over a period of years. As one community development specialist observed, "people may think community development skills come naturally and they don't. People need time to learn how to deal with resources, budgets, conflicts, policies, and community lobbying for support." Another noted that "communities need to have an array of resources at hand when an individual finally recognizes they need help. That includes access to treatment, counseling services for the individual and family, referrals, social support, and so much more. And, not 3 weeks or 3 months from now."

Treatment and Rehabilitation

"We are now seeing families who use solvents recreationally. It's not new, but if we haven't been able to influence their use and behavior then we're talking about intergenerational abuse. How do we deal with those issues?"
Danni Boyd
Saskatchewan Alcohol and Drug Abuse Commission

"Substance abuse, or glue-sniffing or gasoline-sniffing, is one of the biggest problems facing kids right now."
Alex Guy, Chair, Board of Directors
Ranch Ehrio Society, Saskatchewan

Isolated Communities at Risk

The existing levels of alcohol and solvent abuse in some isolated and native communities is a continuing issue for addictions workers, particularly in the West and the Territories. With a range of severe social and economic problems, including inadequate housing and community services, and unemployment as high as 95% in some communities, solvent abuse, for example, is often a way of coping with a painful and seemingly hopeless life for the children, youth, and adults who are affected.

The spectrum of social and economic problems surrounding solvent abuse has made efforts to either treat or prevent it difficult, particularly in those communities where there is widespread and intergenerational abuse. While solvent abuse also exists in urban centers and among all socioeconomic levels of youth, its concentration in some isolated communities is of particular concern. Efforts are continuing to identify those at-risk and to find or develop appropriate intervention and treatment approaches. It is an issue which is raising many questions and one where needs assessment, policy development, and community education and training are still a priority.

There is clear recognition among addictions workers that culturally appropriate and community-based approaches work best in all areas of substance abuse. For example, in the Yukon, the 13 communities of the territory, some primarily native and others primarily nonnative or a mixture, have each developed their own specific action plans for dealing with prevention and treatment. This community-based approach is also well-established in the NWT.

In Saskatchewan, native groups are working with the province to develop a framework for addressing children's issues, including addictions services plus health and education. This community-based focus is becoming entrenched as the best approach to dealing with a spectrum of social and economic issues, of which addiction is only one aspect.

Enforcement and Control

The proceeds of crime issue may be raising expectations about the amount of money which may ultimately be available for sharing with provinces, municipalities, or police forces involved in investigating cases. There is some concern that a media and public belief may be developing that the disposition of the proceeds of crime may bring millions of dollars in revenue to governments at different levels. Observers note, however, that seized property and assets must be retained and managed until a case is completed, which may take years and involve major costs.

Some media reports also have not made clear the distinction between assets and the value of seized drugs. In Winnipeg, for example, a reporter covering the record seizure of marijuana worth over $2.5 million left the impression that the drugs seized could eventually be a source of funds for the local police force.

Enforcement and Control

"Cash-starved municipalities here, as in other provinces, can put to good use their portion of the seized assets."
Editorial, *Halifax Chronicle-Herald*

"It's no secret the city's short of money and they'll take it where they can get it."
Ray Johns, Vice Inspector
Winnipeg

"We care enough about fair competition in sports to make athletes submit to drug-testing—we should be even more concerned when it comes to public safety."
Editorial, *Welland-Port Colborne Tribune*

"The maintenance of public safety would surely be a circumstance justifying such an invasion of privacy (as drug testing)."
Editorial, *London Free Press*

"Ottawa should ban these U.S.-inspired programs instead of waiting for them to be eventually struck down by the courts."
Editorial, *Toronto Star*

The Continuing Media Controversy Over Drug Testing

While not part of Canada's Drug Strategy, the issue of drug testing in private workplaces, government-regulated industries, prisons, and among athletes is still a subject of controversy in media circles, primarily in Ontario. A recent Ontario Law Reform Commission report, for example, recommended that no testing of employees be allowed, on the basis of quotations related to reliability of testing and potential infringement of individual rights, prompting a spate of editorials endorsing the recommendations. While there is no blanket support for workplace testing in public statements and editorials, there is qualified support for testing for those in safety sensitive positions.

International Cooperation

International gang activity is being blamed for the increasing volumes of drugs being smuggled into Canada. As William LeDrew, Director General, Canada Customs Enforcement reported: "We had more cocaine smuggled into Canada in the last 12 months than we had in the last 10 years." At the same time, enforcement officials and coroners have found that the purity of the drugs has also increased, to a point where there has been a noticeable jump in deaths by overdose in Toronto and Vancouver, particularly with heroin.

Of special concern to the enforcement community are organized Asian gangs, which are involved in the production, distribution, and smuggling of heroin. Those close to the issue have been careful to stress that the majority of Asian immigrants are law-abiding citizens. Representatives from within Asian communities in Canada have noted that the gangs are everyone's problem and that cooperation and sharing of information is needed to combat the situation.

Canada has been actively involved with multilateral organizations such as the Caribbean Customs Law Enforcement Council, which includes the United States. Aimed at increasing international cooperation, Canada is assisting with training and development of communications networks.

Coming Soon . . .

- *The Jamais Seul*/Never Alone organization in Québec will launch a permanent television, radio, school, and transit campaign in the spring of 1993, with funding assistance from Canada's Drug Strategy.

- The *Elks Society of Canada* is finalizing a drug awareness campaign which it hopes will involve all member lodges across Canada. The group acts as a resource organization helping other community groups stage drug and alcoholism awareness workshops.

- *The Ranch Ehrlo Society,* with sponsorship from the Rotary Clubs of Regina, will have its substance abuse treatment and rehabilitation program portrayed in a video for use by service clubs and the health industry. The film is expected to be available in mid-1993.

- *The Alcoholism Foundation of Manitoba* recently completed a technical handbook for physicians on chemical abuse, including diagnosis of alcohol abuse among pregnant women. The *Physician's Handbook: A Guide to Chemical Abuse and Dependency, Diagnosis, Treatment and Referral* by A. Hynes, MB, and F. D. Corner, MB, can be made available for reproduction at your cost.

- *Alcohol and Drug Programs of B.C.* is releasing its "Thanks for Caring" information resource package aimed at preventing fetal alcohol syndrome and fetal alcohol effect. This low literacy package includes an awareness raising component, an interactive calendar, appointment cards with healthy recipes, fridge magnets, etc. The intent is to encourage at-risk women to seek health care and to make healthy choices through support and reinforcement.

- A 3-year study now under way with family physicians in Cambridge, Ontario, may help doctors to identify early warning signs of alcohol abuse. Conducted by the *Addiction Research Foundation,* with funding from the Ontario government and the U.S. National Institutes of Health, the 32 family physicians are asking patients to fill in a questionnaire regarding recent accidents. Studies have shown that half of nonfatal falls are related to alcohol.

- Report of the *Vodrey Commission* task force on community issues and concerns about drugs and alcohol in Manitoba is expected in late fall.

Contributors to the Environmental Scan

Health and Welfare Canada

M. Gaston Pelletier
Québec Region Communications

Mr. Pat Brownlow
Maritime Region Communications

Mr. Ken Horseman
Health Promotion Directorate
Prairie Region

Ms. Carole Legge
Health Promotion Directorate
Western Region

Federal Departments/Agencies

Ms. Amanda Maltby
External Affairs

Mr. Michel Perron
Customs and Excise

Ms. Helen Banulescu
Solicitor General

Staff Sgt. Michel Pelletier
RCMP

Mr. Andrew McGillivray
Department of Justice

Provincial Agencies

Ms. Heather MacPherson
Addiction Services of P.E.I.

Mr. Kevin MacPherson/Brian Wilbur
Nova Scotia Commission on Drug Dependency

Ms. Beverley Clark
Alcohol and Drug Dependency Commission of Newfoundland and
    Labrador

Ms. Gina Atkinson
Alcohol and Drug Consultant

Health and Community Services
Government of New Brunswick

Dr. Howard Cappell
Addiction Research Foundation of Ontario

Mr. Dave Kennedy
Alcoholism Foundation of Manitoba

Ms. Danni Boyd
Saskatchewan Alcohol and Drug Abuse Commission

Mr. Len Blumenthal
Alberta Alcohol and Drug Abuse Commission

Mr. Michael Egilson
Alcohol and Drug Programs of B.C.

Mr. John Campbell
Alcohol, Drug and Community Health Services of NWT

Ms. Charlotte Hrenchuck
Yukon Health Services

Information Sources

A great number of large- to small-circulation Canadian daily newspapers, community newspapers, news magazines, and consumer magazines representing a complete cross section of Canadian cities and communities were consulted in the preparation of this report. Other resources consulted included:

Addiction Services of Prince Edward Island, Annual Report 1990-1991

National Drug Intelligence Estimates

Ontario Medicine

Profiles, Alberta Alcohol and Drug Addiction Commission

Social and Health Indicators Profile, AADAC

The newsletter of the Addiction Research Foundation

Speeches, news releases, statements, brochures, and clippings from organizations contributing to this report

Appendix B

Media Analysis
The Debate Over Genetically Modified Organisms
by Aline Michaud

Introduction

This analysis focuses on recent media coverage of issues pertaining to genetically modified organisms (GMOs). The term GMOs refers to food products to which DNA of other organisms (often other species) has been added to provide added benefits. The topic of GMOs has been raised in the media with increasing frequency during the past few months.

The debate surrounding GMOs is multidimensional, involving health, commercial, trade, technological, political, and environmental issues. As the media coverage reveals, these dimensions are interconnected, although the issue of food safety and consumer health underlies all expressed concerns. The Department of Health, which oversees policy and regulatory issues relating to the health of Americans, is a key stakeholder in the current debate.

The period studied encompasses September and October 1999. Six major daily newspapers were scanned for articles on GMOs: the *Chicago Sun-Times,* the *Los Angeles Times,* the *New York Times,* the *Seattle Monitor,* the *Miami Herald,* and the *New Orleans Times-Picayune.* A total of 74 articles were identified and examined for this analysis. Half of the articles were business and news stories, one fourth were opinion (editorial, column, etc.), and one fourth were letters to the editor (Figures B.1 and B.2).

The Framing of GMOs as an International Trade and Cultural Story

In the period under analysis, the GMO story surfaced chiefly as a business item with a focus on trade issues involving North America and Europe. A

AUTHOR'S NOTE: The following media analysis was prepared by Aline Michaud, who is currently studying at the University of Ottawa. It is fictitious.

number of trade-related events spurred the coverage of GMOs, including United Nations-sponsored discussions in Vienna in September, the Seattle meeting of the World Trade Organization (WTO) scheduled for November, and an international meeting on biotechnology trade issues scheduled for January 2000 (Table B.1).

Agriculture in general is high on the agenda of these meetings, particularly that of the Seattle Ministerial, which marks the initiation of the second round of multiyear trade negotiations among WTO member countries. GMOs are expected to generate much attention on account of the enormous pressure exerted by European consumers on their governments. They have demanded that their governments reject GMOs, seen largely as the product of North American agribusiness giants such as Monsanto. American farmers have much at stake in this debate as well.

As a trade story, the issue has international dimensions. The issue has been prominent for more than 2 years in Japan and Europe, with growing public opposition to food imports from North America. On the issue of food safety, the Europeans have shown either distrust or disregard for the scientific arguments and reassurances voiced in favor of GMOs. As one commentator observed, "Europeans believe less than North Americans in the unquestioned benefits of science" (*Los Angeles Times,* October 19, 1999). Anti-GMO activism in Britain is so fervent that protesters have been destroying GMO test crops. While Americans call for more testing and information, Europeans have mounted a strong movement to ban GMOs altogether.

In addition to concerns expressed about food safety, some European countries such as France have objected to the "Americanization" of food. In other words, they have framed the story as a cultural issue. Some commentators see the emergence of this highly charged cultural argument as thinly veiled trade protectionism. Others argue, however, that science alone should be the basis for restrictions in trade. One of the strongest fears, voiced both by proponents of GMOs and those who call for more testing and information, is that the European backlash will ricochet in North America, to the detriment not only of agricultural and commercial concerns, but also of the current and future benefits this area of technology holds for consumers.

Catalysts Driving Domestic Coverage of GMOs

In the period under analysis, the catalysts for domestic media coverage were the following. The ordering reflects the extent to which the events were able to generate publicity (Table B.1):

TABLE B.1 Catalysts, Ranked by Frequency of Mentions

Catalyst	Date	Count
American Health Coalition/200 federal scientists speaking out	October 17, 1999	7
Upcoming WTO ministerial meeting in Seattle	End of November, 1999	6
Article in *Nature* journal	October 7, 1999	4
David Suzuki speaking out	October 17, 1999	4
Monsanto "cave-in"	October 5, 1999	4
NGO coalition campaign	September 1999	3
Monarch butterfly death publicity	Spring 1999	3
European backlash against GMOs	Recent months	2
Breakdown of United Nations trade talks in Vienna	September 1999	2
Gerber and Heinz baby food cave-in	Recent months	2
Bill 311 put on hold	October 19, 1999	2
Japan requiring GMO labeling: Brewers banning GMO corn	Recent months	1
Biotechnology meeting in January 2000	January 2000	1

1. Oppositional statements by the American Health Coalition, which includes 200 scientists and technicians employed by the Health Protection Branch, Department of Health

2. An article published in *Nature*, a reputable science journal, that was critical of GMO

3. The public criticism of GMOs by David Suzuki

4. The decision by Monsanto not to pursue a test seed dubbed the "terminator"

5. An NGO campaign, which generated much coverage

6. The Monarch butterfly death

7. The decision of Gerber and Heinz to eliminate GMOs from baby food

8. The decision to put Bill 311 on hold

The Positioning of Stakeholders and Opinion Leaders

Stakeholders in the debate over GMOs can be divided along the lines of anti- or pro-GMO forces, with NGOs and consumer groups (particularly in Europe) on the "anti" side, and government, industry, and farmers on the "pro" side. Industry includes agribusinesses, food manufacturers, grocery chains, biotechnology companies, biodiversity action networks, and food associations.

The scientific community appears to be divided between the two camps, with opinion leaders such as David Suzuki, Lenny Nelson (spokesperson for the American Food Ethics Council), and Michelle Foster (spokesperson for Department of Health employees) speaking against GMOs and a range of other scientists and scientific organizations speaking in favor of their use.

Lobby groups have also played an influential role. For example, a coalition of nongovernmental organizations launched a public awareness campaign. These NGOs included Greenpeace (the most frequently cited stakeholder), the American Food Ethics Council, the American Health Coalition, and the Millennium Club. Spearheading the NGO campaign has been environmental activist Doug Ellis. The NGO campaign has aimed to get consumers to vote against GMOs with their shopping dollars.

The most prominent journalists speaking out on the topic include Jenepher Tetreault, a business reporter for the *New York Times,* Nancy Cobb of the *New York Times,* Jeremy Best with the *Seattle Monitor,* and Milton Steel, a columnist with the *Los Angeles Times.* (See Tables B.2 and B.3 for a more complete list of stakeholders and opinion leaders.)

In general, discussions have been highly polarized, with a tendency toward the negative: 57% of the articles have argued that GMOs are not safe, 32% have contended that GMOs are safe, and 20% have been either neutral (taking no position) or balanced (showing both sides) (Figure B.1).

Dominant Consumer Concerns

The NGO campaign has focused attention primarily on the safety of GMOs with respect to human health and the environment. For example, the campaign criticized the proposed *Food Safety and Inspection Act,* known as Bill 311, sponsored by the Departments of Health and Agricultural Services.

All six newspapers reported this criticism. Three carried the response of the secretary of health, who defended his departmental policy. Another spokesperson for the department, however, undermined the credibility of this statement when he provided contradictory information. Readers may have been left with the perception that there is confusion, if not mutiny, within the department.

In addition to food safety, other issues raised in the 74 articles can be grouped under need for information, testing and regulating, and labeling (Figure B.2). The mass public has been clamoring for more information and testing, as well as for greater debate on the issue of GMOs and regulations.

TABLE B.2 Stakeholders, Ranked by Frequency of Mentions

Stakeholder	Mentions
Greenpeace	21
Agribusiness companies such as Monsanto	15
Farmers and farmers' organizations	14
Scientific community	12
American public/consumers	12
Food Ethics Council	10
200 employees of Health Protection Branch, Department of Health	9
WTO countries	6
Other	6
Agricultural Services (and/or its secretary)	5
American Health Coalition	5
Millennium Club	5
European public/consumers	5
Media	5
Department of Health (and/or its secretary)	4
Other NGOs	4
Other industry organizations	4
Biotechnology companies or groups	4
Federal government (in general)	3
Grocery chains	3
Food manufacturers	2

TABLE B.3 Opinion Leaders, Ranked by Frequency of Mentions

Opinion Leader	Mentions
David Suzuki	10
Greenpeace representatives	8
Jenepher Tetreault (*New York Times*)	8
American Food Ethics Council (Jenny Nelson)	5
Prince Charles	3
Financial analysts, including Deutsche Bank	3
Jeremy Best (*Seattle Monitor*)	3
Milton Steel (*Los Angeles Times*)	3
Nancy Cobb (*New York Times*)	3
Paul McCartney	2
Nature magazine	2
Doug Ellis (environmental activist)	2
Michelle Foster (former employee of Health Protection Branch)	2
Employees of Health Protection Branch who wrote to Secretary of Health	2
Jimmy Carter	1

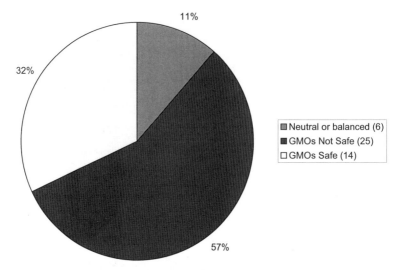

Figure B.1. References to Issues, by Number of Articles

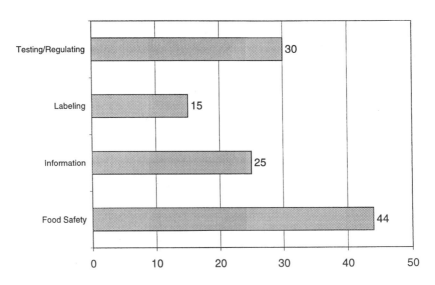

Figure B.2. What is it?

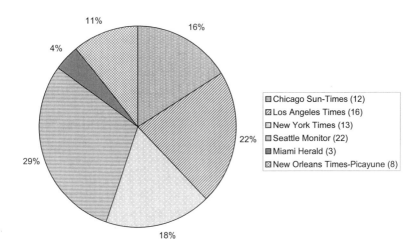

Figure B.3. Number of Articles For and Against Labeling, Expressed in Percentages

People say that they need to believe that what they feed their families every day is nutritious and safe.

In general, most media coverage suggested overwhelming support for labeling. For example, 81% of the articles included in this analysis argued in favor of labeling (Figure B.3). Many advocates simply say they want to know what their food contains. Several articles, however, suggested that existing GMO crops already may have contaminated other crops. On the other side of the debate, some industry detractors argue that if labeling becomes mandatory, eventually it will include all foods that have been subject to "genetic manipulation" (in other words, almost everything we eat). GMOs appear in as much as 60% to 70% of staple products such as potatoes, soy beans, and canola.

Farmers, strong proponents of GMOs, believe that these products offer distinct advantages over their unmodified counterparts. They do not understand why the public do not see the advantages, and a few blame "the government" for not doing its job in informing the public. Because the majority of crops currently planted in the United States do contain GMO seed, the issue that preoccupies farmers is the potential loss of business. For that reason, a growing number of farmers are preparing for the need to label, or worse, for a lack of demand for GMO products. Some have begun to segregate their GMO crops from their non-GMO crops, while others consider the same actions.

Some have translated the problem into a marketing opportunity in the non-GMO niche, and they are gearing up for "organic" farming.

The same issue looms for the agribusiness giants, several of whom have already started to lose share value because of negative publicity surrounding their GMO products. Indeed, some financial analysts, including Deutsche Bank, have advised their clients to "sell." At least two makers of baby food (Heinz and Gerber) have also heeded calls to eliminate GMOs. The decision of Monsanto not to market the "terminator" seed concerned not product safety, but commercial monopoly. The seed in question was genetically programmed for infertility after the initial growth season. Farmer groups rebelled, and at least one litigation resulted.

Critics have dubbed such decisions as a "cave-in" to scaremongerers, who have their own agendas. Milton Steel of the *Los Angeles Times* says that GMO crops are not only safe, but have advantages over non-GMOs: They require fewer pesticides, have higher productivity, and are subject to less crop disease. He talks about the danger of losing out on such benefits if GMOs are banned or if the public is afraid to buy them. "Irrational" fear, he argues, may undermine present and future technological advances. More than one commentator railed against the use of scare tactics to oppose science, while several of the articles made a reference to what may be described as a difference in ideologies. One writer characterized the problem as a battle between "technophiles and technophobes." Whatever the case, the decision to make labeling mandatory, whether taken by the Department of Health or by Agricultural Services, can probably not be delayed much longer.

The debate over labeling of food products with GMOs is taking place only on this side of the ocean. The debate has ended in Europe, where consumers successfully pressured the European Union to make labeling mandatory. The Japanese followed the British example in responding to consumer demands for labeling, and brewers in that country have banned the use of GMO corn. Demands for labeling in Canada are shared by proponents and detractors alike, despite concerns over decreased demand for the products. (The European experience demonstrates that people refuse to buy products containing GMOs.)

Messages Carried in the Media

A primary purpose of this analysis was to ascertain whether the three preferred messages of the Department of Health were carried in the media, namely, (a) the priority of the department is the health of American consumers and the safety of their food supply; (b) the Department of Health ensures, through testing and regulatory controls, that GMOs are safe; and (c) the Department of Health responds effectively to the public's need for information about GMOs and their safety.

There is some doubt as to whether the second and the third messages emerged in this media coverage. Rather, the perception is that not enough is known about GMOs to ensure their safety and that the public is not being given sufficient information about GMOs. In particular, the public wants to know which foods contain GMOs and which do not. They expect the government to provide this information.

Nonetheless, some more specific government messages on the topic of GMOs did emerge. For example, two newspapers uncritically reported the government's decision to put the proposed food safety bill on hold. They also carried the message that health bureaucrats are absolutely confident of the soundness of the country's food testing and regulatory systems. At the same time, government representatives understand the need for more consultation.

In the time period examined, the Department of Health was not directly mentioned until more than halfway through the period (October 8), although many references to "the government" occurred. In the 19 days of coverage that followed the first mention, however, the department was named in one out of three articles that talked about GMOs. The department and its secretary became the central story in the last week or so. If the analysis had continued past October 27, many more references would probably have appeared, as this is an evolving issue that requires close monitoring.

Questions About Roles: Who Owns the Issue?

For the Department of Health, a key issue is the role it should be playing in relationship to Agricultural Services, a second government stakeholder. The latter came under strong criticism because it is perceived to be in conflict of interest vis-à-vis its regulatory responsibility for GMOs and its role as promoter of American agricultural products that include GMOs.

Driving the debate over conflict of interest was publicity generated by the American Health Coalition, as well as the related petition signed by the 200 employees of the Health Protection Branch of the Department of Health. The proposed Bill 311 would entrench the 1990 transfer of responsibility for policing food safety from the Department of Health to the American Food Inspection Agency, which reports to the Secretary of Agricultural Services. The American Health Coalition and Department of Health employees have demanded that the inspection function be reassigned to the Department of Health. Some believe that the political decision to put the bill on hold offers the time for the two government departments to put their houses in order.

The issue of exactly who is responsible for the testing—the federal government or industry—remains unclear and compounds the perception of conflict of interest. Whatever the case, the sense is that the government should be doing more.

References

Aguilar, F. J. (1967). *Scanning the business environment.* New York: Macmillan.

Althaus, S. (1996). Opinion polls, information effects, and political equality: Exploring ideological biases in collective opinion. *Political Communication, 13,* 3-21.

Anderson, D. S. (1992). Identifying and responding to activist publics: A case study. *Journal of Public Relations Research, 4*(3), 151-165.

Ansoff, H. I. (1975). Managing strategic surprise through response to weak signals. *California Management Review, 18*(2), 21-33.

Aristotle. (1962). *The politics of Aristotle* (E. Barker, Trans.). New York: Oxford University Press.

Arundell, E. M. (1988). The publics of public affairs. In W. J. Wright & C. J. DuVernet (Eds.), *The Canadian public affairs handbook: Maximizing markets, protecting bottom lines* (pp. 21-60). Toronto: Carswell.

Asher, H. (1988). *Polling and the public.* Washington, DC: Congressional Quarterly Press.

Atkin, C. K., & Freimuth, V. (1989). Formative evaluation research in campaign design. In R. E. Rice & C. K. Atkin (Eds.), *Public communication campaigns* (pp. 131-150). Newbury Park, CA: Sage.

Axelrod, M. D. (1975, March 15). Ten essentials for good qualitative research. *Marketing News,* p. 11.

Babbie, E. (1990). *Survey research methods* (2nd ed.). Belmont, CA: Wadsworth.

Backer, T. E., Rogers, E. M., & Sopory, P. (1992). *Designing health communication campaigns: What works?* Newbury Park, CA: Sage.

Baker, R., & Ball, S. (Eds.). (1969). *Violence and the media.* Washington, DC: Government Printing Office.

263

Barbour, R. S., & Kitzinger, J. (1998). *Developing focus group research*. London: Sage.

Barker, D. C. (1998). Rush to action: Political talk radio and health care (un)reform. *Political Communication, 15*, 83-97.

Barthes, R. (1988). *The semiotic challenge*. New York: Hill & Wang.

Baskin, O., & Aronoff, C. (1992). *Public relations: The profession and the practice* (3rd ed.). Dubuque, IA: William C. Brown.

Bate, B. (1988). *Communication and the sexes*. New York: Harper & Row.

Bauman, S., & Herbst, S. (1994). Managing perceptions of public opinion: Candidates' and journalists' reactions to the 1992 polls. *Political Communication, 11*(2), 133-144.

Becker, H. P. (1930, November). Distribution of space in the *American Journal of Sociology*, 1895-1927. *American Journal of Sociology*, pp. 461-466.

Becker, H. P. (1932, July). Space apportioned forty-eight topics in the *American Journal of Sociology*, 1895-1930. *American Journal of Sociology*, pp. 71-78.

Benne, K., & Sheats, P. (1948). Functional roles of group members. *Journal of Social Issues, 4*, 41-49.

Bennis, W. (1976). *The unconscious conspiracy: Why leaders can't lead*. New York: AMACOM.

Bentham, J. (1890). *Theory of legislation* (R. Hildreth, Trans.). London: Trubner.

Benton, J. E. (1991). A question order effect in a local government survey. *Public Opinion Quarterly, 55*(4), 640-642.

Berelson, B. (1949). What "missing" the newspaper means. In P. F. Lazarsfeld & F. N. Stanton (Eds.), *Communications research 1948-1949* (pp. 111-129). New York: Harper.

Berelson, B. (1952). *Content analysis in communications research*. Glencoe, IL: Free Press.

Berg, B. L. (1995). *Qualitative research methods for the social sciences*. Boston: Allyn & Bacon.

Berger, A. A. (1991). *Media research techniques*. Newbury Park, CA: Sage.

Berger, J. (1972). *Ways of seeing: The language of advertising 4* [Videotape]. London: British Broadcasting Corporation.

Berger, P., & Luckmann, T. (1967). *The social construction of reality*. Garden City, NY: Doubleday/Anchor.

Bertalanffy, L. Von. (1968). *General systems theory*. New York: Braziller. (Original work published 1937)

Bishop, G., Oldendick, R. W., Tuchfarber, A. J., & Bennett, S. E. (1980). Pseudo-opinions on public affairs. *Public Opinion Quarterly, 44*, 198-209.

Blumer, H. (1972). Symbolic interactionism: An approach to human communication. In R. W. Budd & B. Ruben (Eds.), *Approaches to human communication* (pp. 401-419). New York: Spartan.

Bogardus, E. (1926). The group interview. *Journal of Applied Sociology, 10*, 372-382.

Boorstin, D. J. (1961). *The image: A guide to pseudo events in America.* New York: Atheneum.

Borisoff, D., & Merrill, L. (1992). *The power to communicate: Gender differences as barriers* (2nd ed.). Prospect Heights, IL: Waveland.

Bourque, L. B., & Clark, V. A. (1992). *Processing data: The survey example.* Newbury Park, CA: Sage.

Bourque, L. B., & Fielder, E. P. (1995). *How to conduct self-administered and mail surveys.* Thousand Oaks, CA: Sage.

Brown, J. K. (1979). *This business of issues: Coping with the company's environments.* New York: The Conference Board.

Brown, S. (1980). *Political subjectivity: Applications of Q methodology in political science.* New Haven, CT: Yale University Press.

Brown, S. (1999). *The history and principles of Q methodology in psychology and the social sciences* (pp. 1-22) [On-line]. Available: *http://facstaff.uww.edu/cottlec/QArchive/13Bps. htm*

Bruner, J. (1941, July). The dimensions of propaganda: German shortwave broadcasts to America. *Journal of Abnormal Social Psychology,* pp. 311-337.

BT Organisational Development. (1997). *Focus groups: Involving employees creatively to influence decisions.* London: Industrial House.

Buchholz, R. A., Evans, W. D., & Wagley, R. A. (1985). *Management response to public issues: Concepts and cases in strategy formulation.* Englewood Cliffs, NJ: Prentice Hall.

Budd, R. W., Thorp, R. K., & Donohew, L. (1967). *Content analysis of communications.* New York: Macmillan.

Calder, B. J. (1977). Focus groups and the nature of qualitative marketing research. *Journal of Marketing Research, 14,* 353-364.

Cameron, G. T., & McCollum, T. (1993). Competing corporate cultures: A multi-method, cultural analysis of the role of internal communication. *Journal of Public Relations Research, 5*(4), 217-250.

Canada shackling some deportees: Banning of forcible sedation results in gagging of unwilling passengers. (1991, August 7). *The Globe & Mail,* p. A1.

Cannell, C. F., & Kahn, R. L. (1953). The collection of data by interviewing. In L. Festinger & D. Katz (Eds.), *Research methods in the behavioral sciences* (pp. 327-380). New York: Dryden.

Cantril, H. (1940). *The invasion from Mars: A study in the psychology of panic.* Princeton, NJ: Princeton University Press.

Carter, C., Branston, G., & Allan, S. (Eds.). (1998). *News, gender and power.* London: Routledge.

Cespedes, F. V. (1990). Agendas, incubators, and marketing organizations. *California Management Review, 33,* 27-53.

Chase, W. H. (1984). *Issues management: Origins of the future*. Stamford, CT: Issue Action.

Cleveland, H. (1985). The twilight of hierarchy: Speculations on the global information society. *Public Administration Review, 45*, 185-195.

Clogg, C. C., & Sawyer, D. O. (1981). A comparison of alternative models for analyzing the scalability of response patterns. In S. Leinhardt (Ed.), *Sociological methodology 1981* (pp. 240-280). San Francisco: Jossey-Bass.

Cobb, R., & Elder, C. (1983). *Participation in American politics*. Baltimore, MD: Johns Hopkins University Press.

Cohen, B. C. (1963). *The press and foreign policy*. Princeton, NJ: Princeton University Press.

Cohen, J. (1989). Deliberation and democratic legitimacy. In A. Hamlin & P. Pettit (Eds.), *The good polity: Normative analysis of the state* (pp. 17-34). New York: Basil Blackwell.

Cohen, J., & Davis, R. G. (1991). Third-person effects and the differential impact in negative political advertising. *Journalism Quarterly, 68*(4), 680-688.

Cohen, J., Mutz, D., Price, V., & Gunther, A. (1988). Perceived impact of defamation: An experiment on third-person effect. *Public Opinion Quarterly, 52*, 161-173.

Cohen, R. M. (Producer & Director), & Moyers, B. (Speaker). (1989). *Leading questions: The public mind 4* [Video cassette]. (1991). Toronto: Criterion Video.

Converse, J. M., & Presser, S. (1986). *Survey questions: Handcrafting the standardized questionnaire*. Beverly Hills, CA: Sage.

Converse, P. E. (1964). The nature of belief systems in mass publics. In D. Apter (Ed.), *Ideology and discontent*. New York: Free Press.

Crouse, T. (1972). *The boys on the bus: Riding with the campaign press corps*. New York: Random House.

Curran, J. (1977). Capitalism and control of the press, 1800-1975. In J. Curran, M. Gurevitch, & J. Woollacott (Eds.), *Mass communication and society*. London: Edward Arnold.

Curran, J. (1996a). Rethinking mass communications. In J. Curran, D. Morley, & V. Walkerdine (Eds.), *Cultural studies and communications* (pp. 119-165). London: Edward Arnold.

Curran, J. (1996b). The new revisionism in mass communication research: A reappraisal. In J. Curran, D. Morley, & V. Walkerdine (Eds.), *Cultural studies and communications* (pp. 256-278). London: Edward Arnold.

Curtin, P. A. (1999). Reevaluating public relations information subsidies: Market-driven journalism and agenda-building theory and practice. *Journal of Public Relations Research, 11*, 53-90.

Cutlip, S. M., Center, A. H., & Broom, G. M. (1994). *Effective public relations* (7th ed.). Englewood Cliffs, NJ: Prentice Hall.

Davidson, W. H. (1991). The role of global scanning in business planning. *Organizational Dynamics, 19,* 5-16.

Davis, K. (1953). Management communication and the grapevine. *Harvard Business Review, 31,* 43-49.

Davis, R. (1997). Introduction to understanding broadcast political talk. *Political Communication, 14*(3), 323-332.

Davis, S. (1995). The role of communication and symbolism in interest group competition: The case of the Siskiyou national forest, 1983-1992. *Political Communication Journal, 12,* 27-42.

Davison, W. P. (1983). The third-person effect in communication. *Public Opinion Quarterly, 47,* 1-15.

Day, G. S. (1992). Continuous learning about markets. *Planning Review, 20*(5), 47-49.

DeFleur, M. L., & Dennis, E. E. (1981). *Understanding mass communication.* Boston: Houghton Mifflin.

De Toqueville, A. (1957). *Democracy in America* (R. D. Heffner, Ed.). New York: Mentor Books.

Dozier, D. M., & Ehling, W. P. (1992). Evaluation of public relations programs: What the literature tells us about their effects. In J. E. Grunig (Ed.), *Excellence in public relations and communication management* (pp. 159-184). Hillsdale, NJ: Lawrence Erlbaum.

Dozier, D. M., Grunig, L. A., & Grunig, J. E. (1995). *Manager's guide to excellence in public relations and communication management.* Hillsdale, NJ: Lawrence Erlbaum.

Dozier, D. M., & Repper, F. C. (1992). Research firms and public relations practices. In J. E. Grunig (Ed.), *Excellence in public relations and communication management* (pp. 185-215). Hillsdale, NJ: Lawrence Erlbaum.

Durham, F. D. (1998). News frames as social narratives. TWA Flight 800. *Journal of Communication, 48*(4), 100-117.

Dyer, M. G. (1983). *In-depth understanding: A computer model of integrated processing of narrative comprehension.* Cambridge: MIT Press.

Dyer, S. C. (1996). Descriptive modeling for public relations scanning: A practitioner's perspective. *Journal of Public Relations Research, 8*(3), 137-150.

Easterlin, R. A., & Crimmins, E. M. (1991). Private materialism, personal self-fulfillment, family life, and public interest: The nature, effects, and causes of recent changes in the values of American youth. *Public Opinion Quarterly, 55*(4), 499-533.

Eaton, H., Jr. (1989). Agenda-setting with biweekly data on content of three national media. *Journalism Quarterly, 66*(4), 942-948, 959.

Eco, U. (1976). *A theory of semiotics.* Bloomington: Indiana University Press.

Edwards, J. E., Thomas, M. D., Rosenfeld, P., & Booth-Kewley, S. (1996). *How to conduct organizational surveys: A step-by-step guide.* Thousand Oaks, CA: Sage.

Ekman, P. (1985). *Telling lies: Clues to deceit in the marketplace, politics, and marriage.* New York: Norton.

Entman, R. M., & Rojecki, A. (1993). *Freezing out the public: Elite and media fram*

Enzer, S. (1989). *INTERAX: An interactive model for studying future business environments.* Berkeley: University of California, Graduate School of Business Administration, Center for Futures Research.

Ewing, R. P. (1980). Evaluating issues management. *Public Relations Journal, 36*(6), 14-16.

Ewing, R. P. (1987). *Managing the new bottom line: Issues management for senior executives.* New York: Dow Jones-Irwin.

Fahey, L., & King, W. R. (1977). Environmental scanning for corporate planning. *Business Horizons, 20*(4), 61-71.

Fan, D. P. (1988). *Predictions of public opinion from the mass media: Computer content analysis and mathematical modeling.* New York: Greenwood.

Ferguson, A. (1999, Spring). Interview with former MAPS consultant (Boston research firm) on topic of new techniques used in survey research.

Ferguson, S. D. (1976). *An analysis of the communications of the Latin American military coup d'etat.* Unpublished master's thesis, Indiana University, Bloomington.

Ferguson, S. D. (1993). Strategic planning for issues management: The communicator as environmental analyst. *Canadian Journal of Communication, 18,* 33-50.

Ferguson, S. D. (1994). *Mastering the public opinion challenge.* Burr Ridge, IL: Irwin.

Ferguson, S. D. (1998). Constructing a theoretical framework for evaluating public relations programs and activities. In M. E. Roloff (Ed.), *Communication yearbook 21* (pp. 190-229). Thousand Oaks, CA: Sage.

Ferguson, S. D. (1999). *Communication planning: An integrated approach.* Thousand Oaks, CA: Sage.

Ferguson, S. D., & Ferguson, S. (1988). The systems school. In S. D. Ferguson & S. Ferguson (Eds.), *Organizational communication* (pp. 38-60). Rochelle Park, NJ: Transaction Publishers.

Fern, E. F. (1982). The use of focus groups for idea generation: The effects of group size, acquaintanceship, and moderator on response quantity and quality. *Journal of Marketing Research, 19,* 1-13.

Fink, A. (1995a). *How to analyze survey data.* Thousand Oaks, CA: Sage.

Fink, A. (1995b). *How to ask survey questions.* Thousand Oaks, CA: Sage.

Fink, A. (1995c). *How to design surveys.* Thousand Oaks, CA: Sage.

Fink, A. (1995d). *How to report on surveys.* Thousand Oaks, CA: Sage.

Fink, A. (1995e). *How to sample in surveys.* Thousand Oaks, CA: Sage.

Fink, A. (1995f). *The survey handbook.* Thousand Oaks, CA: Sage.

Fink, A. (1995g). *The survey kit.* Thousand Oaks, CA: Sage.

Fink, A., & Kosecoff, J. (1998). *How to conduct surveys: A step-by-step guide* (2nd ed.). Thousand Oaks, CA: Sage.

Fiske, J. (1982). *Introduction to communication studies*. London: Methuen.

Forbes, P. S. (1992, March). Applying strategic management to public relations. *Public Relations Journal*, pp. 31-32.

Fowler, F., & Mangione, T. (1990). *Standardized survey interviewing: Minimizing interviewer-related errors*. Newbury Park, CA: Sage.

Fowler, F. J., Jr. (1992). How unclear terms affect survey data. *Public Opinion Quarterly, 56*(2), 218-231.

Fowler, F. J. (1993). *Survey research methods*. Newbury Park, CA: Sage.

Fowler, F. J. (1995). *Improving survey questions: Design and evaluation*. Thousand Oaks, CA: Sage.

Frey, J. H. (1989). *Survey research by telephone* (2nd ed.). Newbury Park, CA: Sage.

Frey, J. H., & Oishi, S. M. (1995). *How to conduct interviews by telephone and in person*. Thousand Oaks, CA: Sage.

Friedmann, R. A., & Podolny, J. (1992). Differentiation of boundary spanning roles: Labor negotiations and implications for role conflict. *Administrative Science Quarterly, 37*, 28-47.

Frizzell, A. (1989). The perils of polling. In A. Frizzell & A. Westell (Eds.), *The Canadian general election of 1988*. Ottawa, Ontario, Canada: Carleton University Press.

Fuld, L. (1991). A recipe for business intelligence success. *Journal of Business Strategy, 12*, 12-17.

Gamson, W. A., & Modigliani, A. (1987). The changing culture of affirmative action. In R. G. Braungart & M. M. Braungart (Eds.), *Research in political sociology* (Vol. 3, pp. 137-177). Greenwich, CT: JAI.

Gastil, J., & Dillard, J. P. (1999). Increasing political sophistication through public deliberation. *Political Communication, 16*, 3-23.

Geer, J. G. (1991). Do open-ended questions measure "salient" issues? *Public Opinion Quarterly, 55*(3), 360-370.

Geller, A., Kaplan, D., & Lasswell, H. D. (1942). An experimental comparison of four ways of coding editorial content. *Journalism Quarterly, 19*, 362-370.

Gerbner, G. (1977). Comparative cultural indicators. In G. Gerbner (Ed.), *Mass media policies in changing cultures* (pp. 199-205). New York: John Wiley.

Gerbner, G., & Gross, L. (1976). Living with television: The violence profile. *Journal of Communication, 26*(2), 173-199.

Gerbner, G., Gross, L., Jackson-Beeck, M., Jeffries-Fox, S., & Signorielli, N. (1977). One more time: An analysis of the CBS "Final Comments on the Violence Profile." *Journal of Broadcasting, 21*, 297-304.

Gerbner, G., Gross, L., Morgan, M., & Signorielli, N. (1994). Growing up with television. In J. Bryant & D. Zillmann (Eds.), *Media effects: Advances in theory and research* (pp. 17-42). Hillsdale, NJ: Lawrence Erlbaum.

Gerbner, G., Holsti, O. R., Krippendorff, K., Paisley, W. J., & Stone, P. J. (Eds.). (1969). *The analysis of communication content: Developments in scientific theories and computer techniques.* New York: John Wiley.

Getz, K. (1991). Selecting corporate political tactics. In J. Wall & L. R. Jauch (Eds.), *Academy of Management Best Papers, Proceedings* (pp. 326-330). New York: American Management Association.

Gilad, B. (1991). U.S. intelligence system: Model for corporate chiefs? *Journal of Business Strategy, 12*(3), 20-25.

Ginsberg, B. (1989). How polling transforms the public. In M. Margolis & G. Mauser (Eds.), *Manipulating public opinion: Essays on public opinion as a dependent variable* (pp. 171-193). Pacific Grove, CA: Brooks/Cole.

Glynn, C. J., & Ostman, R. E. (1988). Public opinion about public opinion. *Journalism Quarterly, 65*(2), 299-306.

Gollner, A. (1983). *Social change and corporate strategy.* Stamford, CT: Issue Action.

Granovetter, M. S. (1973). The strength of weak ties. *American Journal of Sociology, 78,* 1360-1380.

Greening, D. (1991). Organizing for public issues: Environmental and organization predictors of structure and process. In J. L. Wall & L. R. Jauch (Eds.), *Academy of Management Best Papers, Proceedings* (pp. 331-335). New York: American Management Association.

Griffin, E. (2000). *A first look at communication theory* (4th ed.). Boston: McGraw-Hill.

Grossman, M., & Kumar, M. (1981). *Portraying the president.* Baltimore, MD: Johns Hopkins University Press.

Grunig, J. E. (1977). Review of research on environmental public relations. *Public Relations Review, 3*(2), 36-58.

Grunig, J. E., & Repper, F. C. (1992). Strategic management, publics, and issues. In J. E. Grunig (Ed.), *Excellence in public relations and communication management* (pp. 117-157). Hillsdale, NJ: Lawrence Erlbaum.

Gunther, A. C., & Mundy, P. (1993). Biased optimism and the third person. *Journalism Quarterly, 70,* 58-67.

Habermas, J. (1989). *The structural transformation of the public sphere* (T. Burger & F. Lawrence, Trans.). Cambridge: MIT Press. (Original work published 1962)

Hall, S. (1986). Media power and class power. In J. Curran, J. Ecclestone, G. Oakley, & R. Richardson (Eds.), *Bending reality.* London: Pluto.

Hall, S., Critcher, C., Jefferson, T., & Roberts, B. (1978). *Policing the crisis.* London: Macmillan.

Hamel, G., & Prahalad, C. K. (1996). *Competing for the future.* Boston: Harvard Business School Press.

Hamilton, A. (1937). Remarks in M. Farrand (Ed.), *The records of the federal convention of 1787* (Vol. 1). New Haven, CT: Yale University Press.

Hanna, M. S., & Wilson, G. L. (1991). *Community in business and professional settings* (3rd ed.). New York: McGraw-Hill.

Hare, A. P., & Davies, M. F. (1994). Social interaction. In A. P. Hare, H. H. Blumberg, M. F. Davies, & M. V. Kent (Eds.), *Small group research: A handbook* (pp. 169-193). Norwood, NJ: Ablex.

Hartley, J. (1982). *Understanding news.* New York: Methuen.

Hauss, D. (1995, May). Technology gives early warning on news breaks. *Public Relations Journal,* pp. 18-22.

Hayes, R. E. (1985). Corporate crisis management. In S. J. Andriole (Ed.), *Corporate crisis management* (pp. 21-37). Princeton, NJ: Petrocelli.

Heath, R. L. (1997). *Strategic issues management.* Thousand Oaks, CA: Sage.

Heath, R. L., & Associates. (1988). *Strategic issues management.* San Francisco: Jossey-Bass.

Heath, R. L., & Nelson, A. (1986). *Issues management: Corporate public policymaking in an information society.* Beverly Hills, CA: Sage.

Hegel, G. W. F. (1952). *The philosophy of right* (T. M. Knox, Trans.). Chicago: Encyclopedia Britannica.

Herbst, S. (1995). On electronic public space: Talk shows in theoretical perspective. *Political Communication, 12*(3), 263-274.

Herman, E. S., & Chomsky, N. (1988). *Manufacturing consent: The political economy of the mass media.* New York: Pantheon.

Herndon, S. L. (1993). Using focus group interviews for preliminary investigation. In S. L. Herndon & G. L. Kreps (Eds.), *Qualitative research: Applications in organizational communication* (pp. 39-45). Cresskill, NJ: Hampton.

Herring, J. P. (1991). Senior management must champion business intelligence programs. *Journal of Business Strategy, 12*(5), 48-52.

Herzog, H. (1940). Professor quiz: A gratification study. In P. F. Lazarsfeld (Ed.), *Radio and the printed page* (pp. 64-93). New York: Duell, Sloan, & Pearce.

Hill, K. A., & Hughes, J. E. (1997). Computer-mediated political communication: The USENET and political communities. *Political Communication, 14,* 3-27.

Hobbes, T. (1963). *Leviathan.* In J. Somerville & R. E. Santoni (Eds.), *Social and political philosophy: Readings from Plato to Gandhi* (pp. 139-168). Garden City, NY: Anchor/Doubleday.

Hogan, J. M., & Smith, T. J., III. (1991). Polling on the issues: Public opinion and the nuclear freeze. *Public Opinion Quarterly, 55,* 534-569.

Holsti, O. R. (1969). *Content analysis for the social sciences and humanities.* Reading, MA: Addison-Wesley.

Hovland, C. J., Lumsdaine, A. A., & Sheffield, F. D. (1965). *Experiments on mass communication: Vol. III. Studies of social psychology in World War II.* New York: John Wiley.

Hoy, C. (1989). *Margin of error.* Toronto: Key Porter Books.

Innes, H. (1950). *Empire and communication.* Toronto: University of Toronto Press.

Isaacs, M. (1998). Two different worlds: The relationship between elite and mass opinion on American foreign policy. *Journal of Communication, 15*(3), 323-345.

Iyengar, S., & Kinder, D. R. (1987). *News that matters: Television and American opinion.* Chicago: University of Chicago Press.

Jackson, W. (1999). *Methods: Doing social research.* Scarborough, Ontario, Canada: Prentice Hall.

Jasperson, A. E., Shah, D. V., Watts, M., Faber, R. J., & Fan, D. P. (1998). Framing and the public agenda: Media effects on the importance of the federal budget deficit. *Political Communication Journal, 15*(2), 205-224.

Jefferson, T. (1963). The Declaration of Independence. In J. Somerville & R. E. Santoni (Eds.), *Social and political philosophy: Readings from Plato to Gandhi* (pp. 239-246). Garden City, NY: Anchor/Doubleday.

Jeffres, L. W. (with Perloff, R. M.). (1997). *Mass media effects* (2nd ed.). Prospect Heights, IL: Waveland.

Jo, E., & Berkowitz, L. (1994). A priming effect analysis of media influences: An update. In J. Bryant & D. Zillmann (Eds.), *Media effects: Advances in theory and research* (pp. 43-60). Hillsdale, NJ: Lawrence Erlbaum.

Johnson, J. D., & Meishoke, H. (1992). Mass media channels: Women's evaluations for cancer-related information. *Newspaper Research Journal, 13*(1/2), 146-159.

Jones, B. L., & Chase, W. H. (1979). Managing public policy issues. *Public Relations Review, 5*(2), 3-23.

Jones, D. A. (1998). Political talk radio: The Limbaugh effect on primary voters. *Journal of Communication, 15*(3), 367-381.

Juniper, D. (1999). Unpublished master's study of Zapatista Internet campaign, University of Northern British Columbia, British Columbia, Canada.

Kahn, R., & Cannell, C. F. (1957). *Dynamics of interviewing.* New York: John Wiley.

Kanter, R. M. (1997). *World class: Thriving locally in the global economy.* New York: Touchstone.

Katz, D., & Kahn, R. L. (1966). *The social psychology of organizations.* New York: John Wiley.

Katz, E., Gurevitch, M., & Haas, H. (1973). On the use of the mass media for important things. *American Sociological Review, 38,* 164-181.

Kaufman, P., Dykers, C., & Caldwell, C. (1993). Why going online can reduce reliability. *Journalism Quarterly, 70*(4), 824-832.

Kern, M., & Just, M. (1995). The focus group method, political advertising, campaign news, and the construction of candidate images. *Political Communication, 12*(2), 127-145.

Kim, Y., Ahn, J., & Song, J. (1991, May). *Perceived media influence on self and others on a controversial issue.* Paper presented at the annual conference of the International Communication Association, Chicago.

Kitzinger, J. (1994). The methodology of focus groups: The importance of interaction between research participants. *Sociology of Health and Illness, 16,* 103-121.

Kitzinger, J., & Williams, K. (1997). Rethinking media influence and power. In J. Eldridge, J. Kitzinger, & K. Williams (Eds.), *The mass media and power in modern Britain* (pp. 160-180). Oxford, UK: Oxford University Press.

Klein, M. W., & Maccoby, N. (1954). Newspaper objectivity in the 1952 campaign. *Journalism Quarterly, 31,* 285-296.

Kodama, F. (1992). Technology, fusion, and the new R&D. *Harvard Business Review, 70*(4), 70-78.

Krippendorff, K. (1980). *Content analysis: An introduction to its methodology.* Beverly Hills, CA: Sage.

Krueger, R. A. (1988). *Focus groups: A practical guide for applied research.* Newbury Park, CA: Sage.

Krueger, R. A. (1993). Quality control in focus group research. In D. L. Morgan (Ed.), *Successful focus groups* (pp. 65-88). Newbury Park, CA: Sage.

Krueger, R. A. (1994). *Focus groups: A practical guide for applied research* (2nd ed.). Thousand Oaks, CA: Sage.

Krueger, R. A. (1997a). *Analyzing and reporting focus group results.* Thousand Oaks, CA: Sage.

Krueger, R. A. (1997b). *Moderating focus groups.* Thousand Oaks, CA: Sage.

Kuklinski, J. H., Metlay, D. S., & Kay, W. D. (1982, November). Citizen knowledge and choices on the complex issue of nuclear energy. *American Journal of Political Science,* 615-642.

Ladd, E., & Benson, J. (1992). The growth of news polls in American politics. In T. E. Mann & G. R. Orren (Eds.), *Media polls in American politics* (pp. 19-31). Washington, DC: Brookings Institution.

Ladd, E. C., & Ferree, G. D. (1981, December/January). Were the pollsters really wrong? *Public Opinion,* pp. 13-14.

Larosa, D. L. (1989). Real and perceived effects of "Amerika." *Journalism Quarterly, 66*(2), 373-378, 529.

Lasswell, H. D. (1948). The structure and function of communication in society. In L. Bryson (Ed.), *The communication of ideas* (pp. 37-51). New York: Harper.

Lasswell, H. D., Leites, N., & Associates. (1949). *The language of politics: Studies in quantitative semantics.* Cambridge: MIT Press.

Lauzen, M. M. (1995). Toward a model of environmental scanning. *Journal of Public Relations Research, 7*(3), 187-203.

Lauzen, M. M. (1997). Understanding the relation between public relations and issues management. *Journal of Public Relations Research, 9,* 65-82.

Lauzen, M. M., & Dozier, D. M. (1994). Issues management mediation of linkages between environmental complexity and management of the public relations function. *Journal of Public Relations Research, 6*(3), 163-184.

Lavine, H., & Latane, B. (1996). A cognitive-social theory of public opinion: Dynamic social impact and cognitive structure. *Journal of Communication, 46*(4), 48-56.

Lavrakas, P. J. (1993). *Telephone survey methods: Sampling, selection, and supervision.* Newbury Park, CA: Sage.

Lazarsfeld, P., Berelson, B., & Gaudet, H. (1948). *The people's choice.* New York: Columbia University Press.

Lazarsfeld, P. F., & Stanton, F. N. (1941). *Radio research.* New York: Duell, Pearce & Sloan.

Lazarsfeld, P. F., & Stanton, F. N. (1944). *Radio research 1942-1943.* New York: Duell, Pearce & Sloan.

Lewis, G. H., & Lewis, J. F. (1980). The dog in the nighttime: Negative evidence in social research. *British Journal of Sociology, 31,* 544-558.

Lewis, I., & Schneider, W. (1982). Is the public lying to the pollsters? *Public Opinion, 5*(2), 42-47.

Likert, R. (1932). A technique for the measurement of attitudes. *Archives of Psychology, 19,* 44-53.

Lipari, L. (1999). Polling as ritual. *Journal of Communication, 49,* 83-102.

Lippmann, W. (1922). *Public opinion.* New York: Free Press.

Litwin, M. S. (1995). *How to measure survey reliability and validity.* Thousand Oaks, CA: Sage.

Liu, W. T., & Duff, R. W. (1972). The strength of weak ties. *Public Opinion Quarterly, 36,* 361-366.

Locke, J. (1952). *A letter concerning civil government.* Chicago: Encyclopedia Britannica. (Original work published 1937)

Lowery, S., & De Fleur, M. L. (1983). *Milestones in mass communication research.* New York: Longman.

Lule, J. (1991). The myth of my widow: A dramatistic analysis of news portrayals of a terrorist victim. In A. O. Alali & K. K. Eke (Eds.), *Media coverage of terrorism: Methods of diffusion* (pp. 86-111). Newbury Park, CA: Sage.

Lunt, P., & Livingstone, S. (1996). Rethinking the focus group in media and communications research. *Journal of Communication, 46*(2), 79-98.

Machiavelli, N. (1963). *The prince.* In J. Somerville & R. E. Santoni (Eds.), *Social and political philosophy: Readings from Plato to Gandhi* (pp. 101-138). Garden City, NY: Anchor/Doubleday.

Madison, J. (1961). *Federalist papers* (No. 10). New York: Mentor Books.

Mahon, J. F., & McGowan, R. A. (1996). *Industry as a player in the political and social arena: Defining the competitive environment.* Westport, CT: Quorum/Greenwood.

Mangiacasale, A. (1992, October 10). The problem with polls. *Ottawa Citizen*, p. B3.

Mangione, T. W. (1995). *Mail surveys: Improving the quality.* Thousand Oaks, CA: Sage.

Mariampolski, H. (1984). The resurgence of qualitative research. *Public Relations Journal, 40*(7), 21-23.

Markham, J. W., & Stempel, G. H., III. (1957). Analysis of techniques in measuring press performance. *Journalism Quarterly, 34,* 187-190.

Marshall, C., & Rossman, G. B. (1989). *Designing qualitative research.* Newbury Park, CA: Sage.

Martino, J. P. (1985). Anticipating technological surprise. In S. J. Andriole (Ed.), *Corporate crisis management* (pp. 49-68). Princeton, NJ: Petrocelli.

Maslow, A. H., & Mintz, N. L. (1956). Effects of esthetic surroundings: I. Initial effects of three esthetic conditions upon perceiving "energy" and "well-being" in faces. *Journal of Psychology, 41,* 247-254.

Masterson, J. (1992, November). Discovering databases. *Public Relations Journal,* pp. 12-19.

Mauser, G. A. (1991). The short-term effect of election polls on foreign exchange rates: The 1988 Canadian federal election. *Public Opinion Quarterly, 55*(2), 232-240.

McCartney, H. P. (1987). Applying fiction conflict situations to analysis of news stories. *Journalism Quarterly, 64,* 163-170.

McCombs, M. (1994). News influence on our pictures of the world. In J. Bryant & D. Zillmann (Eds.), *Media effects: Advances in theory and research* (pp. 1-16). Hillsdale, NJ: Lawrence Erlbaum.

McCombs, M., Einsiedel, E., & Weaver, D. (1991). *Contemporary public opinion: Issues and the news.* Hillsdale, NJ: Lawrence Erlbaum.

McCombs, M. E. (1978). Public response to the daily news. In L. K. Epstein (Ed.), *Women and the news* (pp. 1-14). New York: Hastings House.

McCombs, M. E., & Shaw, D. L. (1972). The agenda-setting function of mass media. *Public Opinion Quarterly, 36*(2), 176-187.

McIver, J. P., & Carmines, E. G. (1981). *Unidimensional scaling.* Newbury Park, CA: Sage.

McKeown, B., & Thomas, D. (1988). *Q methodology.* Newbury Park, CA: Sage.

McLeod, J. M., Kosicki, G. M., & McLeod, D. M. (1994). The expanding boundaries of political communication effects. In J. Bryant & D. Zillmann (Eds.), *Media effects: Advances in theory and research* (pp. 123-162). Hillsdale, NJ: Lawrence Erlbaum.

McLuhan, M. (1964). *Understanding media: The extension of man.* New York: McGraw-Hill.

McQuail, D. (1994). *Mass communication theory: An introduction.* Thousand Oaks, CA: Sage.

McQuail, D., Blumler, J. G., & Brown, J. R. (1972). The television audience: A revised perspective. In D. McQuail (Ed.), *Sociology of mass communications* (pp. 135-165). Middlesex, UK: Penguin.

Mead, G. H. (1934). *Mind, self, and society.* Chicago: University of Chicago.

Meng, M. (1992, March). Early identification aids issues management. *Public Relations Journal, 48*(3), 22-24.

Merriam, J. E., & Makower, J. (1988). *Trend watching: How the media create trends and how to be the first to uncover them.* New York: Tilden Press (American Management Association).

Merton, R. K., & Kendall, P. L. (1946). *The "focussed" interview. A report by the Bureau of Applied Social Research, Columbia University.* New York: Free Press.

Meyrowitz, J. (1994). Visible and invisible candidates: A case study in "competing logics" of campaign coverage. *Political Communication, 11*(2), 145-164.

Millett, S. M., & Leppanen, R. (1991). The business information and analysis function: A new approach to strategic thinking and planning. *Planning Review, 19*(3), 10-15, 36.

Mintz, N. L. (1956). Effects of esthetic surroundings: II. Prolonged and repeated experience in a "beautiful" and "ugly" room. *Journal of Psychology, 41,* 459-466.

Mintzberg, H. (1983). *Power in and around organizations.* Englewood Cliffs, NJ: Prentice Hall.

Molitor, G. T. (1979). The hatching of public opinion. In R. J. Allio & M. W. Pennington (Eds.), *Corporate planning techniques and applications* (pp. 53-62). New York: American Management Association.

Morgan, D. L. (1988). *Focus groups as qualitative research.* Newbury Park, CA: Sage.

Morgan, D. L. (1997). *Focus groups as qualitative research* (2nd ed.). Thousand Oaks, CA: Sage.

Morgan, D. L., & Krueger, R. A. (1997). *The focus group kit: Volumes 1-6.* Thousand Oaks, CA: Sage.

Morley, D. (1996). Populism, revisionism and the "new audience" research. In J. Curran, D. Morley, & V. Walkerdine (Eds.), *Cultural studies and communications* (pp. 279-299). London: Edward Arnold.

Morris, R. (1994). Computerized content analysis in management research. *Journal of Management, 20*(4), 903-931.

Morrison, D. E. (1998). *The search for a method: Focus groups and the development of mass communication research.* Luton, UK: University of Luton Press.

Murdock, G., & Golding, P. (1977). Capitalism, communication and class relations. In J. Curran, M. Gurevitch, & J. Woollacott (Eds.), *Mass communication and society.* London: Edward Arnold.

Naisbitt, J. (1980). *Megatrends: Ten new directions transforming our lives.* New York: Warner Books.

Naisbitt, J., & Aburdene, P. (1991). *Megatrends: Ten new directions for the 1990s*. New York: Avon.

Nakra, P. (1991). The changing role of public relations in marketing communications. *Public Relations Quarterly, 36*, 42-45.

Nelson, B. J. (1984). *Making an issue out of child abuse: Political agenda setting for social problems*. Chicago: University of Chicago Press.

Neuman, W. L. (1997). *Social research methods: Qualitative and quantitative approaches* (3rd ed.). Boston: Allyn & Bacon.

Nicholson-O'Brien, D. (1989, Spring). Interview with the Director General of Communications, Communications Directorate, Department of Justice Canada.

Nie, N. H., & Andersen, K. (1974). Mass belief systems revisited: Political change and attitude structure. *Journal of Politics, 36*, 541-591.

Niemi, R. G., & Weisberg, H. F. (Eds.). (1976). *Controversies in American voting behaviors*. San Francisco, CA: W. H. Freeman.

Nimmo, D., & Combs, J. (1990). *Mediated political realities* (2nd ed.). New York: Longman.

Noelle-Neumann, E. (1993). *The spiral of silence: Public opinion—our social skin* (2nd ed.). Chicago: University of Chicago Press.

Olson, K. M. (1995). The function of form in newspapers' political conflict coverage: The *New York Times'* shaping of expectations in the Bitburg controversy. *Political Communication, 12*, 43-64.

Osgood, C. E., Suci, G. J., & Tannenbaum, P. H. (1957). *The measurement of meaning*. Urbana: University of Illinois Press.

Osgood, C. E., & Walker, E. G. (1959). Motivation and language behavior: Content analysis of suicide notes. *Journal of Abnormal and Social Psychology, 59*, 63.

Oxelheim, L., & Wihlborg, C. G. (1991). Corporate strategies in a turbulent world economy. *Management International Review, 31*(4), 293-315.

Page, B. I., & Tannenbaum, J. (1996). Populistic deliberation and talk radio. *Journal of Communication, 46*(2), 33-54.

Pan, Z., & Kosicki, G. M. (1997). Talk show exposure as an opinion activity. *Political Communication, 14*(3), 371-388.

Pattakos, A. N. (1992). Growth in activist groups: How can business cope? In D. Mercer (Ed.), *Managing the external environment: A strategic perspective* (pp. 107-118). Newbury Park, CA: Sage.

Pavlik, J. V., Vastyan, J., & Maher, M. (1990). Using readership research to study employee views. *Public Relations Review, 16*(3), 250-261.

Pearce, W. B. (1995). A sailing guide for social constructionists. In W. Leeds-Hurwitz (Ed.), *Social approaches to communication?* (pp. 88-113). New York: Guilford.

Pearce, W. B., & Cronen, V. E. (1980). *Communication, action, and meaning: The creation of social realities*. New York: Praeger.

Perloff, R. M. (1989). Ego-involvement and the third-person effect of televised news coverage. *Communication Research, 16*(2), 236-262.

Perloff, R. M. (1993). Third-person effect research, 1983-1992: A review and synthesis. *International Journal of Public Opinion Research, 5,* 167-184.

Peterson, R. C., & Thurstone, L. L. (1933). *Motion pictures and the social attitudes of children.* New York: Macmillan.

Philo, G. (1995). The media in a class society. In G. Philo (Ed.), *Glasgow media group reader* (Vol. 2, pp. 176-183). London: Routledge.

Picard, R. G. (1991). The journalist's role in coverage of terrorist events. In A. O. Alali & K. K. Eke (Eds.), *Media coverage of terrorism: Methods of diffusion* (pp. 40-48). Newbury Park, CA: Sage.

Plato. (1963). *The republic.* In J. Somerville & R. E. Santoni (Eds.) & B. Jowett (Trans.), *Social and political philosophy: Readings from Plato to Gandhi* (pp. 1-45). Garden City, NY: Anchor/Doubleday.

Preble, J. F. (1978). Corporate use of environmental scanning. *University of Michigan Business Review, 30*(5), 12-17.

Presser, S., & Zhao, S. (1992). Attributes of questions and interviewers as correlates of interviewing performance. *Public Opinion Quarterly, 56*(2), 236-240.

Price, V. (1992). *Public opinion.* Newbury Park, CA: Sage.

Pride, R. A. (1995). How activists and media frame social problems: Critical events versus performance trends for schools. *Political Communication, 12,* 5-26.

Ragin, C. (1987). *The comparative method: Moving beyond qualitative and quantitative strategies.* Berkeley: University of California Press.

Reddin, C. (1998, June). *Communicating for productivity.* Paper presented at the annual meeting of the Canadian Communication Association, Learned Societies, Ottawa, Ontario.

Redding, J. C., & Catalanello, R. F. (1994). *Strategic readiness: The making of the learning organization.* San Francisco: Jossey-Bass.

Reed, J. L. (1999, April). *Infobeat* afternoon news edition [On-line]. Available: news@infobeat.com

Reese, S. D. (1991). Setting the media's agenda: A power balance perspective. In J. A. Anderson (Ed.), *Communication yearbook 14* (pp. 309-340). Newbury Park, CA: Sage.

Reid, A. (1988a, October 4). Pollsters often misunderstood, Reid says. *Ottawa Citizen,* p. A4.

Reid, A. (1988b). Public affairs research. In W. J. Wright & C. J. DuVernet (Eds.), *The Canadian public affairs handbook: Maximizing markets, protecting bottom lines* (pp. 117-146). Toronto: Carswell.

Reimann, B. C. (1992). The 1992 strategic management conference: The new agenda for corporate leadership. *Planning Review, 20*(4), 38-46.

Renfro, W. L. (1993). *Issues management in strategic planning.* Westport, CT: Quorum/Greenwood.

Rhee, J. W. (1996). How polls drive campaign coverage: The Gallup/CNN/*USA Today* tracking poll and *USA Today*'s coverage of the 1992 presidential campaign. *Political Communication, 13*(2), 213-229.

Rhee, J. W. (1997). Strategy and issue frames in election campaign coverage: A social cognitive account of framing effects. *Journal of Communication, 47*(3), 26-48.

Riffe, D., Aust, C., & Lacy, S. (1993). The effectiveness of random, consecutive day and constructed week sampling in newspaper content analysis. *Journalism Quarterly, 70,* 133-139.

Ring, P. S., Lenway, S. A., & Govekar, M. (1990, February). Management of the political imperative in international business. *Strategic Management Journal,* pp. 141-151.

Robert, M. M. (1990). Managing your competitor's strategy. *Journal of Business Strategy, 11*(2), 24-29.

Roberts, M., & McCombs, M. E. (1994). Agenda setting and political advertising: Origins of the news agenda. *Political Communication, 11*(3), 249-262.

Robinson, J. P., & Levy, M. R. (1996). News media use and the informed public: A 1990s update. *Journal of Communication, 46*(2), 129-135.

Rogers, E. (1973). *Communication strategies for family planning.* New York: Free Press.

Rogers, E., & Agarwala-Rogers, R. (1976). *Communication in organizations.* New York: Free Press.

Rogers, E. M. (1995). *Diffusion of innovations* (4th ed.). New York: Free Press.

Rogers, E. M., & Dearing, J. W. (1988). Agenda-setting research: Where has it been, where is it going? In J. Anderson (Ed.), *Communication yearbook 11* (pp. 555-594). Thousand Oaks, CA: Sage.

Rogers, E. M., & Shoemaker, F. F. (1971). *Communication of innovations: A cross-cultural approach.* New York: Free Press.

Roth, L. (1993). Mohawk airwaves and cultural challenges: Some reflections on the politics of recognition and cultural appropriation after the summer of 1990. *Canadian Journal of Communication, 18*(3), 315-331.

Roush, G. B. (1991). A program for sharing corporate intelligence. *Journal of Business Strategy, 12,* 4-7.

Rousseau, J. J. (1963). *The Social Contract.* In J. Somerville & R. E. Santoni (Eds.) & C. Frankel (Trans.), *Social and political philosophy: Readings from Plato to Gandhi* (pp. 205-238). Garden City, NY: Anchor/Doubleday.

Rubin, A. M. (1994). Media uses and effects: A uses-and-gratifications perspective. In J. Bryant & D. Zillmann (Eds.), *Media effects: Advances in theory and research* (pp. 417-436). Hillsdale, NJ: Lawrence Erlbaum.

Rucinski, D. M., & Salmon, C. T. (1989). *The other as the "vulnerable voter."* Paper presented at the annual conference of the American Association of Public Opinion Research, St. Petersburg, FL.

Russell, S., & Prince, M. J. (1992). Environmental scanning for social services. *Long Range Planning, 25*(5), 106-113.

Sachsman, D. B. (1976). Public relations influence on coverage of environment in San Francisco area. *Journalism Quarterly, 53,* 54-60.

Sanchez, M. E. (1992). Effects of questionnaire design on the quality of survey data. *Public Opinion Quarterly, 56*(2), 206-217.

Sandell, K. L., Mattley, C., Evarts, D. R., Lengel, L., & Ziyati, A. (1993, May). *The media and voter decision-making in campaign 1992.* Paper presented at the annual meeting of the International Communication Association, Miami, FL.

Saussure, F. de. (1966). *Course in general linguistics* (W. Baskin, Trans.). New York: McGraw Hill.

Saxer, U. (1993). Public relations and symbolic politics. *Journal of Public Relations Research, 5*(2), 127-151.

Scanlon, T. J. (1990, November). Transcript of presentation to the Post-Oka Communications Symposium, hosted by the Department of National Defence, Canada, National Defence Headquarters, Ottawa.

Schaeffer, N. C. (1991). Hardly ever or constantly: Group comparisons using vague qualifiers. *Public Opinion Quarterly, 55*(3), 395-423.

Scheufele, D. A. (1999). Framing as a theory of media effects. *Journal of Communication, 49,* 103-122.

Schramm, W., Lyle, J., & Parker, E. (1961). *Television in the lives of our children.* Palo Alto, CA: Stanford University Press.

Schuman, H., & Presser, S. (1996). *Questions and answers in attitude surveys: Experiments on question form, wording, and context.* Thousand Oaks, CA: Sage.

Scott, S. (1997, April 30). Why poll results can differ: How could three surveys radically differ on federal party standings? Because the findings reflect the individual polling house's questions and methods. *Montreal Gazette,* p. A1.

Sigelman, L., & Yanarella, E. (1986, June). Public information on public information: A multivariate analysis. *Social Science Quarterly,* pp. 402-410.

Simpson, A. L. (1992). Ten rules of research. *Public Relations Quarterly, 37*(2), 27-28.

Singer, E. (1988). Surveys in the mass media. In H. J. O'Gorman (Ed.), *Surveying social life: Papers in honor of Herbert H. Hyman* (pp. 413-436). Middletown, CT: Wesleyan University Press.

Smart, C. F. (1985). Strategic business planning: Predicting susceptibility to crises. In S. J. Andriole (Ed.), *Corporate crisis management* (pp. 9-20). Princeton, NJ: Petrocelli.

Smith, M. J. (1988). *Contemporary communication research methods.* Belmont, CA: Wadsworth.

Sonnenberg, F. K. (1992). Partnering: Entering the age of competition. *Journal of Business Strategy, 13*(3), 49-52.

Squire, P. (1988). Why the 1936 *Literary Digest* failed. *Public Opinion Quarterly,* *52,* 125-133.

Stempel, G. H., III. (1952). Research in brief: Sample size for classifying subject matter in dailies. *Journalism Quarterly, 29,* 333-334.

Stempel, G. H., III. (1989). Content analysis. In G. H. Stempel, III, & B. H. Westley (Eds.), *Research methods in mass communication* (2nd ed., pp. 119-131). Englewood Cliffs, NJ: Prentice Hall.

Stephenson, W. (1953). *The study of behavior: Q-technique and its methodology.* Chicago: University of Chicago Press.

Stewart, D. W., & Shamdasani, P. N. (1990). *Focus groups: Theory and practice.* Newbury Park, CA: Sage.

Stoffels, J. D. (1982). Environmental scanning for future success. *Managerial Planning, 3*(3), 4-12.

Strodtbeck, F. L., & Hook, L. H. (1961). The social dimension of a twelve-man jury table. *Sociometry, 24,* 397-415.

Tannen, D. (1993). *Framing in discourse.* Oxford, UK: Oxford University Press.

Taras, D. (1990). *The newsmakers: The media's influence on Canadian politics.* Scarborough, Ontario: Nelson Canada.

Terkildsen, N., Schnell, F. I., & Ling, C. (1998). Interest groups, the media, and policy debate formation: An analysis of message structure, rhetoric, and source cues. *Political Communication, 15,* 45-61.

Tersine, R. J., & Riggs, W. E. (1988). The Delphi technique: A long-range planning tool. In S. D. Ferguson & S. Ferguson (Eds.), *Organizational communication* (2nd ed., pp. 500-509). New Brunswick, NJ: Transaction Books.

Theus, K. T. (1993). Organizations and the media: Structures of miscommunication. *Management Communication Quarterly, 7,* 67-94.

Thomas, P. S. (1980). Environmental scanning—The state of the art. *Long Range Planning, 13,* 20-28.

Thomsen, S. R. (1995). Using online databases in corporate issues management. *Public Relations Review, 21*(2), 103-122.

TimeWork Web. (1999). *Q methodology: A brief introduction* (pp. 1-2) [On-line]. Available: *http://www.vcn.bc.ca/timework/q.htm*

Tuchman, G. (1978). *A study in the construction of reality.* New York: Free Press.

Tuckel, P. S., & Feinberg, B. M. (1991). The answering machine poses many questions for telephone survey researchers. *Public Opinion Quarterly, 55*(2), 200-217.

Vaughn, S., Schumm, J. S., & Sinagub, J. M. (1996). *Focus group interviews in education and psychology.* Thousand Oaks, CA: Sage.

Walker, G. F. (1994). Communicating public relations research. *Journal of Public Relations Research, 6*(3), 141-162.

Wanta, W., & Hu, Y. (1994). The effects of credibility reliance and exposure on media agenda setting. *Journalism Quarterly, 71,* 90-98.

Watt, J. H., & Van Den Berg, S. A. (1995). *Research methods for communication science.* Boston: Allyn & Bacon.

Weaver, D. (1991). Issue salience and public opinion: Are there consequences of agenda-setting? *International Journal of Public Opinion Research, 3,* 53-68.

Weaver, D. (1994). Media agenda setting and elections: Voter involvement or alienation? *Political Communication, 11*(4), 347-356.

Weber, R. P. (1990). *Basic content analysis* (2nd ed.). Newbury Park, CA: Sage.

Weisberg, H., Krosnick, J. A., & Bowen, B. D. (1996). *An introduction to survey research, polling, and data analysis.* Thousand Oaks, CA: Sage.

Wiemann, G. (1991). The influentials: Back to the concept of opinion leaders. *Journal of Communication, 55*(2), 267-279.

Williams, W., & Semlak, W. (1978). Campaign '76: Agenda setting during the New Hampshire primary. *Journal of Broadcasting, 22*(4), 531-540.

Willnat, L. (1994, August). *Testing the interaction of the third-person effect and spiral of silence in a political pressure cooker: The case of Hong Kong.* Paper presented at the annual conference of the Association for Education in Journalism and Mass Communication, Atlanta.

Wilson, G. L., & Hanna, M. S. (1993). *Groups in context: Leadership and participation in small groups* (3rd ed.). New York: McGraw-Hill.

Wimmer, R. D., & Dominick, J. R. (1992). *Mass media research: An introduction* (3rd ed.). Belmont, CA: Wadsworth.

Wimmer, R. D., & Dominick, J. R. (1997). *Mass media research: An introduction* (5th ed.). Belmont, CA: Wadsworth.

Witte, E. H., & Davis, J. H. (1996). *Understanding group behavior: Small group processes and interpersonal relations* (Vol. 2). Mahwah, NJ: Lawrence Erlbaum.

Wood, J. T. (1996). She says/he says: Communication, caring, and conflict in heterosexual relationships. In J. T. Wood (Ed.), *Gendered relationships* (pp. 149-162). Mountain View, CA: Mayfield.

Yammarino, F. J., Skinner, S. J., & Childers, T. J. (1991). Understanding mail survey response behavior: A meta-analysis. *Public Opinion Quarterly, 55*(4), 613-639.

Yankelovich, D. (1991). *Coming to social judgment: Making democracy work in a complex world.* Syracuse, NY: Syracuse University Press.

Yeric, J. L., & Todd, J. R. (1989). *Public opinion: The visible politics* (2nd ed.). Itasca, IL: F. E. Peacock.

Yeric, J. L., & Todd, J. R. (1996). *Public opinion: The visible politics* (3rd ed.). Itasca, IL: F. E. Peacock.

Zikmund, W. G. (1988). *Business research methods* (2nd ed.). Chicago: Dryden Press.

Author Index

Subject Index

EDITOR'S NOTE: The following typographical conventions used in this index are: *b* identifies
boxes, *f* identifies figures, and *t* identifies tables.

289

About the Authors

Sherry Devereaux Ferguson, PhD, is Professor and Chair of the Communication Department at the University of Ottawa. She is author or editor of five books. Early book projects include *Intercom: Readings in Organizational Communication* (1980) and *Organizational Communication* (1988). She received the National Communication Association PRIDE Award for best book in its class for *Mastering the Public Opinion Challenge* (1994). A recent book is *Communication Planning: An Integrated Approach* (1999). She is presented contracted to produce an edigted volume on Civic Discourse in the Third Millennium as part of the Ablex series edited by Michael Prosser, Rochester Institute of Technology. An article titled "Constructing a Theoretical Framework for Evaluating Public Relations Programs and Activities" appeared in the *Communication Yearbook* (1998). Other recent articles have appeared in Yahya Kamalipour's *U.S. Image Around the World* (1999) and the *Canadian Communication Journal* (1998). She has acted as consultant to many federal government departments, including the Department of Foreign Affairs, the Department of Justice, the Privy Council Office, Health Canada, Secretary of State, Communications Canada, the Canadian Space Agency, the National Research Council, the Department of Fisheries and Oceans, the Bureau of Management Consultants, Indian and Northern Affairs, and Transport Canada.

Other consulting assignments include work for Petro Canada, the Canadian Council of Catholic Bishops, Canadian Satellite Communications, Inc., the Addiction Research Foundation, and the Center for Health Promotion at the University of Toronto. She was an invited faculty member at the annual Management Institute, Canadian Council for Public Affairs Advancement (1997) and priority speaker at sessions sponsored by the International Quality Control and Productivity Center of Chicago (1998) and the International Communications Management conference in Toronto in the spring 1999. She has trained hundreds of managers and executives in issues management and strategic planning and evaluation strategies for more than a decade. Areas of expertise include strategic planning, political communication, issues management, evaluation (specific to communication), public relations, employee communications, and speech communication. She is a member of a La Reléve advisory panel, headed by the Assistant Secretary of Communications to Cabinet, charged with defining curriculum needs for Canadian federal government communication officers. She was a member of a 1998 National Communication Association (United States) task force on communications curricula. She is a member of the Public Awareness Advisory Committee for Amnesty International, Canada.

Alexandra Hendriks is a PhD candidate at the University of Arizona. She specializes in social effects of the media, methodology, and health communication research. She has published articles in the areas of organizational communication, intercultural communication, and advertising. She is currently working with the Communication Health Sciences group at the University of Arizona conducting health-related research. Prior to pursuing her PhD, she worked as a consultant for MaPS, a Boston-based marketing research company, conducting quantitative and qualitative research for *Fortune 100* companies. She acted as a communication consultant for the Federal Communications Council and as a communication officer for the Canadian Human Rights Commission.

AEO-1487